Cultish

Also by Amanda Montell

*Wordslut: A Feminist Guide to Taking
Back the English Language*

Cultish

The Language of
Fanaticism

Amanda Montell

HARPER WAVE
An Imprint of HarperCollins*Publishers*

HarperCollins books may be purchased for educational, business, or sales promotional use. For information, please email the Special Markets Department at SPsales@harpercollins.com.

FIRST EDITION

Designed by Bonni Leon-Berman

Library of Congress Cataloging-in-Publication Data has been applied for.

ISBN 978-0-06-299315-1

21 22 23 24 25 LSC 10 9 8 7 6 5 4 3 2 1

For my dad—the optimist

Contents

Note from the Author

Some names and identifying details have been changed
to protect sources' privacy.

Part 1

Repeat After Me . . .

i.

It started with a prayer.

Tasha Samar was thirteen years old the first time she heard the bewitching buzz of their voices. It was their turban-to-toe white ensembles and meditation malas that first caught her eye, but it was how they spoke that beckoned her through the front door. She heard them through the open window of a Kundalini yoga studio in Cambridge, Massachusetts. "The prayers were so strange, all in another language," Tasha, now twenty-nine, tells me over macadamia milk lattes at an outdoor café in West Hollywood. We're less than a few miles away from the epicenter of the sinister life she led until only three years ago. Judging by her crisp cream buttondown and satiny blowout, you'd never guess she could once tie a turban as naturally as any other young woman in this courtyard could toss her hair into a topknot. "Yeah, I could still do it now, if I had to," Tasha assures me, her meticulous acrylics *clack-clack-clack*ing on her porcelain mug.

Tasha, a first-generation Russian American Jew who experienced an agonizing lack of belonging her entire childhood, was struck by this yoga group's sense of closeness, so she peeked her head into the lobby and asked the receptionist who they were. "The front-desk girl started telling me the basics; the phrase 'the science of the mind' was used a lot,"

Tasha reflects. "I didn't know what it meant, I just remember thinking, 'Wow, I really want to try that.'" Tasha found out when the next yoga class would be, and her parents let her attend. You didn't need to be a permanent member of the group to take a class—the only requirement was an "open heart." Learning and reciting their foreign prayers, all directed toward a man with a long peppery beard whose photograph was plastered throughout the dimly lit studio, cast a spell over tween Tasha. "It felt ancient," she says, "like I was a part of something holy."

Who was this group in all white? The Healthy, Happy, Holy Organization, or 3HO—a Sikh-derived "alternative religion" founded in the 1970s, which hosts Kundalini yoga classes all over the US. The guy with the beard? Their captivating, well-connected leader, Harbhajan Singh Khalsa (or Yogi Bhajan), who claimed—to much contest—to be the official religious and administrative head of all Western Sikhs, and who was worth hundreds of millions of dollars by the time he died in 1993. The language? Gurmukhi, the writing system of modern Punjabi and Sikh scripture. The ideology? To obey Yogi Bhajan's strict New Age teachings, which included abstaining from meat and alcohol,* surren-

---

* Booze was 3HO heresy, so in place of happy hour everyone guzzled gallons of tea. Specifically, members drank Yogi Tea, a multimillion-dollar brand you yourself can find in almost every American grocery store. This was no accident: Yogi Tea was created and owned by Yogi Bhajan. It's not 3HO's only corporate endeavor—among the group's many enterprises is the half-billion-dollar company Akal Security, which holds contracts with everyone from NASA to immigration detention centers. (What's the word for "late capitalism" in Gurmukhi?)

dering to his arranged marriages, waking up at four thirty every morning to read scripture and attend yoga class, and not associating with anyone who didn't follow . . . or who wouldn't be following soon.

As soon as she turned eighteen, Tasha moved to Los Angeles, one of 3HO's home bases, and for eight years, she dedicated her entire life—all her time and money—to the group. After a series of exhaustive trainings, she became a full-time Kundalini yoga instructor and, within months, was attracting big-name, spiritually curious celebrities to her Malibu classes: Demi Moore, Russell Brand, Owen Wilson, Adrien Brody. Even if they didn't become full-time followers, their attendance was good PR for 3HO. Tasha's swamis (teachers) praised her for raking in the dollars and allegiances of the rich, famous, and seeking. At the café, Tasha unsheathes her phone from an inky black clutch to show me old photos of her and Demi Moore, garbed in ghost-white short-shorts and turbans, twirling around a desert retreat, backdropped by Joshua trees. Tasha slowly blinks her eyelash extensions as a bewildered smile blooms across her face, as if to say, *Yeah, I can't believe I did this shit, either.*

Obedience like Tasha's promised to yield great rewards. Just learn the right words, and they'd be yours: "There was a mantra to attract your soul mate, one to acquire lots of money, one to look better than ever, one to give birth to a more evolved, higher-vibration generation of children," Tasha divulges. Disobey? You'd come back in the next life on a lower vibration.

Mastering 3HO's secret mantras and code words made Tasha feel separate from everyone else she knew. Chosen. On a *higher vibration*. Solidarity like this intensified when everyone in the group was assigned a new name. A name-giver appointed by Yogi Bhajan used something called tantric numerology as an algorithm to determine followers' special 3HO monikers, which they received in exchange for a fee. All women were given the same middle name, Kaur, while men were all christened Singh. Everyone shared the last name Khalsa. Like one big family. "Getting your new name was the biggest deal ever," Tasha says. "Most people would change their names on their driver's licenses." Until last year, Tasha Samar's California ID read "Daya Kaur Khalsa."

It might not have been totally apparent, what with the peaceable yoga classes and high-profile supporters, but there was a dangerous undercurrent to 3HO—psychological and sexual abuse by Yogi Bhajan, forced fasting and sleep deprivation, threats of violence toward anyone attempting to leave the group, suicides, even an unsolved murder. Once followers fully adopted the group's jargon, higher-ups were able to weaponize it. Threats were structured in phrases like "Piscean consciousness," "negative mind," "lizard brain." Take a bite of a friend's meaty burger or fail to attend yoga class, and *lizard brain, lizard brain, lizard brain* would play on a loop in your mind. Often, familiar English terms that once held a positive meaning were recast to signify something threatening. "Like 'old soul,'" Tasha tells me. To an average English speaker, "old soul" connotes someone with wisdom beyond their years. It's a compliment. But in 3HO, it incited dread. "It meant someone had been coming back life after life, incarnation after incarnation, and they couldn't get it right," she explains. Even three years after escaping 3HO, Tasha still shudders whenever she hears the phrase.

In 2009, shortly after Tasha arrived in Southern California to give her life to 3HO, another eighteen-year-old moved to LA to start a new life. Her name was Alyssa Clarke, and she'd come down the coast from Oregon to start college. Afraid of gaining the freshman fifteen, Alyssa decided to try joining a gym. She had always struggled with body image, and she was intimidated by LA's formidable fitness scene. So, over holiday break, when she reunited with a family member who'd recently started a new workout program, dropped a ton of weight, and beamed with the honeymoon glow of fresh muscle tone, Alyssa thought, *Damn, I have to check that out.*

The new workout was called CrossFit, and there was a location right near Alyssa's dorm. Upon returning from break, she and her boyfriend signed up for a beginners workshop. The sweaty, sculpted instructors oozed masculine enthusiasm as they introduced Alyssa to a whole new world of terminology she'd never heard before: The gym wasn't called a gym, it was a "box." Instructors weren't teachers or trainers, they were "coaches." Their workouts consisted of "functional movements." You had your *WoD* (workout of the day), which might consist of snatches and clean-and-jerks. You had your *BPs* (bench presses), your *BSs* (back squats), your *C2Bs* (chest-to-bars), and your inevitable *DOMS* (delayed-onset muscle soreness). Who doesn't love a catchy acronym? Alyssa was captivated by how tight-knit all these Cross-Fitters seemed—they had such a culture—and was dead set on mastering their private patois.

A portrait of CrossFit's founder, Greg Glassman (known then to devotees as "The WoDFather," or simply "Coach"), hung on the wall of Alyssa's box next to one of his most famous quotes, a fitness proverb that would soon sear into her brain: "Eat meat and vegetables, nuts and seeds, some fruit, little starch, and no sugar. Keep intake to levels that will support exercise but not body fat. Practice and train major lifts . . . master the basics of gymnastics . . . bike, run, swim, row . . . hard and fast. Five or six days per week." Alyssa was taken with how CrossFit focused on shaping members' mentalities not just inside the box, but everywhere. When driving trainees to work harder, coaches would bellow "Beast mode!" (a motivational phrase that reverberated through Alyssa's thoughts at school and work, too). To help you internalize the CrossFit philosophy, they'd repeat "EIE," which meant "Everything is everything."

When Alyssa noticed everyone at her box was wearing Lululemon, she went out and dropped $400 on designer workout swag. (Even Lululemon had its own distinctive vernacular. It was printed all over their shopping bags, so customers would walk out of the store carrying mantras like, "There is little difference between addicts and fanatic athletes," "Visualize your eventual demise," and "Friends are more important than money"—all coined by their so-called "tribe" leader, Lululemon's founder, Chip Wilson, an aging G.I. Joe type just like Greg Glassman whose acolytes were equally devout. Who knew fitness could inspire such religiosity?)

As soon as Alyssa learned that most CrossFitters followed a Paleo diet, she cut out gluten and sugar. If she made plans to go out of town and knew she wouldn't be able to make her normal workout time, she quickly alerted someone at the box, lest they publicly shame her in their Facebook group for no-showing. Coaches and members were all fooling around with each other, so after Alyssa and her boyfriend split, she started hooking up with a trainer named Flex (real name: Andy; he changed it after joining the box).

So here's the big question: What do Alyssa's and Tasha's stories have in common?

The answer: They were both under cultish influence. If you're skeptical of applying the same charged "cult" label to both 3HO and CrossFit, good. You should be. For now, let's agree on this: Even though one of our protagonists ended up broke, friendless, and riddled with PTSD, and the other got herself a strained hamstring, a codependent friend with benefits, and a few too many pairs of overpriced leggings, what Tasha Samar and Alyssa Clarke irrefutably share is that one day, they woke up on different sides of Los Angeles and realized they were in so deep, they weren't even speaking recognizable English anymore. Though the stakes and consequences of their respective affiliations differed considerably, the methods used to assert such power—to create community and solidarity, to establish an "us" and a "them," to align collective values, to justify questionable behavior, to instill ideology and inspire fear—were uncannily, cultishly similar. And the most compelling techniques had little to do with drugs, sex, shaved heads, remote communes, drapey kaftans, or "Kool-Aid" . . . instead, they had everything to do with language.

ii.

Cultish groups are an all-out American obsession. One of the most gushed-over debut novels of the 2010s was Emma Cline's *The Girls*, chronicling a teenager's summer-long dalliance with a Manson-type cult in the late 1960s. HBO's 2015 Scientology documentary *Going Clear* was critically deemed "impossible to ignore." Devoured with equal gusto was Netflix's 2018 docuseries *Wild Wild Country*, which told of the controversial guru Osho (Bhagwan Shree Rajneesh) and his Rajneeshpuram commune; embellished by an irresistibly hip playlist and vintage footage of his red-clad apostles, the show earned an Emmy and millions of online streams. All any of my friends could talk about the week I started writing this book was the 2019 folk horror film *Midsommar*, about a (fictional) murderous Dionysian cult in Sweden characterized by psychedelic-fueled sex rituals and human sacrifices. And all anyone is talking about now as I edit this book in 2020 are *The Vow* and *Seduced*, dueling docuseries about NXIVM, the self-help scam turned sex-trafficking ring. The well of cult-inspired art and intrigue is bottomless. When it comes to gurus and their groupies, we just can't seem to look away.

I once heard a psychologist explain that rubbernecking results from a very real physiological response: You see an auto accident, or any disaster—or even just news of a disaster, like a headline—and your brain's amygdala, which controls emotions, memory, and survival tactics, starts firing signals to your problem-solving frontal cortex to try to figure out whether this event is a direct danger to you. You enter fight-or-flight mode, even if you're just sitting there. The reason millions of us binge cult documentaries or go down rabbit holes researching groups from Jonestown to QAnon is not that there's some twisted voyeur inside us all that's inexplicably attracted to darkness. We've all seen enough car crashes and read enough cult exposés; if all we wanted was a spooky fix, we'd be bored already. But we're not bored, because we're still hunting for a satisfying answer to the question of what causes seemingly "normal" people to join—and, more important, stay in—fanatical fringe groups with extreme ideologies. We're scanning for threats, on some level wondering, *Is everyone susceptible to cultish influence?* Could it happen to you? Could it happen to me? And if so, how?

Our culture tends to provide pretty flimsy answers to questions of cult influence, mostly having to do with vague talk of "brainwashing." Why did all those people die in Jonestown? "They drank the Kool-Aid!" Why don't abused polygamist sister wives get the hell out of Dodge as soon as they can? "They're mind controlled!" Simple as that.

But it's actually not that simple. In fact, brainwashing is a pseudoscientific concept that the majority of psychologists I interviewed denounce (more on that in a bit). Truer answers to the question of cult influence can only arrive

Cultish

when you ask the right questions: What techniques do charismatic leaders use to exploit people's fundamental needs for community and meaning? How do they cultivate that kind of power?

The answer, as it turns out, is not some freaky mind-bending wizardry that happens on a remote commune where everyone dons flower crowns and dances in the sun. (That's called Coachella . . . which, one could argue, is its own kind of "cult.") The real answer all comes down to words. Delivery. From the crafty redefinition of existing words (and the invention of new ones) to powerful euphemisms, secret codes, renamings, buzzwords, chants and mantras, "speaking in tongues," forced silence, even hashtags, language is the key means by which all degrees of cultlike influence occur. Exploitative spiritual gurus know this, but so do pyramid schemers, politicians, CEOs of start-ups, online conspiracy theorists, workout instructors, even social media influencers. In both positive ways and shadowy ones, "cult language" is, in fact, something we hear and are swayed by every single day. Our speech in regular life—at work, in Spin class, on Instagram—is evidence of our varying degrees of "cult" membership. You just have to know what to listen for. Indeed, while we're distracted by the Manson Family's peculiar outfits* and other flashy

---

* The infatuation with cult garb runs deep: In 1997, thirty-nine members of Heaven's Gate, a UFO fringe religion we'll talk about in part 2, participated in a mass suicide, all wearing matching pairs of black-and-white '93 Nike Decade sneakers. Two surviving Heaven's Gate followers maintain that their leader chose the footwear

"cult" iconography, what we wind up missing is the fact that one of the biggest factors in getting people to a point of extreme devotion, and keeping them there, is something we cannot see.

Though "cult language" comes in different varieties, all charismatic leaders—from Jim Jones to Jeff Bezos to SoulCycle instructors—use the same basic linguistic tools. This is a book about the language of fanaticism in its many forms: a language I'm calling *Cultish* (like English, Spanish, or Swedish). Part 1 of this book will investigate the language we use to talk about cultish groups, busting some widely believed myths about what the word "cult" even means. Then, parts 2 through 5 will unveil the key elements of cultish language, and how they've worked to inveigle followers of groups as destructive as Heaven's Gate and Scientology . . . but also how they pervade our day-to-day vocabularies. In these pages, we'll discover what motivates people, throughout history and now, to become fanatics, both for good and for evil. Once you understand what the language of "Cultish" sounds like, you won't be able to unhear it.

Language is a leader's charisma. It's what empowers them to create a mini universe—a system of values and truths—and then compel their followers to heed its rules. In 1945,

for no particular reason other than that he found a good bulk deal. Nike hastily discontinued the style after the tragedy (nothing like a cult suicide to ruin your product's good name), but that made the sneakers an instant collector's item. At the time of this writing, twenty-two years post–Heaven's Gate, a pair of size 12 Nike Decades from 1993 was listed on eBay for $6,600.

the French philosopher Maurice Merleau-Ponty wrote that language is human beings' element just as "water is the element of fish." So it's not as if Tasha's foreign mantras and Alyssa's acronyms played some small role in molding their "cult" experiences. Rather, because words are the medium through which belief systems are manufactured, nurtured, and reinforced, their fanaticism fundamentally could not exist without them. "Without language, there are no beliefs, ideology, or religion," John E. Joseph, a professor of applied linguistics at the University of Edinburgh, wrote to me from Scotland. "These concepts require a language as a condition of their existence." Without language, there are no "cults."

Certainly, you can hold beliefs without explicitly articulating them, and it's also true that if Tasha or Alyssa did not want to buy into their leaders' messages, no collection of words could've forced them into it. But with a glimmer of willingness, language can do so much to squash independent thinking, obscure truths, encourage confirmation bias, and emotionally charge experiences such that no other way of life seems possible. The way a person communicates can tell us a lot about who they've been associating with, who they've been influenced by. How far their allegiance goes.

The motives behind culty-sounding language are not always crooked. Sometimes they're quite healthy, like to boost solidarity or to rally people around a humanitarian mission. One of my best friends works for a cancer nonprofit and brings back amusing stories of the love-bomb-y buzzwords and quasi-religious mantras they repeat on end to keep fund-raisers hyped: "Someday is today"; "This is our Week of Winning"; "Let's fly above and beyond"; "You are the greatest generation of warriors and heroes in this quest for a cancer cure." "It reminds me of the way multi-level marketing people talk," she tells me (referencing culty direct sales companies like Mary Kay and Amway—more on these later). "It's cultlike, but for a good cause. And hey, it works." In part 5 of this book, we'll learn about all sorts of woo-woo chants and hymns used in "cult fitness" studios that may sound extremist to skeptical outsiders, but aren't actually all that destructive when you take a closer listen.

Whether wicked or well-intentioned, language is a way to get members of a community on the same ideological page. To help them feel like they belong to something big. "Language provides a culture of shared understanding," said Eileen Barker, a sociologist who studies new religious movements at the London School of Economics. But wherever there are fanatically worshipped leaders and belief-bound cliques, some level of psychological pressure is at play. This could be as quotidian as your average case of FOMO, or as treacherous as being coerced to commit violent crimes. "Quite frankly, the language is everything," one ex-Scientologist told me in a hushed tone during an interview. "It's what insulates you. It makes you feel special, like you're in the know, because you have this other language to communicate with."

Before we can get into the nuts and bolts of cultish language, however, we must focus on a key definition: What does the word "cult" even mean, exactly? As it turns out, coming up with one conclusive definition is tricky at best. Over the course of researching and writing this book, my understanding of the word has only become hazier and more fluid. I'm not the only one flummoxed by how to pin down "cult." I recently conducted a small street survey near my home in Los Angeles, where I asked a couple dozen strangers what they thought the word meant; answers ranged from "A small group of believers led by a deceptive figure with too much power" to "Any group of people who are really passionate about something" all the way to "Well, a cult could be anything, couldn't it? You could have a coffee cult, or a surfing cult." And not a single response was delivered with certainty.

There's a reason for this semantic murkiness. It's connected to the fact that the fascinating etymology of "cult" (which I'll chronicle shortly) corresponds precisely to our society's ever-changing relationship to spirituality, community, meaning, and identity—a relationship that's gotten rather . . . *weird*. Language change is always reflective of social change, and over the decades, as our sources of connection and existential purpose have shifted due to phenomena like social media, increased globalization, and withdrawal from traditional religion, we've seen the rise of more alternative subgroups—some dangerous, some not so much. "Cult" has evolved to describe them all.

I've found that "cult" has become one of those terms that can mean something totally different depending on the context of the conversation and the attitudes of the speaker. It can be invoked as a damning accusation implying death and destruction, a cheeky metaphor suggesting not much more than some matching outfits and enthusiasm, and pretty much everything in between.

In modern discourse, someone could apply the word "cult" to a new religion, a group of online radicals, a start-up, and a makeup brand all in the same breath. While working at a beauty magazine a few years ago, I promptly noticed how commonplace it was for cosmetics brands to invoke "cult" as a marketing term to generate buzz for new product launches. A cursory search for the word in my old work inbox yielded thousands of results. "Take a sneak peek at the next cult phenomenon," reads a press release from a trendy makeup line, swearing that the new face powder from their so-called Cult Lab will "send beauty junkies and makeup fanatics into a frenzy." Another pitch from a skincare company vows that their $150 "Cult Favorites Set" of CBD-infused elixirs "is more than skincare, it's the priceless gift of an opportunity to decompress and love oneself in order to handle whatever life throws at them." A priceless opportunity? To handle *anything*? The promised benefits of this eye cream sound not unlike those of a spiritual grifter.

Confusing as this panoply of "cult" definitions might sound, we seem to be navigating it okay. Sociolinguists have found that overall, listeners are quite savvy at making contextual inferences about the meaning and stakes implied whenever a familiar word is used in conversation. Generally, we're able to infer that when we talk about the cult of Jonestown, we mean something different from the "cult" of

CBD skincare or Taylor Swift fans. Of course, there is room for misinterpretation, as there always is with language. But overall, most seasoned conversationalists understand that when we describe certain fitness fiends as "cult followers," we might be referencing their intense, indeed religious-seeming devotion, but we're probably not worried that they're going to drown in financial ruin or stop speaking to their families (at least, not as a condition of their membership). Regarding Swifties or SoulCyclers, "cult" may serve as more of a metaphor, similar to how one might compare school or work to a "prison," as a way to describe an oppressive environment or harsh higher-ups, without raising concerns about literal jail cells. When I sent my initial interview request to Tanya Luhrmann, a Stanford psychological anthropologist and well-known scholar of fringe religions, she responded with "Dear Amanda, I would be happy to talk. I do think that SoulCycle is a cult :-)"—but during our conversation later, she clarified that the statement was more tongue-in-cheek and something she'd never say formally. Which, of course, I already understood. We'll hear more from Tanya later.

With groups like SoulCycle, "cult" works to describe members' fierce fidelity to a cultural coterie that may very well remind us of some aspects of a Manson-level dangerous group—the monetary and time commitment, the conformism, and the exalted leadership (all of which certainly have the potential to turn toxic)—but not the wholesale isolation from outsiders or life-threatening lies and abuse. We know without needing to explicitly state it that the possibility of death or a physical inability to leave is not on the table.

But, like everything in life, there is no good cult/bad cult binary; cultishness falls on a spectrum. Steven Hassan, a mental health counselor, author of *The Cult of Trump*, and one of the country's foremost cult experts, has described an influence continuum representing groups from healthy and constructive to unhealthy and destructive. Hassan says that groups toward the destructive end use three kinds of deception: omission of what you need to know, distortion to make whatever they're saying more acceptable, and outright lies. One of the major differences between so-called ethical cults (Hassan references sports and music fans) and noxious ones is that an ethical group will be up-front about what they believe in, what they want from you, and what they expect from your membership. And leaving comes with few, if any, serious consequences. "If you say 'I found a better band' or 'I'm not into basketball anymore,' the other people won't threaten you," Hassan clarifies. "You won't have irrational fears that you'll go insane or be possessed by demons."†

Or, in the case of our former 3HO member, Tasha, turn into a cockroach. "To my core," Tasha answered, when I

---

† Although "stan culture"—camps of online superfans who religiously worship and defend music stars like Taylor Swift, Lady Gaga, and Beyoncé—has gotten dicier than the celebrity fandom of generations past. In 2014, a psychiatric study found that celebrity stans tend to struggle with psychosocial issues like body dysmorphia, cosmetic surgery obsession, and poor judgment of interpersonal boundaries, as well as mental health conditions like anxiety and social dysfunction. The same study found that stans may also display qualities of narcissism, stalking behavior, and dissociation. We'll talk more about the ups and downs of "pop culture cults" in part 6.

Cultish

asked if she truly believed the group's promise that if she committed a serious offense, like sleeping with her guru or taking her life, she'd come back as the world's most reviled insect. Tasha also believed that if you died in the presence of someone holy, you'd reincarnate higher. Once, she spotted a cockroach in a public restroom and was convinced it was a swami who'd done something awful in a past life and was trying to come back on a higher vibration. "I was like, 'Oh my God, he's trying to die around me because I am an elevated teacher.'" Tasha shivered. When the cockroach scuttled up into the full sink, Tasha opened the plug so it wouldn't have the honor of drowning in her proximity. "I freaked out and ran out of the bathroom," she recounted. "That was probably the pinnacle of my insanity."

By contrast, our CrossFitter Alyssa Clarke told me that the scariest possible outcome for her might be getting called lazy on Facebook if she skipped a workout. Or, if she decided to quit the box and start Spinning instead (heaven forbid), her old pals and paramours might slowly dissolve from her life.

It is to qualify this wide gamut of cultlike communities that we've come up with colloquial modifiers like "cult-followed," "culty," and (indeed) "cultish."

iii.

It's really no coincidence that "cults" are having such a proverbial moment. The twenty-first century has produced a climate of sociopolitical unrest and mistrust of long-established institutions, like church, government, Big Pharma, and big business. It's the perfect societal recipe for making new and unconventional groups—everything from Reddit incels to woo-woo wellness influencers—who promise to provide answers that the conventional ones couldn't supply seem freshly appealing. Add the development of social media and declining marriage rates, and culture-wide feelings of isolation are at an all-time high. Civic engagement is at a record-breaking low. In 2019, *Forbes* labeled loneliness an "epidemic."

Human beings are really bad at loneliness. We're not built for it. People have been attracted to tribes of like-minded others ever since the time of ancient humans, who communed in close-knit groups for survival. But beyond the evolutionary advantage, community also makes us feel a mysterious thing called happiness. Neuroscientists have found that our brains release feel-good chemicals like dopamine and oxytocin when we partake in transcendent bonding rituals, like group chanting and singing. Our nomadic hunter-gatherer ancestors used to pack their village squares to engage in ritualistic dances, though there was no practical need for them. Modern citizens of countries like Denmark and Canada, whose governments prioritize community connection (through high-quality public transportation, neighborhood co-ops, etc.), self-report higher degrees of satisfaction and fulfillment. All kinds of research points to the idea that humans are social and spiritual by design. Our behavior is driven by a desire for belonging and purpose. We're "cultish" by nature.

This fundamental human itch for connection is touching, but when steered in the wrong direction, it can also cause an otherwise judicious person to do utterly irrational things. Consider this classic study: In 1951, Swarthmore College psychologist Solomon Asch gathered together half a dozen students to conduct a simple "vision test." Asch showed four vertical lines to the participants, all but one of whom were in on the experiment, and asked them to point to the two that were the same length. There was one obviously correct answer, which you needed zero skills other than eyesight to figure out, but Asch found that if the first five students pointed to a blatantly wrong answer, 75 percent of test subjects ignored their better judgment and agreed with the majority. This ingrained fear of alienation, this compulsion to conform, is part of what makes being part of a group feel so right. It's also what charismatic leaders, from 3HO's Yogi Bhajan to CrossFit's Greg Glassman, have learned to channel and exploit.

It was once true that when in need of community and answers, people defaulted to organized religion. But increasingly this is no longer the case. Every day, more and more Americans are dropping their affiliations with mainstream churches and scattering. The "spiritual but not religious" label is something most of my twentysomething friends have claimed. Pew Research data from 2019 found that four in ten millennials don't identify with any religious affiliation; this was up nearly 20 percentage points from seven years prior. A 2015 Harvard Divinity School study found that young people are still seeking "both a deep spiritual experience and a community experience" to imbue their lives with meaning—but fewer than ever are satisfying these desires with conventional faith.

To classify this skyrocketing demographic of religious disaffiliates, scholars have come up with labels like the "Nones" and the "Remixed." The latter term was coined by Tara Isabella Burton, a theologian, reporter, and author of *Strange Rites: New Religions for a Godless World*. "Remixed" describes the tendency of contemporary seekers to mix and match beliefs and rituals from different circles (religious and secular) to come up with a bespoke spiritual routine. Say, a meditation class in the morning, horoscopes in the afternoon, and then ultra-Reform Friday night Shabbat with friends.

Spiritual meaning often doesn't involve God at all anymore. The Harvard Divinity School study named SoulCycle and CrossFit among the groups giving America's youth a modern religious identity. "It gives you what religion gives you, which is the feeling that your life matters," Chani Green, a twenty-six-year-old actress and die-hard SoulCycler living in Los Angeles, told me of the exercise craze. "The cynicism we have now is almost antihuman. We need to feel connected to something, like we're put on earth for a reason other than just dying. At SoulCycle, for forty-five minutes, I feel that."

For those who bristle at the idea of comparing workout classes to religion, know that as tricky as it is to define "cult," scholars have been arguing even harder for centuries over how to classify "religion." You might have a feeling that Christianity is a religion, while fitness is not, but even experts have a tough time distinguishing exactly why. I like Burton's way of looking at it, which is less about what religions are and more about what religions do, which is to provide the following four things: meaning, purpose, a sense of community, and ritual. Less and less often are seekers finding these things at church.

Modern cultish groups also feel comforting in part because they help alleviate the anxious mayhem of living in a world that presents almost too many possibilities for who to be (or at least the illusion of such). I once had a therapist tell me that flexibility without structure isn't flexibility at all; it's just chaos. That's how a lot of people's lives have been feeling. For most of America's history, there were comparatively few directions a person's career, hobbies, place of residence, romantic relationships, diet, aesthetic— everything—could easily go in. But the twenty-first century presents folks (those of some privilege, that is) with a Cheesecake Factory–size menu of decisions to make. The sheer quantity can be paralyzing, especially in an era of radical self-creation, when there's such pressure to craft a strong "personal brand" at the very same time that morale and basic survival feel more precarious for young people than they have in a long time. As our generational lore goes, millennials' parents told them they could grow up to be whatever they wanted, but then that cereal aisle of endless "what ifs" and "could bes" turned out to be so crushing, all they wanted was a guru to tell them which to pick.

"I want someone to tell me what to wear every morning. I want someone to tell me what to eat," Phoebe Waller-Bridge's thirty-three-year-old character confesses to her priest (the hot one) in season 2 of her Emmy-winning series *Fleabag*. "What to hate, what to rage about, what to listen to, what band to like, what to buy tickets for, what to joke about, what not to joke about. I want someone to tell me what to believe in, who to vote for, who to love, and how to tell them. I just think I want someone to tell me how to live my life."

Following a guru who provides an identity template—from one's politics to one's hairstyle—eases that chooser's paradox. This concept can be applied to spiritual extremists like Scientologists and 3HO members, but also to loyalists of social media celebrities and "cult brands" like Lululemon or Glossier. Just being able to say "I'm a Glossier girl" or "I follow Dr. Joe Dispenza" (a dubious self-help star we'll meet in part 6) softens the burden and responsibility of having to make so many independent choices about what you think and who you are. It cuts the overwhelming number of answers you need to have down to a manageable few. You can simply ask, "What would a Glossier girl do?" And base your day's decisions—your perfume, your news sources, all of it—on that framework.

The tide of change away from mainstream establishments and toward nontraditional groups is not at all new. It's something we've seen all over the world at several different junctures in human history. Society's attraction to so-called cults (both the propensity to join them and the anthropological fascination with them) tends to thrive during periods of broader existential questioning. Most alternative religious leaders come to power not to exploit their followers, but instead to guide them through social and political turbulence. Jesus of Nazareth (you may be familiar) arose during what is said to be the most fraught time in Middle Eastern history (a fact which speaks for itself). The violent, encroaching Roman Empire left people searching for a nonestablishment guide who could inspire and protect them. Fifteen hundred years later, during the tempestuous European Renaissance, dozens of "cults" cropped up in rebellion against the Catholic Church. In seventeenth-century India, fringe groups grew out of the social discord that resulted from the shift to agriculture, and then as a reaction to British imperialism.

Compared to other developed nations, the US boasts a particularly consistent relationship with "cults," which speaks to our brand of distinctly American tumult. Across the world, levels of religiosity tend to be lowest in countries with the highest standards of living (strong education levels, long life expectancies), but the US is exceptional in that it's both highly developed and full of believers—even with all our "Nones" and "Remixed." This inconsistency can be explained in part because while citizens of other advanced nations, like Japan and Sweden, enjoy a bevy of top-down resources, including universal healthcare and all sorts of social safety nets, the US is more of a free-for-all. "The Japanese and the Europeans know their governments will come to their aid in their hour of need," wrote Dr. David Ludden, a language psychologist at Georgia Gwinnett College, for *Psychology Today*. But America's laissez-faire atmosphere makes people feel all on their own. Generation after generation, this lack of institutional support paves the way for alternative, supernaturally minded groups to surge.

This pattern of American unrest was also responsible for the rise of cultish movements throughout the 1960s and '70s, when the Vietnam War, the civil rights movement, and both Kennedy assassinations knocked US citizens unsteady. At the time, spiritual practice was spiking, but the overt reign of traditional Protestantism was declining, so new movements arose to quench that cultural thirst. These included everything from Christian offshoots like Jews for Jesus and the Children of God to Eastern-derived fellowships like 3HO and Shambhala Buddhism to pagan groups like the Covenant of the Goddess and the Church of Aphrodite to sci-fi-esque ones like Scientology and Heaven's Gate. Some scholars now refer to this era as the Fourth Great Awakening. (The first three were a string of zealous evangelical revivals that whirred through the American Northeast during the 1700s and 1800s.)

Different from the earlier Protestant awakenings, the fourth was populated by seekers looking toward the East and the occult to inspire individualistic quests for enlightenment. Just like twenty-first-century "cult followers," these seekers were mostly young, countercultural, politically divergent types who felt the powers that be had failed them. If you subscribe to an astrology app or have ever attended a music festival, odds are that in the 1970s, you'd have brushed up against a "cult" of some kind.

Ultimately, the needs for identity, purpose, and belonging have existed for a very long time, and cultish groups have always sprung up during cultural limbos when these needs have gone sorely unmet. What's new is that in this internet-ruled age, when a guru can be godless, when the barrier to entry is as low as a double-tap, and when folks who hold alternative beliefs are able to find one another more easily than ever, it only makes sense that secular cults—from obsessed workout studios to start-ups that put the "cult" in "company culture"—would start sprouting like dandelions. For good or for ill, there is now a cult for everyone.

iv.

A couple of years ago, amid a conversation about my decision in college to quit the competitive (and quite cultish) theater program at my university in favor of a linguistics major, my mother told me that my change of heart really came as no surprise to her since she'd always considered me profoundly "un-culty." I chose to take this as a compliment, since I definitely wouldn't want to be characterized the opposite way, but it also didn't fully digest as praise. That's because, juxtaposed with the dark elements, there's a certain sexiness surrounding cults—the unconventional aspect, the mysticism, the communal intimacy. In this way, the word has almost come full circle.

"Cult" hasn't always carried ominous undertones. The earliest version of the term can be found in writings from the seventeenth century, when the cult label was much more innocent. Back then, it simply meant "homage paid to divinity," or offerings made to win over the gods. The words "culture" and "cultivation," derived from the same Latin verb, *cultus*, are "cult"'s close morphological cousins.

The word evolved in the early nineteenth century, a time of experimental religious brouhaha in the United States. The American colonies, which were founded upon the freedom

Cultish

to practice new religions, gained a reputation as a safe haven where eccentric believers could get as freaky as they liked. This spiritual freedom opened the door for a stampede of alternative social and political groups, too. During the mid-1800s, well over one hundred small ideological cliques formed and collapsed. When the French political scientist Alexis de Tocqueville came to visit the US in the 1830s, he was astonished by how "Americans of all ages, all stations in life, and all types of disposition [were] forever forming associations." "Cults" of the time included groups like the Oneida Community, a camp of polyamorous communists in upstate New York (sounds fun); the Harmony Society, an egalitarian fellowship of science lovers in Indiana (how lovely); and (my favorite) a short-lived vegan farming cult in Massachusetts called Fruitlands, which was founded by philosopher Amos Bronson Alcott, an abolitionist, women's rights activist, and father of *Little Women* author Louisa May Alcott. Back then, "cult" merely served as a sort of churchly classification, alongside "religion" and "sect." The word denoted something new or unorthodox, but not necessarily nefarious.

The term started gaining its darker reputation toward the start of the Fourth Great Awakening. That's when the emergence of so many nonconformist spiritual groups spooked old-school conservatives and Christians. "Cults" soon became associated with charlatans, quacks, and heretical kooks. But they still weren't considered much of a societal threat or criminal priority . . . not until the Manson Family murders of 1969, followed by the Jonestown massacre of 1978 (which we'll investigate in part 2). After that, the word "cult" became a symbol of fear.

The grisly death of over nine hundred people at Jonestown, the largest number of American civilian casualties prior to 9/11, sent the whole country into cult delirium. Some readers may recall the subsequent "Satanic Panic," a period in the '80s defined by widespread paranoia that Satan-worshipping child abusers were terrorizing wholesome American neighborhoods. As sociologist Ron Enroth wrote in his 1979 book *The Lure of the Cults*, "The unprecedented media exposure given Jonestown . . . alerted Americans to the fact that seemingly beneficent religious groups can mask a hellish rot."

Then, as these things tend to go, as soon as cults became frightening, they also became cool. Seventies pop culture didn't wait long to birth terms like "cult film" and "cult classic," which described the up-and-coming genre of underground indie movies like *The Rocky Horror Picture Show*. Bands like Phish and the Grateful Dead came to be known for their peripatetic "cult followings."

A generation or two after the Fourth Great Awakening, the era began to take on a nostalgic cool factor among cult-curious youth. Fringe groups from the '70s now boast a sort of perversely stylish vintage cachet. At this point, being obsessed with the Manson Family is akin to having an extensive collection of hippie-era vinyl and band tees. At an LA salon the other week, I eavesdropped on a woman telling her stylist that she was going for a "Manson girl" hair look: overgrown, brunette, middle-parted. A twentysomething acquaintance of mine recently hosted a cult-themed birthday party in New York's Hudson Valley—the site of numerous historical "cults" (including The Family,* NXIVM, and countless witches), as well as the Woodstock music festival. The dress code? All white. Filtered photographs of guests sporting ivory slips and glassy-eyed "oops, I didn't know I was haunted" expressions flooded my Instagram feed.

Over the decades, the word "cult" has become so sensationalized, so romanticized, that most experts I spoke to don't even use it anymore. Their stance is that the meaning of "cult" is too broad and subjective to be useful, at least in academic literature. As recently as the 1990s, scholars had no problem tossing around the term to describe any group "considered by many to be deviant." But it doesn't take a social scientist to see the bias built into that categorization.

A few scholars have tried to get more precise and identify specific "cult" criteria: charismatic leaders, mind-altering behaviors, sexual and financial exploitation, an us-versus-them mentality toward nonmembers, and an ends-justify-the-means philosophy. Stephen Kent, a sociology professor at the University of Alberta, adds that "cult" has typically been applied to groups that have some degree of supernat-

---

* There are several cultish groups who hide behind the vague moniker "The Family." This one was a '60s-born New Age doomsday commune run by a sadistic Australian yoga instructor named Anne Hamilton-Byrne, who (common story) claimed messiah status and was busted in the late '80s for kidnapping over a dozen children and abusing them in aberrant ways, like forcing them to take ritualistic heaps of LSD.

ural beliefs, though that isn't always the case. (Angels and demons don't usually make their way into, say, cosmetics pyramid schemes. Except when they do . . . more on that in part 4.) But Kent says the result of all these institutions is the same: a power imbalance built on members' devotion, hero worship, and absolute trust, which frequently facilitates abuse on the part of unaccountable leaders. The glue that keeps this trust intact is members' belief that their leaders have a rare access to transcendent wisdom, which allows them to exercise control over their systems of rewards and punishments, both here on earth and in the afterlife. Based on my conversations, these qualities seem to encapsulate what many everyday folks view as a "real cult" or "the academic definition of a cult."

But as it turns out, "cult" doesn't have an official academic definition. "Because it's inherently pejorative," Rebecca Moore, a religion professor at San Diego State University, clarified during a phone interview. "It's simply used to describe groups we don't like." Moore comes to the subject of cults from a unique place: Her two sisters were among those who perished in the Jonestown massacre; in fact, Jim Jones enlisted them to help pull off the event. But Moore told me she doesn't use the word "cult" in earnest because it's become inarguably judgment-laden. "As soon as someone says it, we know as readers, listeners, or individuals exactly what we should think about that particular group," she explained.

Equally, "brainwashing" is a term that is tossed around incessantly by the media, but that almost every expert I consulted for this book either avoids or rejects. "We don't say that soldiers are brainwashed to kill other people; that's basic training," offers Moore. "We don't say that fraternity members are brainwashed to haze† their [pledges]; that's peer pressure." Most of us tend to take "brainwashing" literally, imagining that some neurological rewiring occurs during cult indoctrinations. But brainwashing is a metaphor. There is nothing objective about it.

Moore would be the perfect candidate to believe in literal brainwashing, considering her two sisters' role in the Jonestown tragedy. But she still refutes the concept because, for one, it disregards people's very real ability to think for themselves. Human beings are not helpless drones whose decision-making skills are so fragile that they can be wiped clean at any time. If brainwashing were real, says Moore, "we would expect to see many more dangerous people running around, planning to carry out reprehensible schemes." Simply put, you cannot force someone to believe something

---

† Here's a fun little story: In 1959, a Southern California cult conducted an unusual initiation ceremony. Men who wished to be part of the clan had to prove their devotion by ingesting a nightmarish buffet of pig's head, fresh brains, and raw liver. In his attempts to complete the challenge, one young recruit named Richard kept vomiting up the concoction, but desperate for acceptance, he eventually forced it down. Promptly, a hulking mass of liver became wedged in his windpipe and he choked on it; by the time he reached the hospital, he was dead. But no criminal charges were ever filed, because this wasn't actually a "cult"—it was a fraternity at USC, enacting just one of countless pledge-hazing rituals, which are often far more disgusting, outlandish, and deadly and involve more vomit (and other bodily fluids) than anything you'll find in most alternative religions.

they absolutely do not on any level want to believe by using some set of evil techniques to "wash" their brain.

Secondly, Moore argues, brainwashing presents an untestable hypothesis. For a theory to meet the standard criteria of the scientific method, it has to be controvertible; that is, it must be possible to prove the thing false. (For example, as soon as objects start traveling faster than the speed of light, we'll know that Einstein got his Theory of Special Relativity wrong.) But you can't prove that brainwashing doesn't exist. The minute you say someone is "brainwashed," the conversation ends there. No room is left to explore what might actually be motivating the person's behavior—which, as it turns out, is a much more interesting question.

When tossed around to describe everyone from a political candidate's supporters to militant vegans, the terms "cult" and "brainwashing" acquire a sort of armchair-therapist éclat. We all love a chance to feel psychologically and morally superior without having to think about why, and calling a whole bunch of people "brainwashed cult followers" does just that.

This negative bias is detrimental because not all "cults" are depraved or perilous. Statistically, in fact, few of them are. Barker (our London School of Economics sociologist) says that out of the thousand-plus alternative groups she's documented that have been or could be described as "cults," the vast majority have not been involved with criminal activity of any kind. Moore and Barker note that fringe communities only gain publicity when they do something awful, like Heaven's Gate and Jonestown. (And even those groups didn't set out with murder and mayhem in mind. After all, Jonestown started out as an integrationist church. Things escalated as Jim Jones grew hungrier for power, but most "cults" never spiral as catastrophically as his did.) A feedback loop of scandal is created: Only the most destructive cults gain attention, so we come to think of all cults as destructive, and we simultaneously only recognize the destructive ones as cults, so those gain more attention, reinforcing their negative reputation, and so on ad infinitum.

Equally troubling is the fact that the word "cult" has so frequently been used as permission to trash religions that society just doesn't approve of. So many of today's longest-standing religious denominations (Catholics, Baptists, Mormons, Quakers, Jews, and most Native American religions, to name a few) were once considered unholy blasphemies in the United States—and this was a nation founded on religious freedom. Today, American alternative religions (oppressive and not), from Jehovah's Witnesses to Wiccans, are widely regarded as "cults." The Chinese government insistently decries the cultish evils of new religion Falun Gong, despite its peaceful tenets, which include patience and compassion through meditation. Barker has noted that official reports out of majority-Catholic Belgium condemn the Quakers (just about the chillest religion ever) as a "cult" (or *secte* actually, as the word *culte* in French has held on to its neutral connotations).

Throughout the world, cultural normativity still has so much to do with a religious group's perceived legitimacy . . .

no matter if its teachings are any weirder or more harmful than a better-established group. After all, what major spiritual leader doesn't have some trace of blood on their hands? As the religion scholar Reza Aslan famously stated, "The biggest joke in religious studies is that cult + time = religion."

In the US, Mormonism and Catholicism have been around long enough that they've been given our stamp of approval. Having earned the status of religion, they enjoy a certain amount of common respect and, importantly, protection under the Constitution's First Amendment. Because of this protection variable, labeling something a "cult" becomes not just a value judgment, but an arbiter of real, life-or-death consequences. To quote Megan Goodwin, a researcher of American alternative religions at Northeastern University, "The political ramifications of identifying something as a cult are real and often violent."

What do these ramifications look like? Dig no deeper than Jonestown. Once the press identified Jonestown's victims as "cultists," they were instantly relegated to a subclass of human. "This made it easier for the public to distance themselves from the tragedy and its victims, dismissing them as weak, gullible, unsuited to life, and unworthy of postmortem respect," wrote Laura Elizabeth Woollett, author of the Jonestown-inspired novel *Beautiful Revolutionary*. "Bodies weren't autopsied. Families were denied the timely return of their relatives' remains."

Perhaps the most significant fiasco that resulted from demonizing "cult followers" was the case of the Branch Davidians—the victims of the notorious Waco siege of

1993. Founded in 1959, the Branch Davidians were a religious movement descended from the Seventh-day Adventist Church. At its peak in the early 1990s, the group had about one hundred members, who lived together on a settlement in Waco, Texas, preparing for the Second Coming of Jesus Christ under the abusive governance of David Koresh, who claimed to be a prophet (as solipsistic new religious leaders often do). Reasonably perturbed and in urgent need of help, followers' families tipped off the FBI, who, in February 1993, seized the Branch Davidian compound. Several dozen agents arrived, armed with rifles, tanks, and tear gas, to "save" the "brainwashed cult followers." But the invasion didn't go to plan. Instead, it led to a fifty-one-day standoff, which ended only after a few hundred more FBI agents showed up and used tear gas to flush their targets out of hiding. In the mayhem, a fire broke out, resulting in the deaths of nearly eighty Branch Davidians.

Koresh was not innocent in all this. He was maniacal and violent (in fact, he may have lit the fatal flame), and his stubbornness was part of what led to so many casualties. But so was the fear surrounding the word "cult." If the FBI had applied such excessive violence to a more socially accepted religion, one that benefited from the First Amendment safeguard, there likely would have been much more of an uproar. Their attack on the Branch Davidian base, by contrast, was both legally sanctioned and socially condoned. "Religion is a constitutionally protected category . . . and the identification of Waco's Branch Davidians as a cult places them outside the protections of the state," explains

Catherine Wessinger, a religion scholar at Loyola University in New Orleans. The FBI may have gone to "save" the Branch Davidians, but when they killed them instead, few Americans cared, because they weren't a church—they were a "cult." Alas, the semantics of sanctimony.

In a classic 1999 study, the famous Stanford psychologist Albert Bandura revealed that when human subjects were labeled with dehumanizing language such as "animals," participants were more willing to harm them by administering electric shocks. It seems that the "cult" label can serve a similar function. This is not to say that some groups that have been or could be called cults aren't hazardous; certainly, plenty of them are. Instead, because the word "cult" is so emotionally charged and up for interpretation, the label itself does not provide enough information for us to determine if a group is dangerous. We have to look more carefully. We have to be more specific.

In an attempt to find a less judgy way to discuss nonmainstream spiritual communities, many scholars have used neutral-sounding labels like "new religious movements," "emergent religions," and "marginalized religions." But while these phrases work in an academic context, I find they don't quite capture the CrossFits, multilevel marketing companies, college theater programs, and other hard-to-categorize points along the influence continuum. We need a more versatile way to talk about communities that are cult-like in one way or another but not necessarily connected to the supernatural. Which is why I like the word "cultish."

V.

I grew up entranced by all things "cult," mostly because of my father: As a kid, he was forced to join one. In 1969, when my dad, Craig Montell, was fourteen, his absentee father and stepmother decided they wanted in on the blossoming countercultural movement. So they moved young Craig and his two toddler-age half sisters onto a remote Socialist commune outside San Francisco called Synanon. In the late 1950s, Synanon started as a rehabilitation center for hard-drug users, labeled "dope fiends," but later extended to accommodate non-drug-addicted "lifestylers." In Synanon, children lived in barracks miles away from their parents, and no one was allowed to work or go to school on the outside. Some members were forced to shave their heads; many married couples were separated and assigned new partners. But everyone on the Synanon settlement, no exceptions, had to play "the Game."

The Game was a ritualistic activity where every evening, members were divided into small circles and subjected to hours of vicious personal criticism by their peers. This practice was the centerpiece of Synanon; in fact, life there was divided into two semantic categories: *in the Game* and *out of the Game*. These confrontations were presented as group therapy, but really, they were a form of social control. There was nothing fun about the Game, which could be hostile or humiliating, yet it was referred to as something you "played." It turns out that this type of extreme "truth-telling" activity is not uncommon in cultish groups; Jim Jones hosted similar events called Family Meetings or Catharsis Meetings, where followers would all gather in the Mother Church on Wednesday nights. During these meetings, anyone who had offended the group in some way was called to the Floor so their family and friends could malign them to prove their greater loyalty to the Cause. (More on all that in part 2.)

I cut my teeth on Synanon tales from my father, who escaped at seventeen and went on to become a prolific neuroscientist. Now his very job is to ask hard questions and seek proof at every turn. My dad was always so generous with his storytelling, indulging my wide-eyed curiosity by repeating the same stories of Synanon's dismal living quarters and conformist milieu, of the biologist he met there who tasked him with running the commune's medical lab at age fifteen. While his peers outside Synanon were fretting over puppy-love squabbles and SAT prep, my dad was culturing followers' throat swabs and testing food handlers' fingertips for tuberculosis microbes. The lab was a sanctuary for my dad, a rare space on Synanon's grounds where the rules of empirical logic applied. Paradoxically, it's where he found his love of science. Hungry for an education outside the commune's closed system—and desperate for a legitimate diploma that would allow him to attend college—when he wasn't in a white coat (or playing the Game) he was sneaking off the settlement to attend an accredited high school in San Francisco, the only Synanon child to do so. He stayed quiet, flew under the radar, and privately interrogated everything.

Even when I was a little kid, what always gripped me most about my dad's Synanon stories was the group's special language—terms like "in the Game" and "out of the Game," "love match" (meaning Synanon marriages), "act as if" (an imperative never to question Synanon's protocols, to simply "act as if" you agreed until you did), "demonstrators" and "PODs" (parents on duty, the rotation of adults randomly selected to chaperone the children's "school" and barracks), and so many more. This curious lingo was the clearest window into that world.

As the daughter of scientists, I figure some combination of nature, nurture, and Synanon stories caused me to become a rather incredulous person, and since early childhood, I have always been keenly sensitive to cultish-sounding rhetoric— but also beguiled by its power. In middle school, my best friend's mother was a born-again Christian, and I'd sometimes secretly skip Hebrew school on Sundays to accompany the family to their evangelical megachurch. Nothing enraptured me more than the way these churchgoers spoke— how, upon setting foot in the building, everyone slipped into a dialect of "evangicalese." It wasn't King James Bible English; it was modern and very distinct. I started using their glossary of buzzwords whenever I attended services, just to see if it affected how the congregants treated me. I picked up phrases like "on my heart" (a synonym for "on my mind"), "love up on someone" (to show someone love), "in the word" (reading the Bible), "Father of Lies" (Satan, the evil that "governs the world"), and "convicted" (to be divinely moved to do something). It was like the code language of an exclusive clubhouse. Though these special terms didn't communicate anything that couldn't be said in plain English, using them in the right way at the right time was like a key unlocking the group's acceptance. Immediately, I was perceived as an insider. The language was a password, a disguise, a truth serum. It was so powerful.

Creating special language to influence people's behavior and beliefs is so effective in part simply because speech is the first thing we're willing to change about ourselves . . . and also the last thing we let go. Unlike shaving your head, relocating to a commune, or even changing your clothes, adopting new terminology is instant and (seemingly) commitment-free. Let's say you show up to a spiritual meeting out of curiosity, and the host starts off by asking the group to repeat a chant. Odds are, you do it. Maybe it feels odd and peer pressure-y at first, but they didn't ask you to fork over your life savings or kill anyone. How much damage can it do? Cultish language works so efficiently (and invisibly) to mold our worldview in the shape of the guru's that once it's embedded, it sticks. After you grow your hair out, move back home, delete the app, whatever it is, the special vocabulary is still there. In part 2 of this book, we'll meet a man named Frank Lyford, a survivor of the 1990s "suicide cult" Heaven's Gate, who, twenty-five years after defecting and disowning its belief system, still calls his two former leaders by their monastic names, Ti and Do; refers to the group as "the classroom"; and describes its members' haunting fate with the euphemism "leaving Earth," just as he was taught to do over two decades ago.

The idea to write this book occurred to me after my best friend from college decided to quit drinking and go to Alcoholics Anonymous. She lived three thousand miles away from me at the time, so I only saw her a few times a year, and from afar, I couldn't tell how committed she was to this no-drinking thing, or really what to make of it. That is, until the first time I went to visit her after she got sober. That night, we were having trouble figuring out dinner plans, when the following sentence exited her mouth: "I've been *HALTing* all day, I *caught a resentment* at work, but trying not to *future-trip*. Ugh, let's just focus on dinner: *First things first*, as they say!"

I must have looked at her as if she had three heads. "HALT"? "Future-trip"? "Caught a resentment"? What on earth was she saying?* Three months in AA, and this person who was so close to me I could've accurately distinguished the meanings of her different exhalations was suddenly speaking a foreign language. Instantly, I had a heuristic reaction—it was the same instinct I felt looking at

---

* I'd quickly learn that "HALT" stands for Hungry, Angry, Lonely, and Tired; "future-tripping" is stressing out over potential events you can't control; "caught a resentment" means to be overcome by disdain for someone; and "first things first" is a self-proclaimed AA "cliché" that means just what it sounds like. Admittedly, these are extremely useful mottos (as are most of the zingers in AA's clever lexicon).

those old photos of Tasha Samar in the desert; the same response my dad had the day he first stepped onto Synanon's grounds. A Jonestown survivor once told me, "They say that a cult is like pornography. You know it when you see it." Or, if you're like me, you know it when you hear it. The exclusive language was the biggest clue. AA wasn't Synanon, of course; it was changing my friend's life for the better. But its conquest of her vocabulary was impossible to unhear.

Instincts aren't social science, though—and in truth, I didn't actually "know" AA was a "cult." But I had a strong inkling that there was something mighty and mysterious going on there. I had to look deeper. I had to understand: How did the group's language take such rapid hold of my friend? How does language work, for better and for worse, to make people submerge themselves in zealous ideological groups with unchecked leaders? How does it keep them in the whirlpool?

I began this project out of the perverse craving for cult campfire tales that so many of us possess. But it quickly became clear that learning about the connections across language, power, community, and belief could legitimately help us understand what motivates people's fanatical behaviors during this ever-restless era—a time when we find multilevel marketing scams masquerading as feminist start-ups, phony shamans ballyhooing bad health advice, online hate groups radicalizing new members, and kids sending each other literal death threats in defense of their favorite brands. Chani, the twenty-six-year-old SoulCycler, told me she once saw one teenager pull a weapon on another over the last pair of sneakers at an LA hypebeast sample sale. "The next Crusades will be not religious but consumerist," she suggested. Uber vs. Lyft. Amazon vs. Amazon boycotters. TikTok vs. Instagram. Tara Isabella Burton put it well when she said, "If the boundaries between cult and religion are already slippery, those between religion and culture are more porous still."

The haunting, beautiful, stomach-twisting truth is that no matter how cult-phobic you fancy yourself, our participation in things is what defines us. Whether you were born into a family of Pentecostals who speak in tongues, left home at eighteen to join the Kundalini yogis, got dragged into a soul-sucking start-up right out of college, became an AA regular last year, or just five seconds ago clicked a targeted ad promoting not just a skincare product but the "priceless opportunity" to become "part of a movement," group affiliations—which can have profound, even eternal significance—make up the scaffolding upon which we build our lives. It doesn't take someone broken or disturbed to crave that structure. Again, we're wired to. And what we often overlook is that the material with which that scaffolding is built, the very material that fabricates our reality, is language. "We have always used language to explain what we already knew," wrote English scholar Gary Eberle in his 2007 book *Dangerous Words*, "but, more importantly, we have also used it to reach toward what we did not yet know or understand." With words, we breathe reality into being.

A linguistic concept called the theory of performativity says that language does not simply describe or reflect who we are, it creates who we are. That's because speech itself has the capacity to consummate actions, thus exhibiting a level of intrinsic power. (The plainest examples of performative language would be making a promise, performing a wedding ceremony, or pronouncing a legal sentence.) When repeated over and over again, speech has meaningful, consequential power to construct and constrain our reality. Ideally, most people's understandings of reality are shared, and grounded in logic. But to enmesh in a community that uses linguistic rituals—chants, prayers, turns of phrase—to reshape that "culture of shared understanding" Eileen Barker spoke of can draw us away from the real world. Without us even noticing, our very understanding of ourselves and what we believe to be true becomes bound up with the group. With the leader. All because of language.

This book will explore the wide spectrum of cults and their uncanny lexicons, starting with the most famously blatantly dreadful ones and working its way to communities so seemingly innocuous, we might not even notice how cultish they are. In order to keep the scope of these stories manageable (because goodness knows I could spend my whole life interviewing people about "cults" of all kinds), we're going to focus mainly on American groups. Each part of the book will focus on a different category of "cult," all the while exploring the cultish rhetoric that imbues our everyday lives: Part 2 is dedicated to notorious "suicide cults" like Jonestown and Heaven's Gate; part 3 explores controversial religions like Scientology and Children of God; part 4 is about multilevel marketing companies (MLMs); part 5 covers "cult fitness" studios; and part 6 delves into social media gurus.

The words we hear and use every day can provide clues to help us determine which groups are healthy, which are toxic, and which are a little bit of both—and to what extent we wish to engage with them. Within these pages lies an adventure into the curious (and curiously familiar) language of Cultish.

So, in the words of many a cult leader: Come along. Follow me . . .

Part 2

Congratulations—You Have Been Chosen to Join the Next Evolutionary Level Above Human

i.

"Drinking the Kool-Aid."

This is a phrase you know. Having taken a seat at the table of everyday idioms, it's probably come up on at least a few dozen occasions over the course of your English-speaking life. The last time I overheard the expression was only about a week ago, as I caught someone casually describe their allegiance to Sweetgreen, the trendy chopped-salad chain: "I guess I've just drunk the Kool-Aid," they said with a side smile, taking their quinoa to go.

I, too, once uttered this remark just as reflexively as any other familiar stock saying—"speak of the devil," "hit the nail on the head," "can't judge a book by its cover." But that was before I knew the stories.

Today, "drinking the Kool-Aid" is most often used to describe someone mindlessly following a majority, or as shorthand for questioning their sanity. In 2012, *Forbes* christened it a "top annoying cliché" used by business leaders. Bill O'Reilly has invoked the saying to write off his critics ("The Kool-Aid people are going nuts," he's told listeners). I've even found it in contexts as glib and self-deprecating as "Yeah, I finally bought a Peloton. I guess I drank the Kool-Aid!" or "He's obsessed with Radiohead—he drank the Kool-Aid back in the nineties" (and then of course the Sweetgreen thing).

Most speakers use the idiom without batting an eye, but there are a select few who grasp its gravity. "One of the most vile phrases in the English language" is how seventy-one-year-old Tim Carter describes it. Tim told me this on a long call from San Francisco, talking a mile a minute, as if he couldn't get his repugnance out fast enough. "People have no idea what they're even saying." Decades ago, an old neighbor of Tim's named Odell Rhodes voiced the same sentiment in an exposé for the *Washington Post*: "The whole 'drinking the Kool-Aid' saying is so odious . . . so completely wrong." Teri Buford O'Shea, a sixty-seven-year-old poet who once knew both Tim and Odell, made a similar comment on the phrase: "It makes me shudder."

Tim, Odell, and Teri have a unique perspective on "drinking the Kool-Aid," because in the 1970s, they were all members of the Peoples Temple. The group went by many names—a congregation, a movement, a lifestyle, an agricultural project, an experiment, a Promised Land. This was not unintentional. Shadowy groups are expert rebranders, benefiting from the confusion, distraction, and secrecy a revolving door of puzzling new labels can incite.

The Peoples Temple started as a racially integrated church in Indianapolis in the 1950s. A decade later, it moved to Northern California, where it evolved to become more of a progressive "socio-political movement." That's according to the FBI reports. But it wasn't until 1974, when the Peoples Temple relocated to a remote stretch of land in South America, that it became the "cult" known as Jonestown.

Mythologized by many but understood by few, Jonestown

was an arid 3,800-acre settlement in northwestern Guyana that housed about a thousand occupants at the time of its denouement in 1978. The place was named after its inglorious leader, Jim Jones. He also went by many names. In Indianapolis, when the group still had religious leanings, followers addressed Jones as "God" or "Father" ("Father's Day" was celebrated on May 13, his birthday). By the time the group reached Guyana and secularized, his moniker evolved to the cozier "Dad." Eventually, members also started calling him "the Office" by way of metonymy, like how a king might be referred to as "the crown." And in his later years, Jones insisted on the courtly title "Founder-Leader."

Jones moved his followers from Redwood City, California, to Guyana, promising a Socialist paradise outside the evils of what he saw as an encroaching fascist apocalypse in the United States. Grainy film prints of the place depict a veritable Eden—children of all races blissfully play as their parents braid each other's hair and befriend the neighboring wildlife. In one image, a twenty-five-year-old woman named Maria Katsaris (one of Jones's lovers and a member of his innermost circle) grins while placing a genial index finger on the tip of a toucan's beak. Scrap the historical context, and it looks like the sort of humble, off-the-grid elysium where I could've seen any number of my progressive LA pals going to escape the Trump administration. A pet toucan sounds nice.

Today, most Americans have at least heard of Jonestown, if not the name, then the iconography: a commune in the jungle, a manic preacher, poisoned punch, corpses piled in the grass. Jonestown is best known for the mass murder-suicide of over nine hundred followers on November 18, 1978. Most of the victims, including more than three hundred children, met their fate after consuming a lethal concoction of cyanide and trace amounts of tranquilizers, which were mixed into vats of grape-flavored juice made from the powdered fruit concentrate Flavor Aid. "Drinking the Kool-Aid" is a metaphor derived from this tragedy. Our culture erroneously remembers the elixir as Kool-Aid, not Flavor Aid, due to the former's status as a genericized trademark (like how some people call all tissues "Kleenex," even though there are also Puffs and Angel Soft). But Jonestownians died by the cheaper shelf-brand version, which they ingested—most orally, some by injection, and many against their will—under extreme pressure from Jones, who claimed "revolutionary suicide" was their only option for "protesting the conditions of an inhumane world."

Folks didn't go to Guyana to die a bizarre death; they went in search of a better life: to try Socialism on for size, or because their churches back home were failing, or to evade the racist American police (sound familiar?). With the Promised Land, Jim Jones guaranteed a solution for every walk of life—and with all the right words delivered just so, people had reason to believe him.

Jones, whose character alone has been the subject of several dozen books, made famous what are now recognized as all the classic red flags of a dangerous guru: On the surface, he seemed a prophetic political revolutionary, but underneath, he was a maniacal, lying, paranoid narcissist. As the story tends to go, his devotees didn't find that out until it was too late. In the beginning, more than one survivor swore to me, there seemed nothing not to love.

Born and raised in Indiana, Jim Jones was a promising new pastor in his twenties when he created his first congregation there. A rock-ribbed integrationist, he and his wife were the first white couple in the state to adopt a Black child, and they soon filled their home with many other nonwhite kids. Jones called his household the "Rainbow Family," which sent a message that he walked the walk of racial justice not only at church, but in his personal life, too.

Jones's image wasn't just progressive and pious, though. He was handsome, too—an Elvis doppelgänger in his youth. Personally, I don't see the appeal (unpopular opinion, I guess, but Jones's blocky, cartoonish features have always reminded me a little of Biff Tannen, the bully from *Back to the Future*). I suppose deranged murderers might just not be my type, though I know that hybristophilia, an attraction to brutish criminals, is a very real thing. Jones, Ted Bundy, and Charles Manson all had groupies. Even the famous psychologist Philip Zimbardo, the guy known for the Stanford Prison Experiment, openly commented on Jones's irresistible "sexual appeal."

But sex appeal isn't just looks—it's an ability to craft the illusion of intimacy between yourself and your fans. That's what Jonestown expats remember. Each one I spoke to rhapsodized about the man's impossible charm, his knack for seamlessly relating to anyone, from white upper-middle-class

Congratulations—You Have Been Chosen . . . .

bohemians to Black folks active in the church. With twenty-something San Francisco progressives, Jones waxed Socialist, seducing them with professorial Nietzsche quotes; with older Pentecostals, he used Bible verses and the familiar timbre of a reverend. Multiple survivors told me that the first time they spoke to Jones, it felt as if he had known them their whole lives—that he "spoke their language." This kind of intense validation later traded for control is what some social scientists term "love-bombing."

"He appealed to anyone on any level at any time," explained Leslie Wagner Wilson, a public speaker, memoirist, and survivor of Jonestown. "He could quote scripture and turn around and preach socialism." Leslie didn't just live to tell the tale of Jonestown—the morning of the massacre, she escaped by darting into the jungle. At just twenty-two, a young Black woman with round glasses and cherubic cheeks, Leslie trekked thirty miles through the gnarled vegetation, her three-year-old son strapped to her back with a bedsheet. Her mother, sister, brother, and husband did not survive.

Flashback nine years: Leslie was in junior high when her mother, who was raising a house full of kids on her own and searching for support, joined the Peoples Temple in Redwood City. Since she was thirteen years old, the Peoples Temple was Leslie's whole world. Jones was Father and Dad to her. He called her his "little Angela Davis." Talk about love-bombing: For the teenager, whose identity was still forming, a comparison to the radical activist and role model strengthened her trust in Jones. Every time he used the nickname, it reinforced that commitment. "Ever the savvy showman, Jones successfully manipulated the revolutionary aspirations of young African Americans reeling from the fading promise of the Black Power movement," wrote Sikivu Hutchinson, feminist author of *White Nights, Black Paradise*. Naturally, Leslie wanted to believe she was the next Angela Davis. She was understandably motivated to think she could offer her community that kind of hope.

In this way, it wasn't Jones's looks, family optics, or even his ideas that hooked people; it was his way with words. "The way that he spoke—he was a great orator," said Leslie. "It moved you, it inspired you. . . . I was just enthralled." Jones didn't convince all the people Leslie loved—bright, family-oriented folks who objectively had nothing in common with the guy—to follow him to the ends of the earth using some form of cryptic mind magic. "It was with language," another Jonestown survivor told me fervently. "That's how he gained and kept control."

Boasting the intonation and passion of a Baptist preacher, the complex theorizings of an Aristotelian philosopher, the folksy wit of a countryside fabler, and the ferocious zeal of a demented tyrant, Jim Jones was a linguistic chameleon who possessed a monster arsenal of shrewd rhetorical strategies, which he wielded to attract and condition followers of all stripes. This is what the most cunning cultish leaders do: Instead of sticking to one unchanging lexis to represent a unified doctrine, they customize their language according to the individual in front of them. Known for quotes like "Socialism is older than the Bible by far" and "A capitalist mentality [is] the lowest vibration at which one could operate in this already dense plane of existence," Jones's Frankensteinian oratory often referenced political theory and metaphysics in the same breath. "His vocabulary could change quickly from being rather backwoods and homey to being quite intellectual," recalled Garry Lambrev, a poet and Peoples Temple vet from back in its Redwood City days. "He had an enormous vocabulary. He read an unbelievable amount. I don't know where he found the time."

A quick-changing vocabulary used for social capital: A linguist might tell you Jones was a sly practitioner of code-switching, or fluidly alternating between multiple language varieties. Among the nondiabolical, code-switching is an efficient (and usually unconscious) way of using every linguistic resource at your disposal to handle a verbal exchange most effectively. One might code-switch between dialects or languages from one setting to the next, or even within a single conversation, to express a specific mood, emphasize a statement, adapt to a social convention, or communicate a certain identity. The stakes of code-switching can be as high as ensuring respect and even survival, as is the case for speakers of certain marginalized ethnolects, like African American English, who learn to shift to "Standard English" in settings where they could be judged or persecuted otherwise. And then, in a kind of opposite way, code-switching can be used to connivingly gain trust. This was Jim Jones's specialty. Like a Machiavellian version of my twelve-year-old self slipping into evangelicalese at my friend's megachurch, Jones learned how to meet each follower on their linguistic level, which sent an instant signal that he understood them and their backgrounds uniquely.

Starting early in life, Jones carefully studied the speech stylings of compelling populist pastors and politicians from Dr. Martin Luther King Jr. and Father Divine (a Black spiritual leader and mentor to Jones) to Hitler. He stole the best bits and added his own Jonesian twist. He learned to modulate his voice in the manner of a Pentecostal preacher and picked up phrases that white people weren't supposed to know . . . like "Jack White preachers," an in-group label used in some Black church groups to criticize scammy white televangelists. By the time the Peoples Temple reached Guyana, it had become about three-quarters African American, although Jones's inner circle was almost entirely young white women (like Maria Katsaris), which is a pattern in power abuse: an older man at the top, and by his side, a clique of fair-skinned twenty- and thirtysomething women who acquiesce to exchanging their whiteness and sexuality for a few more grains of power.

By invoking politicized buzzwords—like "bourgeois bitches," a term Jones coined to forbid white followers from attending certain meetings, and "churchianity," a portmanteau condemning phony white Christians—Jones created the illusion that the Black majority had more privilege than they did. "He would visit Black churches, stand at the back door, and look at the preacher, who had mesmerized a crowd of a hundred people," recalled Jonestown survivor Laura Johnston Kohl. At seventy-two years old, Laura sports a fair sloping face and inch-long silver hair, but the same hopeful eyes that met Jim Jones's five decades ago and thought, *this man is onto something great.* In retrospect, of course, she sees him more clearly: "Jim didn't care about religion. He studied those people because he thought, 'That's the job I want and more.'"

Laura Johnston Kohl found the Peoples Temple as a twenty-two-year-old civil rights demonstrator. Born to a progressive, politically active single mom in a still-segregated DC suburb, she grew up witnessing racial injustice all around her. Laura dropped out of college in 1968 and moved to California to pursue activism full-time. "I wanted to live in a community that was a mix of all races, all financial levels, all economic levels. I joined Peoples Temple for the political part," Laura told me on one of our many phone calls. She longed for societal equality, and was down to get experimental to find it. Jones's plans for a rural settlement overseas made her pupils dilate with possibility. She packed a single duffel bag and moved to Guyana eagerly.

Laura lived to tell her story because on the day of the massacre, she wasn't in Jonestown. She was one of a lucky few who'd been sent to Georgetown, Guyana's capital, on an assignment. Laura was tasked with greeting Congressman Leo Ryan, a California rep who'd come to investigate Jonestown, having caught word from members' families that the place was suspicious. Still an enthusiastic Peoples Temple loyalist, Laura was sure to make a good impression. One hundred fifty miles east of Jonestown, she missed the carnage entirely. You'd think narrowly escaping such an event might turn one off to remote utopias, but two years later, in 1980, Laura joined another one: Synanon, the very same group my dad had escaped eight years before.

Her involvement in two infamous cults notwithstanding, Laura seemed totally level-headed when we spoke. Energetic and curious, she reminded me of half the girls I went to liberal arts college with. She spoke of her childhood as a popular girl, her well-adjusted family, her days hosting Black Panther meetings in her kitchen, her love for communal living. "In the seventies we had a saying: One person can only whisper. You need to be in a group to stand strong," Laura told me. So when she moved to San Francisco in her early twenties and met a passionate organizer named Jim, who told her he detested white supremacy and wanted to create a Socialist haven outside of it, she thought, *Where do I sign?* Never did she predict her political hero would murder all her friends under the guise of "revolutionary suicide."

This term is one of many Jones distorted in order to emotionally wrangle his followers. "Revolutionary suicide" was, in fact, the very last phrase he uttered before their deaths. Coined by Black Panther Party leader Huey Newton in the late 1960s, "revolutionary suicide" initially described the act of a demonstrator dying at the hands of their oppressor. The idea was that if you took to the streets to protest the Man, the Man might shoot you down, but the rebel behind you would pick up the banner and keep going. They might get shot down, too, but the movement would continue, until one day, one of your successors would carry that banner all the way to freedom. "Revolutionary suicide," as Newton meant it, was a phrase most Peoples Temple followers could

Cultish

get on board with, so Jones slowly perverted it, using it in various contexts depending on what he wanted out of them. On some occasions, Jones described revolutionary suicide as an appropriate alternative to being taken prisoner or being enslaved by the Man. Other times he used it to describe the act of walking into a crowd of enemies wearing a bomb and detonating it. But most famously, Jones invoked the phrase on the day of the massacre, framing death for his followers as a political statement against the *Hidden Rulers* (evil secret heads of government), rather than a coerced fate they had no say in.

By March 18, 1978, many of Jones's followers had already lost faith in him. His mental and physical health had long been in decline; he'd been abusing a cocktail of pharmaceuticals and suffered from a host of medical ailments (which are hard to keep track of, since he exaggerated and lied about a great many of them, including telling acolytes he had lung cancer and then "curing" himself of it). Not to mention Jonestown's brutal living conditions. As it turned out, the "Promised Land" followers expected to find in Guyana was not conducive to growing crops. Children were starving and their parents were brutally overworked, sleep deprived, and desperate to leave. That's why Congressman Ryan came to town.

Having received tips from followers' families that they were being held captive against their will, Ryan decided to fly down and check in, and he brought a few reporters and some delegates along with him. Jones, impresario that he was, did everything to conceal the rotten truths of the place while putting on a show for the Congressman (a lavish dinner, confident banter). But Jones knew there was no way they'd let him off the hook. At the end of the visit, Ryan and his crew returned to the small Jonestown airstrip to leave, and several residents followed them, trying to escape. Jones had ordered his militia to tail the defectors, and as soon as they began to board, thinking they were in the clear, the squad turned on them. They opened fire and killed five people: one Jonestown defector, three journalists, and Congressman Ryan.

This event sparked the infamous "suicide." Contrary to popular belief, the tragedy wasn't premeditated, at least not how the press painted it to be. And most of its victims did not die voluntarily. Popular Jonestown coverage spun a story that Jones regularly hosted ghoulish suicide rehearsals known as White Nights, where his mind-controlled minions would line up like lobotomized communicants and swallow cups of punch in preparation for the "real" suicide on November 18, 1978. But this wasn't what happened at all.

Surviving Peoples Templers contend that the real White Nights were much subtler events, and you didn't have to be "mind controlled" to participate. Originally, Jones used the phrase "White Night" to denote any sort of crisis, and the possibility of death as a result of that crisis. He chose this particular phrase to subvert the fact that our language tends to equate the color black with negativity: blacklist, blackmail, black magic. He decided the phrase "White Night" destabilized that concept. Not a bad point, but a really bad motive. Over time, as Jones grew more deranged and power-starved, the term evolved to mean a slew of insidious things. Some say White Night described occasions when Jones convinced followers to arm themselves with makeshift weapons and stay up for days on end, prepared to defend their Promised Land to the death against attacks he swore were coming but never did. Others remember the term referencing the dozen or so meetings when people approached a microphone and declared their willingness to die—that very night, if necessary—for the Cause (the Peoples Temple term for living in service of the group, not the self). There's also the story that White Nights were weekly events when Jones would keep the group up all night to discuss community concerns. And then there are those who've said a White Night was simply any meeting in which Jones mentioned death.

The congressman's visit confirmed what Jones had suspected for a long time: He couldn't keep this thing up forever. Jonestown was a failure. Too many people were trying to leave. He was doomed to be found out and dethroned. So he gathered everyone in the main pavilion and told them the enemy was on their way to ambush them. "They'll shoot some of our innocent babies. . . . They'll torture our people. They'll torture our seniors. We cannot have this," he announced. It was too late to escape: "We can't go back. They won't leave us alone. They're now going back to tell more lies, which means more congressmen. And there's no way, no way we can survive." Then he made known his wish: "My opinion is that we be kind to children and be kind to seniors and take the potion like they used to take in ancient Greece, and step over quietly because we are not committing suicide. It's a revolutionary act." The words were smooth, as they had always been, but surrounded by armed guards, residents were presented with two options: die by poison* or be shot trying to escape.

This is what every leader of the half dozen "suicide cults" in history have done: Taking an apocalyptic stance on the universe, with them at its center, they believe their imminent demise means everyone else must go down, too. For them, followers' lives are chips on the table—and if they're going to lose either way, they might as well go all in. But hands-on killing is a dirty job. They're in the business of opportunism and manipulation, not murder. So as soon as they feel their grasp on power start to slip, they bear down on forecasts that the world is coming to a gruesome, unstoppable end. The only solution, the leader preaches, is suicide, which, if conducted in a specific way at a certain time, will at the very least render you a martyr and at most literally transport you to the kingdom of God. Their loyalists back them up, echoing their words, pressuring any doubters to follow along.

A few gutsy Peoples Templers tried to argue with Jones that day. One of them was Christine Miller, a Black senior member who frequently stood up to Jones. A poor Texas

---

* Where and when did Jones get all that cyanide? According to a CNN report, he'd been secretly stockpiling the stuff for years, preparing for the day he'd need to use it, whenever that might be. Allegedly, Jones obtained a jeweler's license in order to purchase the chemical, which can be used to clean gold.

girl who grew up to become a successful LA County clerk, Christine had opened her purse countless times for Jones, in whom she placed ardent faith. But her willingness to compromise with him had limits. By the time she reached Guyana, where members were supposed to live simply and communally, sixty-year-old Christine refused to give up wearing the jewelry and furs she'd worked so hard for. Known for her unyielding frankness, she and Jones had a love-hate relationship that often turned tense. At one meeting, Jones became so exasperated by Christine's opposition that he pulled a gun on her. "You can shoot me, but you are going to have to respect me first," she retorted—and he backed down. If there were a time for Jones to heed Christine again, it'd be on March 18, 1978. Christine approached the mic at the front of the pavilion and tried to defend her fellow members' right to live, suggesting they look for alternative outs, spare the children, flee to Russia maybe. "It's not that I am afraid to die, but . . . I look at the babies and I think they deserve to live, you know?" she contested. "I still think as an individual I have a right to say what I think, what I feel. . . . We all have a right to our own destiny as individuals. . . . I feel like as long as there's life, there's hope."

Jones let her speak; he even complimented her "agitation." But ultimately, the choice was made for her. "Christine," he said. "Without me, life has no meaning. I'm the best thing you'll ever have." Later that afternoon, everyone under that canopy—including Christine, the guards, and eventually Jones himself, who took a pistol to his head—was gone.

You can get just the tiniest sense of Jones's coercive preaching style in a piece of audio known as the Jonestown Death Tape. The forty-five-minute recording captures the final speech Jones gave in the pavilion. "Death is not a fearful thing, it's living that's cursed," he proclaimed from his pulpit, as parents, by his command, squirted fluid-filled syringes into their babies' mouths, then had no choice but to administer their own doses or have someone else finish the job for them. Upon swallowing the bitter punch, followers were escorted outside one by one, where they perished, bodies convulsing, collapsing, and coming to stillness on the lawn.

Forever a peacock, Jones made the Death Tape himself; now it's public record, and you can listen to it online. Survivors like Odell Rhodes, who was one of only thirty-three to evade the poisoning that day (he hid under a building until nightfall), maintain that Jones doctored the tape, stopping and starting to whiteout bursts of protest, commotion, and cries of agony. The Death Tape is a subject of intense fascination; at least half a dozen different people, including religion scholars and FBI agents, have taken cracks at transcribing it, eyes pinched shut, headphones turned all the way up, trying to catch and confirm every last line.

If listening to nearly a thousand people squabble with Jones and each other mere moments before the infamous tragedy weren't hair-raising enough, the Death Tape's haunting soundtrack makes it stranger than fiction. There's a score of faint music playing underneath all the talking, which sounds like it was added later for effect; as it turns out, the tape originally contained a series of soul tunes. Jones taped over them, resulting in a "ghost recording" of muffled, tempo-warped melodies. At the very end, after the speech is over, you can hear "I'm Sorry," a 1968 R&B song by the Delfonics, played at half speed like a church organ.

Even in this brief excerpt of the Death Tape, you can get a chilling impression of Jones's rhythmic repetition and deceptive hyperbole.

> *If we can't live in peace, then let's die in peace. . . . We have been betrayed. We have been so terribly betrayed. . . . I've never lied to you. . . . The best testimony we can make is to leave this goddamn world. . . . I'm speaking as a prophet today. I wouldn't sit up in this seat and talk so serious if I did not know what I was talking about. . . . I don't want to see you go through this hell no more, no more, no more, no more. . . . [Death] is not to be feared, not be feared. It's a friend, it's a friend. . . . Let's get gone, let's get gone, let's get gone. . . . Death is a million times more preferable than 10 more days in this life. . . . Hurry, my children. . . . Sisters, good knowing you. . . . No more pain now, no more pain. . . . Free at last.*

The Death Tape is a poem, a curse, a mantra, a betrayal, a haunting. And proof of language's lethal power.

ii.

I was a spooky kid who grew up on cult tales, so I've been tuned in to Jonestown stories ever since I can remember. My dad often compared Jim Jones to Chuck Dietrich, the manic leader of Synanon. Though Dietrich never led a "mass suicide," my dad's half sister Francie, who spent her elementary school years in Synanon, told me that if Dietrich had stayed in power a little longer, she could've seen it happening. Synanon wasn't physically violent while my dad was there, but like Jones, Dietrich grew more bloodthirsty over the years. By the late 1970s, he'd appointed a militarized coalition called the Imperial Marines, which carried out dozens of violent crimes, like mass beatings against defectors, whom Dietrich labeled "splittees." One splittee was pummeled so hard, his skull was fractured; he subsequently contracted bacterial meningitis and fell into a coma. Just a few weeks before the Jonestown mass death in 1978, a lawyer named Paul Morantz, who'd helped a few splittees sue Synanon, was bitten by a rattlesnake Dietrich's Imperial Marines had placed in his mailbox. Dietrich was arrested after that, then went bankrupt, and by 1991, Synanon had crumbled. Like most leaders of fringy communes, Dietrich never got as far as Jones.

But nineteen years after Jonestown, someone got close.

In late March 1997, another cult suicide made headlines, reminding everyone of the tragedy in Guyana. This ordeal transpired in Rancho Santa Fe, California, where thirty-eight members of Heaven's Gate, a group of UFO-believing doomsdayers, systematically took their lives over a three-day period. Their deaths came by ingesting a mixture of applesauce, vodka, and barbiturates before tying plastic bags around their heads. They completed the act within the 9,200-square-foot mansion they shared, under the direction of their grandfatherly leader, Marshall Applewhite, who perished alongside his supporters in the same bizarre, theatrical manner. A sixty-five-year-old seminary school dropout who went on to obtain a master's degree in musical theater, Applewhite boasted a snow-white buzz cut, saucerlike eyes, and a passion for sci-fi tales. Like many power abusers in his category, Applewhite claimed prophet status—more specifically, that he and his by then deceased coleader, Bonnie Nettles (who passed away from liver cancer in 1985), were elevated, extraterrestrial souls temporarily inhabiting earthly bodies.

Jim Jones had lost the loyalty of many of his nine-hundred-plus followers by the time of their deaths, but Applewhite retained his small congregation's steadfast support through the end. On the day of the Heaven's Gate mass suicide, all thirty-eight followers remained convinced of the following scenario: A heaven-bound spacecraft trailing the Comet Hale–Bopp was going to bypass Earth in March 1997, allowing followers a chance to leave this "temporal and perishable world," board the flying saucer, and transport themselves to a distant space dimension Applewhite swore was the Kingdom of God.

Using a soft but firm, paternalistic tone of voice, Applewhite spoke in long strings of esoteric space talk and Latin-derived syntax to make his small, pseudo-intellectual following feel elite. According to his credo, the earth as we know it was on the verge of being recycled, or *spaded under*, so that the planet might be *refurbished*. "The human 'weeds' have taken over the garden and disturbed its usefulness beyond repair," avows the Heaven's Gate website. As of 2020, the site remains upkept by two surviving followers, though it doesn't seem to have undergone much of a redesign (it reads emphatically GeoCities; let's just say there's some cherry-red Comic Sans happening).

But Applewhite had a way out—all his followers had to do to "overcome their genetic vibrations" was "exit their vehicles" so their spirits could reemerge aboard the spacecraft and carry them to a physical and spiritual Evolutionary Kingdom Level Above Human. Earthly bodies were merely "containers" that could be disregarded for a higher existence. The souls who did not "graduate" along with them would inevitably reach "a certain degree of corruption" and ultimately initiate "a self-destruct mechanism at the Age's end" (aka, the apocalypse). For the exclusive Away Team, death was not only "nothing to fear," but a "once-in-a-lifetime opportunity" to enter a world that was "everlasting and noncorruptible."

Like Jones, Nettles and Applewhite also went by many names: The most famous were "the Two," Bo and Peep, and

Ti and Do (pronounced *tee* and *doe*, like the notes on a scale). In Heaven's Gate, every student chose a new first name as well (and renounced their last name), which, per Applewhite's instructions, ended in the suffix *−ody*. There was Thurstonody, Sylvieody, Elaineody, Qstody, Srrody, Glnody, Evnody, etc. Scholars theorize the suffix was a quasi-portmanteau of Do and Ti, and it served as linguistic proof that members had been rhetorically reborn of their leaders.

"The language was symbolic of who we were becoming," recollects Frank Lyford, aka Andody, who belonged to Heaven's Gate for eighteen years. Frank initially joined the group as a shaggy-haired twenty-one-year-old on a spiritual journey alongside his long-term girlfriend Erika Ernst, who became Chkody. They both exemplified the typical Heaven's Gate joinee: white, ex-Christian, New Age–minded, middle-class, unmarried. For the first half of Frank's membership, Ti and Do proclaimed that the transition from the "human level" to the "next level" would take place while everyone in the group was alive and well. "So it would be a conscious transition," Frank, now sixty-five, explained to me in an interview. "That didn't really start to change until after Ti passed on." The way Frank remembers it, Ti's death had a traumatic effect on Do; he started to become more controlling, and his ideas about how to graduate to the next level morphed. That's when ending their human lives crept into the picture.

By the 1990s, Frank was starting to have doubts. At the time, Heaven's Gate members were allowed to have normal jobs outside the Rancho Santa Fe mansion to earn money for the group, and Frank was employed as a software developer. He loved the work—it was creative and stimulating, and whenever he did something right, his boss gave him full credit. But having an independent purpose beyond the Away Team went totally against Heaven's Gate dogma. After nearly two decades of suppressing his entire identity in service of Ti and Do, Frank got the sense that being a cog in a wheel, especially this wheel, was not the answer. He defected in 1993, and though he begged Chkody to leave with him, she couldn't be convinced. Two years later, she "exited her vehicle" along with the rest of the Away Team.

Now a much older man, with a thin melancholy face and rimless rectangular glasses, Frank lives in Kansas, where he works as a personal life coach for a mostly remote clientele. From the comfort of home, he shares the fruits of his undeniably unique—and ongoing—spiritual adventures. "I believe all of us came here with a specific path, a purpose to learn things at the soul level," he told me, his voice a soft, fluttery tenor. Frank struggles with his speech—not quite a stutter, words tend to get caught somewhere between his soft palate and the air in front of him. It's an impediment he attributes to Heaven's Gate: Once, Applewhite mocked the morning huskiness in Frank's voice (he'd just woken up) with such humiliating scorn that over time, he developed what he calls a "severe inability to speak." It's a linguistic poltergeist that vexes him even after all these years. Still, he continues: "Our experiences may look like trauma or something horrendous. But no matter what we go through, there is knowledge to be gained."

Like Jim Jones, Ti and Do vehemently denounced mainstream Christianity and the United States government, calling both "totally corrupt." They also shared Jones's claim of being the only ones who could solve the epic calamity that was modern life on Earth. But that's about where their similarities end. By the Heaven's Gate era, the stick-it-to-the-man '70s were long gone; instead, Applewhite's rhetoric was heavily influenced by the 1990s' UFO mania. It was a decade defined by shows like *The X-Files* and Fox's alien autopsy hoax. People were just starting to grasp digital technology, but before widespread internet and smartphones, not everybody had access to it, so it carried a certain mystery and, for followers of Heaven's Gate, new answers to life's oldest questions. Applewhite was obsessed with the television series *Star Trek: The Next Generation*, particularly the show's hive mind of alien antagonists called the Borg. The Borg had a favorite saying: "Resistance is futile. You will be assimilated." "Do loved that," Frank Lyford recalled. "He espoused that hive mentality."

To match his credo, Applewhite concocted a whole Heaven's Gate vocabulary of niche, sci-fi-esque terms. There was a severe regimentation of daily life in the mansion, and the lingo helped keep things in order. The kitchen was the "nutra-lab," the laundry room was the "fiber-lab," and meals were called "laboratory experiments." The group as a whole was "the classroom," followers were "students," and teachers like Ti and Do were known as "Older Members" and "clinicians." If followers were off doing something in normal society, that was "out of craft." If they were in the house they shared, that was "in craft." "The special talk put them in a rhetorical place where they could imagine themselves in the specific world where they wanted to be," analyzed Heaven's Gate scholar Benjamin E. Zeller, a religion professor at Lake Forest College. By marinating in this specific, thematic vernacular every day for years, followers began to picture life on that spacecraft, drifting toward the Kingdom of God. "It was doing real religious work," said Zeller. "It wasn't just gobbledygook."

On the day of their suicide, the Away Team was not only at peace with their imminent graduation, they were giddy about it. You can see it yourself in the "Exit Statements," a series of goodbye interviews Applewhite's disciples filmed in the hours preceding the suicide and published on their website. (I found the clips edited together on YouTube.) In these tapes, Heaven's Gate members all sport the same centimeter-long crew cuts, billowy tunics, and placid expressions, backdropped by an idyllic outdoor setting. Birds chirp perversely offscreen. For the camera, followers reflect on their experiences in Heaven's Gate and justify why they're ready to enter the next level, seeming not fearful or confused, but genuinely, gleefully committed to their plan. "I just want to . . . say how grateful and thankful I am to be in this class," a camera-shy newer recruit tells the lens, "and to thank my Older Member Do and his Older Member Ti for . . . offering us the chance to overcome this world and . . . to enter the true Kingdom of God, the evolutionary level above human, and become a next-level member."

Nearly a week after these videos were recorded, police

found all thirty-nine members' bodies, including Apple-white's, neatly posed—and decomposing—in their bunk beds. Each was dressed in an identical uniform: black sweat suit, fresh black-and-white Nike Decades, and an armband patch reading "Heaven's Gate Away Team." Members' pockets each contained a precise sum of cash: one $5 bill and three quarters ("toll money," apparently). Purple shrouds cloaked each body's torso and face.

Jonestown and Heaven's Gate were entirely unrelated groups whose members shared almost nothing in terms of politics, religion, age, race, and general life experience. The worlds each leader concocted for their followers were very different, and so, too, was the rhetoric that narrated them. But these groups' grotesque codas placed them in the same unique genre of cult, garnering worldwide fascination from scholars, reporters, artists, and everyday onlookers, desperate to understand how someone could become so "brainwashed" that they'd take their own life. Finally, an answer . . .

iii.

Within and outside cultish environments, language can accomplish real, life-or-death work. Volunteering at a youth suicide lifeline, I learned firsthand that when used in a certain carefully considered manner, speech can help someone not die. Conversely, language can also prompt someone to die. The causal relationship between a charismatic figure's speech and another person's suicide was judicially confirmed in 2017 during the controversial Michelle Carter court case, where a young woman was convicted of manslaughter for convincing her high school boyfriend to kill himself via text message—an act described as "coerced suicide." The Michelle Carter case inspired the nation to have one of its first serious, country-wide debates about the deadliness of words alone.

Year after year, we ask: What makes people join cults like Jonestown and Heaven's Gate? What makes them stay? What makes them behave in wild, baffling, sometimes gruesome ways? Here's where the answer starts: Using systematic techniques of conversion, conditioning, and coercion, with language as their ultimate power tool, Jones and Applewhite were able to inflict unforgettable violence on their followers without personally laying a finger on them.

Across the influence continuum, cultish language works to do three things: First, it makes people feel special and understood. This is where the love-bombing comes in: the showers of seemingly personalized attention and analysis, the inspirational buzzwords, the calls for vulnerability, the "YOU, just by existing, have been tagged to join the elite Away Team destined for the Kingdom of God." For some people, this language will instantly sound like a scammy red flag, and others will decide it just doesn't resonate; but a few will have this transformative experience where all of a sudden, something "clicks." In a moment, they become filled with the sense that this group is their answer, that they can't not come back. This tends to happen all at once, and it's what makes a person "join." This is called conversion.

Then, a different set of language tactics gets people to feel dependent on the leader, such that life outside the group doesn't feel possible anymore. This is a more gradual operation, and it's called conditioning—the process of subconsciously learning a behavior in response to a stimulus. It's what makes people stick by the group far longer than anyone on the outside can understand. And last, language convinces people to act in ways that are completely in conflict with their former reality, ethics, and sense of self. An ends-justify-the-means ethos is embedded, and in the worst cases, it results in devastation. This is called coercion.

The first key element of cultish language? Creating an us-versus-them dichotomy. Totalitarian leaders can't hope to gain or maintain power without using language to till a psychological schism between their followers and everyone else. "Father Divine said to always establish a 'we/they': an 'us,' and an enemy on the outside," explained Laura Johnston Kohl, our Jonestown vet. The goal is to make your people feel like they have all the answers, while the rest of the world is not just foolish, but inferior. When you convince someone that they're above everyone else, it helps you both distance them from outsiders and also abuse them, because you can paint anything from physical assault to unpaid labor to verbal attacks as "special treatment" reserved only for them.

This is part of why cults have their own jargon in the first place: elusive acronyms, insider-y mantras, even simple labels like "fiber-lab." It all inspires a sense of intrigue, so potential recruits will want to know more; then, once they're in, it creates camaraderie, such that they start to look down on people who aren't privy to this exclusive code. The language can also highlight any potential troublemakers, who resist the new terms—a hint that they might not be fully on board with the ideology and should be watched.

But for most committed members, the special language feels fun and sacred, like a snazzy new uniform. Followers shed their old vocabularies with enthusiasm. "The goal was to substitute terms for everyday concepts that might be a reminder of our previous identities," Frank Lyford, the former Heaven's Gate member, told me. "In my way of thinking, that was a good thing." This goal of isolating followers from the outside while intensely bonding them to each other is also part of why almost all cultish groups (as well as most monastic religions) rename their members: Ti, Do, Andody, Chkody. The ritual signifies a member's shedding of their former skin and submitting wholly to the group.

It's not just followers who gain new names; outsiders get them, too. Jones's and Applewhite's vocabularies were chockablock with inflammatory nicknames used to exalt devotees and villainize everyone else. A Heaven's Gate member might be called a "student of the Kingdom of Heaven," a "recipient of the gift of recognition," or a "child of a Member of the Level Above Human." By contrast, mainstream Christians belonged to a "Luciferian program" and a "counterfeit God," having succumbed to the "lower forces." Ti and Do encouraged their students to distance from souls who hadn't received the "deposit of knowledge." According to Heaven's Gate teachings, mere possession of "the Truth" would make separating from the rest of society "inevitable."

In the Peoples Temple, "my children" was the coveted title Jones bestowed upon obedient supporters, while "outside forces" naturally applied to anyone who didn't follow. Even more loaded, "traitors" meant defectors, like Garry Lambrev, who'd seen the light but turned away. The "Hidden Rulers" referred to what some might later call the "deep state." The odious "Sky God" (the bogus Christian deity) described the enemy to "God in the Body," aka Father Jones.

But the words themselves only did half the job; the other half was the performance. As anyone who ever attended one of Jim Jones's sermons remembers vividly, the guy had a flair for the dramatic. On the pulpit, he'd pound out short, hyperbole-laden phrases to get his congregation fired up.

Once the group energy was high, it did the work for him. Every time Jones gave a sermon, he'd pick one fact from the news, or a historical event, and catastrophize it. Jonestown survivor Yulanda Williams recalls Jones showing the Redwood City congregation a film called *Night and Fog* about the Nazi concentration camps. "He said, 'This is what they have planned for people of color. We've got to build our land up over there in Jonestown, we've got to get over there. We've got to move fast, we've got to move swiftly, we've got to pool our resources together,'" she explained. Garry Lambrev couldn't forget Jones's rococo preaching style if he tried: "He'd say things like, 'The paper idle' [his term for the Bible] 'is useful for one thing,' and he'd point to his ass— toilet paper," Garry narrated. "He would tear it up theatrically on the podium and let the pages fly all over. Then he'd say things like, 'Nobody touch it, it's damned,' he'd cackle away, and we'd all laugh."

This phenomenon of listeners mistaking say-it-like-it-is honesty (which of course isn't actual honesty, just a lack of filter) for the refreshing voice of antiestablishment dissent might feel familiar to anyone who's lived through the reign of a problematic populist: Italy's Silvio Berlusconi, Slovakia's Vladimír Mečiar, Donald Trump. It would be irresponsible, I think, not to mention the oratorical similarities between Trump and Jim Jones, who shared the same love of coining zingy, incendiary nicknames for their opponents. ("Fake News" and "Crooked Hillary" were Trump's analogs to Jones's "Hidden Rulers" and "Sky God.") Even when their statements didn't contain any rational substance, the catchy phrases and zealous delivery were enough to win over an audience. It's riveting to watch someone on a podium speak from a place so animalistic that most of us don't let ourselves behave that way even with our closest friends. As *Atlantic* staff writer George Packer wrote in 2019, the strength of Trump's populist language lies in its openness: "It requires no expert knowledge. . . . It's the way people talk when the inhibitors are off."

Over time, the memorable nicknames and insider-y terminology acquire a strong emotional charge. When a word or phrase takes on such baggage that its mere mention can spark fear, grief, dread, jubilation, reverence (anything), a leader can exploit it to steer followers' behavior. This lingo is what some psychologists call loaded language.

Sometimes loaded language works by twisting the meaning of existing words until the new significance eclipses the old one. Like how 3HO redefined "old soul" from a compliment to something dreadful. Or how the megachurchgoers from my childhood talked about being "convicted." Or how Jim Jones warped the meanings of "revolutionary suicide" and "the Cause," or how he defined "accidents" as "things that never happen unless we deserve them." If Jones were to say something like, "We need to do everything we can to prevent accidents," an everyday listener would understand that sentence to have a fairly innocuous meaning, according to the shared rules of semantics and reality that most speakers agree upon. The loaded charge it carried for Jones's followers would be lost, because for the majority of us, "accidents" is a simple word with no identity or sky-high stakes attached.

Other times, loaded language comes in the form of misleading euphemisms. Certainly it's no secret that when authority figures use too many vague turns of phrase, it can be a sign of missing logic, or that something inauspicious is hiding in a pocket of subtext. It's also entirely true that euphemisms can soften unpleasant truths without being intentionally pernicious. Everyday speakers have plenty of them for taboo concepts, like death ("passed away," "lost their life," "didn't make it"), which we might use to be polite, avoid discomfort, and maintain a certain degree of denial.

But Jones's and Applewhite's euphemisms recast death as something actively aspirational. Jones referred to the macabre reality as "the transition" or, during his more manic moods, "the Great Translation." On the Death Tape, he calls dying a minor matter of "stepping over quietly to the next plane." Applewhite never used the words "dying" or "suicide," either—instead, he referred to these matters as "exiting your vehicle," "graduation," "a completion of the changeover," or "overcoming containers to inherit next-level bodies." These terms were conditioning tools—invoked to make followers cozy up to the idea of death, to dismiss their ingrained fears of it.

There's a companion tool to loaded language that can be found in every cultish leader's repertoire: It's called the thought-terminating cliché. Coined in 1961 by the psychiatrist Robert J. Lifton, this term refers to catchphrases aimed at halting an argument from moving forward by discouraging critical thought. Ever since I learned of the concept, I now hear it everywhere—in political debates, in the hashtag wisdom that clogs my Instagram feed. Cultish leaders often call on thought-terminating clichés, also known as semantic stop signs, to hastily dismiss dissent or rationalize flawed reasoning. In his book *Thought Reform and the Psychology of Totalism*, Lifton writes that with these stock sayings, "the most far-reaching and complex of human problems are compressed into brief, highly selective, definitive-sounding phrases, easily memorized and easily expressed. They become the start and finish of any ideological analysis." So while loaded language is a cue to intensify emotions, semantic stop signs are a cue to discontinue thought. To put it most simply, when used in conjunction, a follower's body screams "Do whatever the leader says," while their brain whispers "Don't think about what might happen next"—and that's a deadly coercive combination.

Thought-terminating clichés are by no means exclusive to "cults." Ironically, calling someone "brainwashed" can even serve as a semantic stop sign. You can't engage in a dialogue with someone who says, "That person is brainwashed" or "You're in a cult." It's just not effective. I know this because every time I witness it happen on social media, the argument comes to a standstill. Once these phrases are invoked, they choke the conversation, leaving no hope of figuring out what's behind the drastic rift in belief.

Contentious debates aside, thought-terminating clichés also pervade our everyday conversations: Expressions like

"It is what it is," "Boys will be boys," "Everything happens for a reason," "It's all God's plan," and certainly "Don't think about it too hard" are all common examples. Among New Age types, I've also heard semantic stop signs come in the form of wily maxims like "Truth is a construct," "None of this matters on a cosmic level," "I hold space for multiple realities," "Don't let yourself be ruled by fear," and dismissing any anxieties or doubts as "limiting beliefs." (We'll discuss more of this rhetoric in part 6.)

These pithy mottos are effective because they alleviate cognitive dissonance, the uncomfortable discord one experiences when they hold two conflicting beliefs at the same time. For example, I have an acquaintance who recently got laid off from her job, and she was lamenting to me about how beside the point it felt when people responded to her bad news with "Everything happens for a reason." The layoff was due to a mix of crappy, complicated factors like the tanking economy, poor company management, implicit sexism, and her boss's mercurial temperament—there was no one "reason." But her roommates and old coworkers didn't want to think about those things, because doing so would make them anxious, suddenly hyperaware of the fact that life fundamentally bends toward entropy, which would conflict with their goal of appearing sympathetic. So they fed her a line—"Everything happens for a reason"—to simplify the situation and put everyone's cognitive dissonance to bed. "It's work to think, especially about things you don't want to think about," confessed Diane Benscoter, an ex-member of the Unification Church (aka the Moonies, an infamous '70s-era religious movement). "It's a relief not to have to." Thought-terminating clichés provide that temporary psychological sedative.

Jones had a whole repertoire of these phrases, which he'd whip out whenever a follower's question or concern needed silencing. "It's all the media's fault—don't believe them" was a go-to whenever someone brought up a piece of news that challenged him. On the day of the tragedy, he delivered phrases like "It's out of our hands," "[The] choice is not ours now," and "Everybody dies" to shut down dissenters like Christine Miller.

In Heaven's Gate, Ti and Do frequently repeated rote sayings like "Every religion is less than the Truth" to halt consideration of other belief systems. To muzzle accusations that their theories were illogical, they argued that if "the TRUTH about the Evolutionary Level Above Human" was not yet clear to you, it wasn't their fault. You simply hadn't been "bestowed the gift of recognition."*

Having thought-terminating clichés like these meant that whenever difficult queries arose—like, how can Jonestown be our only good option if we're all starving? Or, is there a way to achieve enlightenment without killing ourselves?—you had a simple, catchily packaged answer telling you not to worry about it. Digging for more information is poison to a power abuser; thought-terminating clichés squash independent thinking. This simultaneously puts the follower in their place and lets them off the hook. If "It's all the media's

---

* And in Synanon, any impulse to challenge Dietrich or his bizarre rules could be snuffed out with the maxim "act as if."

fault" is burned into your brain, you quickly learn to use the media as a scapegoat and not consider any other causes for your suffering. If raising too many questions means you simply don't have the gift of recognition, then eventually you're going to stop asking, because the gift of recognition is what you want more than anything in the world.

In the most oppressive cultish environments, even if followers pick up on these tactics and want to speak out against them, there are strategies in place to make sure they are silenced. Both Applewhite and Jones kept their followers from conversing not only with the outside world but also with each other. It didn't take long after settling in Jonestown for Peoples Templers to notice that this Promised Land was a sham. But bonding over their shared misery? Not allowed. Jones enforced a "quiet rule," so whenever his voice played over the camp PA system (which was often), no one was allowed to talk. In Heaven's Gate, too, followers' speech was heavily monitored. Frank Lyford remembers that everyone was expected to speak at a low volume, or not at all, so that they wouldn't disturb other members. No communication, no solidarity. No chance to figure a way out.

iv.

Cultish language isn't a magic bullet or lethal poison; it's more like a placebo pill. And there are a host of reasons why it might be likelier to "work" on certain people and not others. We'll investigate some of these factors throughout this book, but one of them has to do with a type of conditioning most of us have experienced: the conditioning to automatically trust the voices of middle-aged white men.

Over the centuries, we've been primed to believe that the sound of a Jim Jones–type voice communicates an innate power and capability—that it sounds like the voice of God. In fact, during the heyday of television broadcasting, there was a known style of delivery labeled "the voice of God," which applied to the deep, booming, exaggerated baritones of newscasters like Walter Cronkite and Edward R. Murrow. It doesn't take much analysis to notice that the voices of history's most destructive "cult leaders" largely fit this description. That's because when a white man speaks confidently in public about big topics like God and government, many listeners are likely to listen by default—to hear the deep pitch and "standard" English dialect and trust it without much questioning. They fail to nitpick either the delivery or the content, even if the message itself is suspect.

In Lindy West's essay collection *The Witches Are Coming*,

there is a chapter titled "Ted Bundy Wasn't Charming—Are You High?," which criticizes America's frightfully low standards for men's charisma. As long as someone is white, male, and telling us to pay attention to him, we'll follow even "the most obviously bumbling con artist dumbass ever birthed by the universe," West says. Even rude, mediocre, murderous Ted Bundy. Even buffoonish Fyre Festival fraudster Billy McFarland. Even racist fascist misogynist Donald Trump. Even diabolical despotic Jim Jones.

Admittedly, it isn't always productive to make blanket statements equating Donald Trump (or any problematic leader) to Jim Jones. That's chiefly because it's not the most useful way to evaluate their specific danger. Jonestown, cult scholars agree, was a singularly extraordinary tragedy, which had never happened before and remains unreplicated to this day. And yet policy makers and media professionals across the political spectrum have been guilty of tossing around "Jonestown" and "Kool-Aid" as omens to warn against all kinds of people they disagree with, from PETA members to abortion rights activists and right back at the anti-PETA and antiabortion protesters screaming at them about Kool-Aid. I am not the first person to point out the similarities between Jones and Trump, but I highlight their overlapping oratories more as an invitation to consider the precise language forms that contributed to Trump's deceptive and violent charisma, not to drum up fear that the man is capable of orchestrating a mass poisoning in Guyana (I doubt Trump could even name which continent Guyana is on). To think this reductively creates a false dilemma—a scenario where something is either just like Jonestown or otherwise totally fine. Which is obviously not the case; there are nuances. And isn't cultish rhetoric worth a look even when the stakes aren't literally Jonestown?

In every corner of life, it's true that the way we interpret someone's speech corresponds precisely to the amount of power we think they ought to have. When it comes to "suicide cult" leaders, I can think of just one woman who's gained any significant amount of attention and authority. Her name is Teal Swan, and at the time of this writing, she is very much still alive. Swan is a thirtysomething self-help guru who operates mostly on social media. To her loyalists, she is known as the "spiritual catalyst"; to her critics, she's the "suicide catalyst." On the cultish continuum, Swan seems to fall about halfway between Gwyneth Paltrow and Marshall Applewhite—the midpoint between a self-serving "wellness" influencer and a bona fide sociopath.

Most people who find Swan do so on YouTube. There, her "personal transformation" videos offer tutorials on everything from how to overcome addiction to how to open your third eye. She started posting videos in 2007, and altogether they have received tens of millions of views. Swan utilizes SEO strategies to target the lonely internet searches of people struggling with depression and suicidal thoughts. A person might search "I'm all alone" or "Why does this hurt so much," and those keywords could lead them to her content. Not everyone who "follows" Swan becomes a *follower-*follower, but those who do might receive an invitation to the Teal Tribe, her exclusive Facebook group dedicated to her most committed adherents. Eventually, they might attend one of her in-person workshops or fly down to her pricey retreat center in Costa Rica to undergo the Completion Process, her signature trauma-healing technique.

Swan has no mental health accreditation; she uses an assortment of dubious psychological treatments, like "recovered memory therapy" (the controversial practice of unearthing "repressed memories," which was popular during the Satanic Panic and which Swan claims to have undergone as a child to uncover lost flashbacks of "Satanic ritual abuse"). Most modern psychologists say this exercise actually implants false memories and can be deeply traumatic for patients.

But Swan's unique vocabulary of "Tealisms" helps her establish herself as a trustworthy spiritual and scientific authority. Like Jim Jones, who could use the Bible to preach socialism, Swan invokes Eastern metaphysics to diagnose mental health disorders. She blurs mystical talk of "synchronicity," "frequency," and "the Akashic records" with the formal language of the *DSM*: borderline, PTSD, clinical depression. For people struggling with their mental health, who haven't found a solution through traditional therapy and pharmaceuticals, her brand of occultic psychobabble creates the impression that she is tapped into a power higher than science. (This marriage of medical jargon with supernatural-speak is nothing new, either; it's a strategy problematic gurus from Scientology's L. Ron Hubbard to NXIVM's Keith Raniere have employed for decades. In the social media age, a throng of shady online oracles have followed in Swan's footsteps, using this speech style to capitalize on Western culture's resurrected interest in the New Age. We'll meet some of her controversial contemporaries in part 6.)

Swan hasn't caused any mass suicides, but at least two of her mentees have taken their own lives. Critics attribute these tragedies to the fact that Swan uses a range of highly triggering terms to talk about suicide: "I can see your vibrations, and you're passively suicidal" and "The hospitals and suicide helpline do nothing" are a sampling of her signature thought-terminating clichés. Although she claims not to support or encourage suicide, Swan touts these sayings in combination with emotionally loaded metaphors like "Death is a gift you give yourself" and "Suicide is pushing the reset button." As Swan posted on her blog, suicide happens because "we all intuitively (if not mentally) know what is waiting for us after death is the pure positive vibration of source energy." Suicide, she pens, is a "relief."

In the early 2010s, one of Swan's longtime mentees named Leslie Wangsgaard stopped taking her antidepressants, started having thoughts of suicide, and approached Swan for guidance. After Swan, this guru she'd trusted for years, told Leslie she didn't seem to "want" her methods to work and that she either had to "commit fully to life or commit fully to death," Leslie completed suicide in May 2012. Later, Swan stated that there was "nothing that any healer could ever do for [Leslie's] type of vibration." Not her, not anyone.

Perversely aligned with her reputation as the "suicide catalyst," Teal Swan, like Jim Jones, also became a sex symbol. There have been countless articles written about her "goddesslike" beauty—her long dark hair, her piercing green eyes, her skincare routine ("I can't stop thinking about her pores," reads a line from one *New York* magazine essay). And most of all, her voice, which sounds like a siren's hypnotic lullaby in videos of her saying it feels "delicious to die." Normatively feminine and soothing, almost motherly sounding, Swan's voice carries a private, homey form of power, especially since it's something you consume alone in your house. "I've talked to people who said they would just listen to her all night," said Jennings Brown, host of the investigative podcast *The Gateway*. Swan makes no effort to approximate male authority, but for her particular brand of nurturing "personal transformation" guru, it works. She's not your politician or prophet; she's your DIY self-actualization mom. She's seeking exactly the breed of cultish leadership deemed acceptable for a beautiful, thirtysomething white woman—no more, no less. And to that extent, people follow.

V.

Techniques like us-versus-them labels, loaded language, and thought-terminating clichés are absolutely crucial in getting people from open, community-minded folks to victims of cultish violence; but importantly, they do not "brainwash" them—at least not in the way we're taught to think about brainwashing.

Jim Jones certainly tried to use language to brainwash his followers. Among the techniques he studied was Newspeak, the make-believe language George Orwell created for his dystopian novel *1984*. In the book, Newspeak is a euphemistic, propaganda-filled language that authoritarian leaders force their citizens to use as "mind control." À la Newspeak, Jones attempted to mind control his followers by, for example, requiring them to give him daily thanks for good food and work, even though the labor was backbreaking and the food scarce.

1984 was a work of fiction, but with Newspeak, Orwell satirized a very real and widely held belief of the twentieth century: that "abstract words" were the cause of World War I. The theory was that the misuse of abstract words like "democracy" had a brainwashing effect on the world population, single-handedly spawning the war. To prevent it from ever happening again, a pair of language scholars named C. K. Ogden and I. A. Richards wrote a book called *The Meaning of Meaning* and launched a program to reduce English to strictly concrete terms. No euphemisms, no hyperbole, no room for misinterpretation or mind control. They called it Basic English.

But odds are you've never heard of Basic English, because it never caught on or fulfilled its intended purpose. That's because language doesn't work to manipulate people into believing things they don't want to believe; instead, it gives them license to believe ideas they're already open to. Language—both literal and figurative, well-intentioned and ill-intentioned, politically correct and politically incorrect—reshapes a person's reality only if they are in an ideological place where that reshaping is welcome.

Not to disappoint any aspiring cult leaders, but there's a linguistic theory about the relationship between language and thought called the Sapir–Whorf hypothesis, which says that while language does influence our ability to conceive of ideas, it does not determine it. That is to say, we are still able to conceive of thoughts that don't match the language available to us. For example, just because one person might not know the color terms "cyan" and "cerulean" (both vibrant blues) does not mean their visual systems cannot physically perceive the difference between the two. Someone very charismatic could try to convince them the two shades are the same, referencing their lack of language as proof, but if the person knows in their gut that these nameless blues look different, they couldn't be "brainwashed" to believe otherwise.

So when Jones invoked phrases like "revolutionary suicide" on the Death Tape, they only succeeded in reminding those who still had faith in him that what they were doing was right and good. They didn't work on Christine Miller anymore. By then, it was too late to get out alive. But it was never too late to resist.

To this point, research consistently shows that "even if you've got a gun to your head, people can resist if they want to." That quote comes from our British sociologist Eileen Barker, who's been analyzing cult membership for the past half century. Barker was one of the first scholars to publicly question the scientific validity of "brainwashing." Mind control first emerged in the 1950s in press coverage of the torture techniques North Korea reportedly used in the Korean War. By the 1970s, brainwashing was a mainstream idea and served as a defense for the sketchy practice of deprogramming—attempts to "save" new religion converts that often involved illegal kidnapping and worse.* "The excuse was the person wouldn't be able to leave of their own free will," says Barker. But instead, what she found was this: Out of 1,016 study subjects who'd been involved with the Moonies, 90 percent of those who'd been interested enough

---

* Some '70s-era "anti-cult" movements were just as unhinged as the groups they were combatting. Throughout its two-decade practice, an organization called the Cult Awareness Network (CAN) kidnapped and tortured dozens of "cult followers" in an attempt to deprogram them. One of CAN's founders, Ted Patrick, got himself into trouble after two parents, concerned about their adult daughter's involvement with left-wing politics, paid him $27,000 to abduct her and handcuff her to a bed for two weeks.

to attend one of the workshops where this so-called brain-washing occurred decided that the whole thing wasn't really their cup of tea and quickly ended their Moonie careers. They couldn't be converted. Of the remaining 10 percent who joined, half left on their own steam within a couple of years.

So what made the other 5 percent stay? Prevailing wisdom would tell you that only the intellectually deficient or psychologically unstable would stick by a "cult" that long. But scholars have disproven this, too. In Barker's studies, she compared the most committed Moonie converts with a control group—the latter had gone through life experiences that might make them very "suggestive" ("Like having an unhappy childhood or being rather low-intelligence," she said). But in the end, the control group either didn't join at all or left after a week or two. A common belief is that cult indoctrinators look for individuals who have "psychological problems" because they are easier to deceive. But former cult recruiters say their ideal candidates were actually good-natured, service-minded, and sharp.

Steven Hassan, an ex-Moonie himself, used to recruit people to the Unification Church, so he knows a little something about the type of individual cults go for. "When I was a leader in the Moonies we selectively recruited . . . those who were strong, caring, and motivated," he wrote in his 1998 book *Combatting Cult Mind Control*. Because it took so much time and money to enlist a new member, they avoided wasting resources on someone who seemed liable to break down right away. (Similarly, multilevel marketing higher-ups agree that their most profitable recruits aren't those in urgent need of cash but instead folks determined and upbeat enough to play the long game. More on that in part 4.) Eileen Barker's studies of the Moonies confirmed that their most obedient members were intelligent, chin-up folks. They were the children of activists, educators, and public servants (as opposed to wary scientists, like my parents). They were raised to see the good in people, even to their own detriment.

In this way, it's not desperation or mental illness that consistently suckers people into exploitative groups—instead, it's an overabundance of optimism. It's not untrue that cultish environments can appeal to individuals facing emotional turmoil. Love-bombing will feel especially good to those weathering stressful life transitions. But the attraction is often more complex than ego or desperation, having more to do with a person's stake in the promises they were originally told.

In Jonestown, for instance, the reason why Black women perished in disproportionate numbers on that fateful day in 1978 was not that their despair made them easier to "brainwash." The targets of a complicated political storm, Black women in the '70s had an extremely hard time amplifying their voices above those of the white (often unwelcoming) second-wave feminist activists, as well as the civil rights movement's mostly male leaders. Jim Jones, who had ties to all the right people (Angela Davis, the Black Panthers, the American Indian Movement, the reactionary Nation of Islam, many left-leaning Black pastors in San Francisco, not to mention his own "Rainbow Family"), seemed to offer a rare opportunity to be heard. "Black women were especially vulnerable because of their history of sexist/racist exploitation, as well as their long tradition of spearheading social justice activism in the church," explains Sikivu Hutchinson. The reason so many of these women died was because they had so much to gain from a movement that turned out to be a lie.

Laura Johnston Kohl readily admitted that no one forced her to buy what Jim Jones was selling; she willingly heard the buzzwords and thought-terminators she wanted to hear and tuned out the rest. "I was [in Jonestown] for political reasons, so Jim thought, 'Every time I see Laura sitting in a meeting, I have to address politics.' I let him address my priorities, and put blinders on for other things," she told me.

Letting people tell us only what we want to hear is something we all do. It's classic confirmation bias: an ingrained human reasoning flaw defined by the propensity to look for, interpret, accept, and remember information in a way that validates (and strengthens) our existing beliefs, while ignoring or dismissing anything that controverts them. Experts agree that not even the most logical minds—not even scientists—can escape confirmation bias completely. Common human irrationalities like hypochondria, prejudice, and paranoia are all forms of confirmation bias, where every little thing that happens can be interpreted as an illness, a reason to deride a whole demographic of people, or proof that something is out to get you. This phenomenon also explains why, to a willing listener, even the vaguest astrological horoscopes, psychic readings, and indistinctly "relatable" social media posts seem to resonate uniquely.

Cultish leaders all rely on the power of confirmation bias by presenting a one-sided version of information that supports their ideology and that their followers actively want to hear; after that, confirmation bias does the work for them. Enhanced by peer pressure, it becomes all the harder to resist. Confirmation bias also explains why cultish leaders' rhetoric is so vague—the loaded language and euphemisms are made purposefully amorphous to mask off-putting specifics about their ideology (and to leave space for that ideology to change). Meanwhile, followers project whatever they want onto the language. (For instance, whenever Jones used the phrase "White Night," followers like Laura interpreted it how they wished, neglecting the possibility of more violent implications.) For most people, the fallout of confirmation bias isn't Jonestown-level urgent, but it's not the woefully naive or desperate among us who get that far. In many cases, it's the extraordinarily idealistic.

In her post-commune years, Laura became a public school teacher, a Quaker, an atheist, and an immigrant rights activist. "I have not become less political, but I have become less mesmerized by [the] words somebody says," she told a reporter in 2017. Still, Laura never stopped searching for a way to achieve what the Peoples Temple originally promised. Even after all the violence, hope remained. "If there were any way for me to live in a community today, I would do it in a hot second," she told me. "It just has to be leaderless, and it has to be diverse." Easier imagined than found;

Laura let loose a wistful sigh. "I just haven't found a safe community that has the things I want. But I am a communalist, always have been. I've had a wild life, but I don't want to sit with people who have had my same kind of wildness. So I did really love living in Peoples Temple. Jonestown was the highlight of my life."

Frank Lyford, who lost his entire early adulthood and beloved partner to Marshall Applewhite, doesn't stew in regret, either. "My view of my experience is, I incarnated with the goal of going through Heaven's Gate. The deeper we go into darkness, the higher we go back into the light like a slingshot," he professed. "If I hadn't experienced the darkness and suppression, the diminishing of self, I wouldn't have had the impetus to move into this self-awareness I have now." Indeed, while love-bombing can attract the broken, it's those like Laura and Frank—those buoyed by enough idealism to trust that the act of committing wholeheartedly to this group will bring them miracles and meaning, to believe it's worth the leap—who stay.

"For me to have a positive outlook on life, I do my own brainwashing," Laura told me matter-of-factly. "You look at the news. I'm fighting cancer now. We all have things in our lives that suck, things that try to keep us in bed or not fighting back. I definitely believe in brainwashing, or I guess you could call it 'positive vibes' in some settings. But I think we all brainwash ourselves. Sometimes we have to."

After our last interview, Laura and I remained in touch, emailed back and forth, swapping Synanon stories. One night she got together with some old Synanon pals for dinner, and with a guy named Frankie she wrote down a list of all the special jargon she remembered from back in those days. "Frankie thinks he remembers your dad—he was a youngster in Synanon at that time too," she wrote to me, the glossary enclosed. "Funny, the synchronicity of life when you don't expect it." Two months later, Laura passed away from cancer, surrounded by so many of the companions she'd collected over the course of her wild life.

I can think of so many motives explaining why someone might enter a community like the Peoples Temple or Heaven's Gate. Maybe it's because life is hard and they want to make it better. Because someone promised they could help. Maybe they want their time on Earth to feel more meaningful. Maybe they're sick of feeling so alone. Maybe they want new friends. Or a new family. Or a change of scenery. Maybe someone they love is joining. Maybe everybody is joining. Maybe it just seems like an adventure.

The majority leave before things get deadly, but the reasons some don't might also sound familiar. They're the same reasons you might put off a necessary breakup: denial, listlessness, social stresses, fear they might seek revenge, lack of money, lack of outside support, doubt that you'll be able to find something better, and the sheer hope that your current situation will improve—go back to how it was at the start—if only you hold on a few more months, commit a fraction more.

The behavioral economic theory of loss aversion says that human beings generally feel losses (of time, money, pride, etc.) much more acutely than gains; so psychologically, we're willing to do a lot of work to avoid looking defeats in the eye. Irrationally, we tend to stay in negative situations, from crappy relationships to lousy investments to cults, telling ourselves that a win is just around the corner, so we don't have to admit to ourselves that things just didn't work out and we should cut our losses. It's an emotional example of the sunk cost fallacy, or people's tendency to think that resources already spent justify spending even more. We've been in it this long, we might as well keep going. As with confirmation bias, not even the smartest, most judicious people are immune to loss aversion. It's deeply embedded. I've been in my fair share of toxic one-on-one relationships, and noticing the similarities between abusive partners and cultish leaders has been, to say the least, humbling.

So while power abuse can look like poisoned punch and purple shrouds, the linchpin is what it sounds like. If a form of language cues you to have an instant emotional response while also halting you from asking further questions, or makes you feel "chosen" just for showing up, or allows you to morally divorce yourself from some one-dimensionally inferior other, it's language worth challenging. The labels and euphemisms probably won't kill you, but if you're after more than just basic survival, surely the most fulfilling life is the one you narrate yourself.

"Our inner guidance is the best possible navigation any of us has," Frank Lyford told me. This doesn't mean we can't look outward (or upward) for help through the chaos. "But to me," he continued, "a good coach is one who does not guide, but shines light on a person's deepest desires and blocks." Not a guide, not a prophet, not a guru telling you just what to say. But a candle in the dimly lit library of existence. The only dictionary you need is already open.

Part 3

Even YOU Can Learn to Speak in Tongues

i.

My favorite story to tell is the one about how I got kidnapped by the Scientologists.

I was nineteen years old, spending a lonely summer in Los Angeles with a crappy part-time job, a mild depression, and not much I could bring myself to do except pal around with the one person I knew in town: an aspiring young actress named Mani. We'd met freshman year at NYU. Mani was living in the Valley while on break from school, sharing an apartment with her mom and kid sister, auditioning for commercials and starring in USC student films. Mani was spellbinding: She had long blond hair and catlike Ukrainian features, wore baggy T-shirts with fishnets, and owned a pet snake. Her full name was Amanda, like mine, but freespirited and untamable as she was, she went by the more exotic-sounding nickname: *Mah-nee*. We'd carry out our days doing whatever she wanted. Mani would say the word, and—mesmerized in that way insecure teenage girls always are by self-possessed ones—we'd do it: I would drive from Santa Monica to Studio City to pick her up in my Honda Civic, and we'd go thrift shopping, or diner hopping, or horseback riding on Tuesday afternoons in the hills ($12 for two hours). Or, on one day, against my better judgment, accepting an invitation to take a "personality test" at the colossal Church of Scientology in Hollywood.

On this particular July afternoon, Mani and I were frolicking about town, on our way to procure a Jamba Juice, when two twentysomethings standing on Sunset Boulevard, dressed for a high school orchestra performance (white button-downs, black slacks), held out a pair of pamphlets and asked, "Do you want to take a personality test?" I was a self-absorbed youth who loved nothing more than flipping to the quiz sections of *Seventeen* and *Cosmopolitan* to find out who my *Gilmore Girls* heartthrob was or what fall fashion trend I should try according to my zodiac sign. But I had also spent two semesters in New York City, and so had Mani, so you can imagine my surprise when, instead of bullishly power walking right past this street team as if they belonged to a species below human, Mani stopped, smiled, and said, "That sounds FUN."

Once we examined the literature and discovered it was branded with Scientology insignia, I thought for certain Mani would agree to steer clear of these wackadoodles. Get the smoothies. Drive home. But no, Mani was cool and beautiful and afraid of nothing, so the Scientology thing only intrigued her more. "We have to do it," she declared, batting her gigaparsec-length eyelashes.

Trying to be as down for anything as Mani was, I consented. We put our quest for frozen fructose on pause, climbed back into my Civic, drove four blocks, and turned down L. Ron Hubbard Way. After parking in a spacious lot, we sauntered up to the 377,000-square-foot cathedral, which I'd only ever seen from afar. You might have come across photos of this place in a documentary or a Wikipedia black hole—it's that famous building with the Grecian-looking facade embossed with a story-tall Scientology cross (featuring eight points instead of four). It's mecca for the twenty-five thousand Scientologists living in the US,* most of whom reside (troublingly) within twelve square miles of my current home in Los Angeles.

Here in LA, Scientologists hide in plain sight: They're your baristas, your yoga teachers, your favorite CW-drama side characters, and—especially—all those twinkly-eyed transplants hoping to strike it big in Tinseltown. Wannabe film stars find ads in issues of *Backstage* magazine promising career-making crash courses in entertainment, or they attend artist workshops secretly backed by Scientology. Others accept street team invitations to take a personality test. Some spend an afternoon touring the impressive campus (it's open to the public) or attend an intro course as a joke. Some do it with a genuinely open mind, and most get the hell out of Dodge long before they're really in. But a select few look at celebrities like Tom Cruise, John Travolta, and Elisabeth Moss—Scientology's mascots—and tell themselves, *That could be me.*

You can't clock a Scientologist in the wild by the way they dress or act—only by how they speak, and only if you know what to listen for. "If you were ever in Scientology,

---

* This stat is according to the Institute for Advanced Study, though Corporate Scientology claims a staggering ten million members worldwide.

you could have a conversation with someone and know what they were by the way they talked," an ex-Scientologist named Cathy Schenkelberg told me in an interview. Now in her forties, Cathy has been out of Scientology for nearly two decades and lives part-time in Ireland, working as a small-time actress. In 2016, Cathy gained some media attention after coming forward with a story about how she once auditioned for what she thought was a Scientology training video, but turned out to be an interview for the role of Tom Cruise's girlfriend. When they asked her seemingly at random what she thought of the movie star, she told them frankly, "I can't stand him, I think he's a narcissistic baby. I'm really bummed about him splitting with Nicole." Needless to say, she didn't get the gig, and not long after, Katie Holmes was cast instead.

These days, Cathy performs a one-woman traveling comedy show about her Scientology experience called *Squeeze My Cans*. It's a cheeky reference to Hubbard's famous E-Meter, a lie detector–esque machine resembling an oversize portable CD player from the '90s. An E-Meter is used to "audit" (spiritually counsel) PCs ("pre-clears," or auditing subjects), though even the Church of Scientology admits that the device "itself does nothing." A few years ago, half a decade after she'd escaped the church, Cathy was doing a voice-over gig for McDonald's when she met a director named Greg, and within five minutes of conversing, alarm bells sounded in her brain. "He was giving me directions, and he used certain words," she said . . . like "enturbulated," meaning upset, and "Dev-T," which stands for Developed Traffic and means "cause for delay." "So I said to him, 'Greg, are you a Scientologist?' And he goes, 'Yeah, I was wondering the same thing about you.' He ended up killing himself, but that's another story. Yeah, he lost everything."

Having big dreams makes you vulnerable; Scientologists know this, and they claim to hold the keys to help you unlock your potential. "They call it a postulate," Cathy told me on a phone call from Galway, referencing Scientology's special label for a personal resolution, or what your average LA stargazer might call a "manifestation." Even deep into her Scientology membership, after she'd lost entire homes and savings accounts and relationships, after the church had taken up so much of her time that she was barely auditioning anymore, Cathy never gave up on her ambitions of making it. "I just wanted to do the levels and move back to New York and be a musical theater actress," she recounted dolefully. "But of course that didn't happen."

Promises for an extraordinary life are how they roped in Cathy, who stayed in the church for eighteen years, long after she was desperate to leave it. In 1991, Cathy was a twenty-three-year-old entertainer on the rise living in Chicago. She was starting to book big commercials and voice-over jobs ("I don't know if you've heard 'SC Johnson: A Family Company,' or 'Applebee's: Eatin' Good in the Neighborhood,'" she performed for me over the phone). That year, Cathy met a sweet fellow actress who told her about an amazing artists group she was part of, full of up-and-comers just like her. It was called Scientology. Cathy had never heard of the group, but it sounded legit. It had "science" in the name, after all. Cathy started accompanying the actress to local meet-ups, which she later learned were organized by the church. "Like, 'See? We're not so crazy. We're artists,'" Cathy explained of their motives. "Art is the universal solvent! L. Ron Hubbard said that."

In the beginning, Cathy seemed like the perfect recruit—bright-eyed, dedicated, making a good living, and eager to do good in the world. "Like lots of people in their early twenties, I wanted to join the Peace Corps or Habitat for Humanity, some type of group where I could contribute in a way that wasn't being a self-centered performer," she explained. And she was searching, spiritually. A cradle Catholic from Nebraska who grew up one of ten kids, Cathy lost an older brother suddenly in a car crash when she was thirteen. "That was a turning point for me," said Cathy, who stopped going to her home church after they tried convincing her God had "chosen" her brother to die young, because he was "ready to be with God." It was a thought-terminating cliché, and Cathy wasn't buying it: "I thought, 'Well then that's not the kind of God I want anything to do with.'" She spent the next decade seeking a higher power elsewhere—everything from crystal meditation workshops to churches where they spoke in tongues. Nothing stuck.

Originally, Scientology was pitched to Cathy as a non-denominational group whose primary goal was to "spread hope for mankind." She recalls, "Everyone I talked to said the same thing, 'Oh, you can practice whatever you like,' and I believed them. They play it cool." But once inside, Cathy quickly learned that partaking in other religions was absolutely not allowed. "They call it 'squirreling,'" she told me. "One day you look up and you realize you're in a room of five hundred people hip-hip-hooraying for a bronze bust of L. Ron Hubbard at the front of the room."

ii.

Back in Los Angeles, Mani skipped (as I trudged) into the elephantine lobby of Scientology HQ, where we were greeted by a too-smiley white gentleman in his forties. He was wearing a crisp, cornflower-blue suit and a meticulous silver coif, and he spoke perfect Spanish to his largely Latinx staff. "Thank you for joining us, follow me," he said, ushering us deeper into the building. Mani shot me a blithe smile, while I marked every nearby exit.

In all, Mani and I spent more than three hours within Scientology's walls, zigzagging through a Byzantine sequence of their introductory grooming tactics. First, we killed forty-five minutes in their museum hall, meandering between exhibits of E-Meter devices and propaganda videos of world religious leaders saying vague things about L. Ron Hubbard, edited together to paint him as God's gift to humanity. Then we were shepherded into a classroom where the grinning man in the blue suit handed us each a thick paper packet, a Scantron sheet, and a tiny golf pencil. We used these to complete a ninety-minute personality assessment. When at long last we finished, Mani and I wearily exited the room and waited another half century while our results were tabulated. By midafternoon, Mr. Blue Suit materialized and separated us to deliver our results. Mani went first; I loafed about for another ungodly half hour, and then it was my turn to reenter the classroom.

While Mani sat five yards away, having been passed on to a different employee, engaged in a conversation I couldn't hear, Mr. Blue Suit proceeded to undress my personality. My test revealed the faults that were holding me back in life—stubbornness, fear of vulnerability (fair enough, though I quietly wondered what Mani's had been). After every critique the man repeated the same line, his eyes sparkling: "Scientology can help you with that." Once his spiel ended, he ushered me over to join Mani and the other employee. Here came the hard sell. This second guy, a spray-tanned D-list actor I thought I recognized, proceeded to pitch us a series of self-improvement courses—books and workshops— nothing religious, just "tools" to help us live better lives. For us, hardworking students with so much promise, they'd cost just $35 a class. If we committed today, he could take us to another wing of the building and show us a preview of what we'd learn right now.

"They get you with the small basic courses," Cathy explained to me, eight years after my Scientology tryst. "That's the bait and switch of it all. They start you out with these courses on 'communication' or 'ups and downs in life,' and you go, 'Wow, this really helps.'" Unlike me, Cathy didn't grow up with a father who openly talked about the cult he was forced into; she was open-minded and optimistic, and, most important, she didn't know anything about Scientology before she got involved. "It was 1991, before Google, so it's not like I could look it up," she contextualized. "I was just basing it on this actress I liked who was in it." After Cathy started paying for courses and further intertwining her life with Scientology, she certainly didn't do any independent digging, because the rules explicitly forbid it. "I was told not to look on the internet, the newspaper, or any 'black PR' on Scientology," Cathy said. "All of those people and journalists were just trying to destroy Scientology because they know it's the only hope for mankind." Now, every time Cathy entered a counseling session (always prepaid, of course), the first questions asked were: Did you look at the internet? Has anyone said anything bad to you about Scientology? Have you had an affair? Have you been taking drugs? Have you talked to a journalist? Are you connected to someone in an embassy or the government, or politics, or a lawyer? "It was madness," Cathy says in retrospect—though at the time, these just seemed like routine precautions.

Very quickly, Cathy's new circle started using us-versus-them verbiage to isolate her from those on the outside. "They had ways of making you look at people who weren't in Scientology as less-than," she remembers. Any criticisms of the organization were labeled "hidden crimes." A person or behavior that threatened Scientology in some way—like associating with an SP (suppressive person: a bad influence, like a journalist or skeptical family member)—was instantly labeled PTS, potential trouble source. There is a long list of PTS Types in Scientology. These classifications—Types 1–3 and Types A–J—all refer to different enemies of the church: doubters, criminals, people who've publicly denounced or sued Scientology, people too closely connected with an SP, people who've undergone a "psychotic break." PTS Types covered the array of potential "thems" and were used to legitimize the slander or persecution of anyone who didn't fall in line.

"My Scientology friend, Greg, the creative director on that McDonald's commercial? After he killed himself, they said he was PTS Type 3, which meant he had a psychotic break," Cathy told me. "But really, Greg had spent all his money and his father's money, sold his house, lost his job. He was destitute." It wasn't "PTS"; Scientology had ruined the guy's life. Cathy sighed into the receiver. "Now that I think about it, I wasted two decades of my life with that place." But back then, she thought it was her eternity. "With this knowledge, I was going to be able to come back the next lifetime and handle stuff other people couldn't, you know?"

Scientology operates on the logic that because L. Ron Hubbard's "tech" (belief system) is flawless, if you're in the church and unhappy, then you clearly did something to "pull it in." This is a classic Scientology thought-terminating cliché meaning that whatever negative experience you're having, it's no one's responsibility but yours. "You made it happen," Cathy explained. "If I tripped on the sidewalk and sprained my ankle, it wasn't the crack in the sidewalk that did it, it's because I *pulled it in*." Perhaps you were entertaining doubts or associating too closely with an SP. In Scientology, if you have an issue with your marriage, with a friend group, or at work, you need to either disconnect, or "handle" (meaning convince them to agree with the doctrine), or "get them on the bridge"—convert them to Scientology.

While Mani nodded her head agreeably at the spray-tanned half celebrity, a table of books and DVDs before us, I remembered a lecture my mother had given me in high school after we'd decided to take up a family friend's invitation to spend spring break at a beach resort in Mexico. "As soon as we arrive, they're going to bring us into a little room, and they're going to try to sell us a timeshare," my mother warned me, soberly. "They're going to feed us snacks, and compliment us, and make it sound amazing. But the LAST THING you EVER want to do is buy a timeshare. It will ruin your life. So we are going to say 'no thank you' over and over again. And then they're going to try to take us into another little room to show us a video presentation. No matter what, we CANNOT let them take us into that next room. We are going to stand up, and we are going to leave."

When I was nineteen, approaching my fourth hour behind those Scientology HQ doors, I had no idea the millions of dollars and psychological trauma this "church" had wrung out of everyday people under false promises that started with $35 self-improvement workshops. All I knew was that this felt like a timeshare sell. And I couldn't let them take us to that next room.

So I stood up. I said, "NO THANK YOU. WE ARE NOT YOUR TARGET AUDIENCE. PLEASE LET US GO. MANI, WE'RE LEAVING." Spray Tan made eye contact with Mr.

Blue Suit, exhaled, and gestured toward the door. I grabbed Mani by the hand, and we ran—properly sprinted—out of the classroom, through the museum hall, across the lobby, and out the door, then swooped into my Civic and sped away, never to turn down L. Ron Hubbard Way again.

"Kidnapped" might be a smidge over the top in describing my interaction with the Scientologists . . . but I wouldn't put it past them to engage in such activities. Years later, I would learn that if I had let them take it one step further by agreeing to purchase one of those courses, I would've been led into a movie theater and shown a Scientology welcome video, with the door locked behind me. If I had continued on with Scientology from there, signed up for more courses and one-on-one sessions, I would have sunk thousands of dollars, if not millions, whatever I had, into my churchly commitment.

Because my ultimate goal as a Scientologist would be to "go clear"—to ascend to L. Ron Hubbard's highest level of enlightenment. The church dangles this ambition above all its members, but its convoluted hierarchy of levels—which secretly go on forever—ensures that going clear is not actually possible. After Cathy had spent a few years in Scientology, she made it to a level called Dianetic Clear, which, to her knowledge, was the finish line. "I thought, 'Oh my gosh, this is great. I'm clear, I have no more reactive mind, I'm going to go out into the world with this newfound awareness,'" she recounted. But in Scientology, as soon as you arrive at what you've been led to believe is the top, they reveal that there's more. This is just the beginning, actually, because now you've opened up a whole other spiritual can of worms. Now you have no choice but to climb to the next level, then the next. And whereas before it might have cost $5,000 or $10,000 to level up, now it could be $100,000 or more.

As I continued to traverse Scientology's Bridge to Total Freedom (the path to going clear), I'd come to learn about supernatural concepts like Xenu the galactic overlord and invisible "body thetans" (spirits of ancient aliens that cling to humans and cause destruction). It would have been lunacy. But I'd have to keep going. The sunk cost fallacy and loss aversion would tell me I can't quit. Not this far in. Plus, my superiors would insist, if I leave right now in the middle of an upper level of auditing, I could pull in misfortune. I could pull in disease, even death. One ex-Scientologist named Margery Wakefield, a longtime officer in the OSA (Office of Special Affairs, Scientology's "intelligence agency"), wrote about how she was off-loaded (kicked out) in the early '80s for her perceived decline in mental state. After more than a decade of membership and intense conditioning, Margery was convinced that it was so energetically perilous to be off-loaded in the middle of her current level that she would surely die within twelve days. (She was flabbergasted when she, in fact, survived.)

If I'd gotten as far as Margery and joined the OSA or the SEA-Org (Scientology's paramilitary group), I would have signed a Billion-Year Contract of spiritual allegiance and undergone training to help the church execute federal crimes: breaking and entering, stealing government documents, wiretapping, destroying criminal evidence, lying under oath, whatever was deemed necessary to protect the church. Once, Margery alleges, she witnessed church officials plan the murders of two people. One was a defector, who'd been caught by the OSA and taken prisoner in a motel room. "The next day they were going to take him out to sea and deep six him—tie weights to him and dump him overboard," she wrote in a 1990 affidavit. The other was a journalist who'd written a book that spoke critically of Scientology (a fact I try my best to forget).

Because, as I would eventually learn, Scientology law > wog law ("wog" meaning outsider; it may be connected to an outdated racial slur, but etymologists aren't sure). According to multiple ex-Scientologists, there's a whole course on how to lie to wogs. It's called TR-L, which stands for Training Routine Lie. Purportedly, in TR-L, Scientologists learn the skill of lying with unwavering confidence, even under extreme stress. In her affidavit, Margery Wakefield details an incident from her time in the OSA when she was forced to make false allegations of sexual misconduct against a judge. The judge was slated to preside over a case dealing with Scientology, but allegedly, the church didn't like him and wanted him removed, so they assigned Margery to claim he'd sexually harassed her. Before testifying, Margery remembers asking one of her superiors about lying under oath and was answered with a quote from a Hubbard policy called "the greatest good for the greatest number of dynamics."* It meant that whatever it took to ensure Scientology's survival must be done. It meant to call on her TR-L and obey. It meant the ends justified the means.

By that point, I would have become so absorbed in Scientology's doctrine that I would not even be able to communicate with anyone outside the church. "I don't know if you've ever listened to a conversation between two high-ranking Scientologists," Steven Hassan, our ex-Moonie psychologist, told me, "but you won't understand anything they're talking about." Because with Scientology, as with all cultish religions, language is the beginning and end of everything. In a sense, it's God itself.

---

* A "dynamic" in Scientology refers to some element of the universe, starting with the self, then extending to your family, the community, the species as a whole, and all the way to God or infinity. Hubbard described eight total dynamics, to which Scientologists refer using acronyms; so, you might call your spouse your "2D" and your group of friends your "3D."

iii.

This is the power of religious language: Whether it's biblical words we've grown up with and know so well we never consider anything different (God, commandment, sin), or alternative phrases from a newer movement (audit, PC, Bridge to Total Freedom), religious speech packs a unique punch. Remember the theory of linguistic performativity, the one about how language doesn't just reflect reality, it actively creates reality? Religious language, some scholars say, is the single most intensely performative kind of speech there is. "Much religious language 'performs' rather than 'informs,' [rousing us] to act out the best or the worst of our human nature," wrote Gary Eberle in his book *Dangerous Words.*

Religious utterances cause events to transpire in a way that feels incomparably profound for believers. "We used chants to manifest things, to make things happen, to make ourselves believe in things," said Abbie Shaw, a twenty-seven-year-old social worker and ex-member of Shambhala, a controversial offshoot of Tibetan Buddhism, whom I met at a party in LA and interviewed a few days later. "Some of the language I loved and call on to this day, and some of it caused the most bizarre trauma I've ever experienced."

Think of all the performative verbs that come up in religious scenarios: bless, curse, believe, confess, forgive, vow, pray. These words trigger significant, consequential changes in a way that nonreligious language just doesn't. The phrase "In the name of God" can allow a speaker to wed, divorce, even banish someone in a way that "In the name of Kylie Jenner" cannot (unless you truly do worship at the altar of Kylie Jenner, believing she has sole jurisdiction over your life and afterlife, in which case, I stand corrected, and I wish I'd interviewed you for this book). You could very well say "In the name of God" (and certainly "In the name of Kylie Jenner") in a nonreligious way. Scriptural phrases pervade our daily secular lives—just think of Bible-themed slang like #blessed. But these expressions assume a special, supernatural force when stated in a religious context, because the speaker is invoking what they believe to be the ultimate authority to imbue their declaration with meaning.

"Religious language involves us in the largest context of all," Eberle writes. It's beyond the domain of the workplace or politics; if someone really believes, it's beyond all of space and time. Eberle continues: "While a baseball umpire calling 'Y'er out' is performative within the ballpark in the context of the game, religious language involves the performance of a person's whole self and very existence."

There's a reason most religions encourage prayer: Language strengthens beliefs. In her studies of contemporary witches and "charismatic Christians" (if they do say so themselves*), psychological anthropologist Tanya Luhrmann found that if one wants to know their higher power—if they want that deity to seem real—they have to open their mouths and speak to them. The theological vocabulary between the Christians and witches Luhrmann observed was quite different, but for both, repeatedly engaging in prayers or spells "sharpened their mental imagery" of the figure on the receiving end. Practice talking to a spiritual authority over and over again, and in time, you'll conjure the experience that Yahweh or the alien overlords or whoever you're chatting with is talking back. Eventually, when certain spontaneous thoughts pop into your mind during the conversation (or what Luhrmann calls an "imaginal dialogue")—say, a certain person's face or a scene that seems to answer a question you've been pondering—these thoughts will seem not self-authored but instead as though they are coming straight from your higher power. People need something to help make the supernatural feel real, Luhrmann told me, and language does precisely that.

In order to keep the tremendous power of religious language healthy and ethical, it must be confined to a limited "ritual time." This refers to a metaphorical domain in which

* The word "charisma" actually has centuries-old ties to Christianity. It derives from the ancient Greek word for "gift or favor," and by the mid-1600s, it'd come to mean "God-given abilities," like teaching and healing. It wasn't until the 1930s that the word evolved to connote an earthly knack for leadership, and only in the late '50s was it used in the more pedestrian sense of "personal charm."

using Biblical words like "covenant" or Tibetan chants suddenly seems completely appropriate. To enter ritual time, some symbolic action typically must take place, like singing a song, lighting a candle, or clipping on your SoulCycle shoes (really). Rituals like these signal that we're separating this religious thing we're doing from the rest of our daily life. And there's often an action at the end, too (blow out the candle, repeat "namaste," unclip the shoes) to get us out of ritual time and back to everyday reality. There's a reason the word "sacred" literally means "set aside."

But an oppressive group doesn't let you leave ritual time. There is no separation, no going back to a reality where you have to get along with people who might not share your beliefs, where you understand that performing a mantra or citing the Ten Commandments in the middle of lunch would be a violation of the unspoken rules for how to be. With destructive groups like Scientology, the Moonies, the Branch Davidians, 3HO, The Way International (a fundamentalist Christian cult we'll talk about later), and so many others, there is no longer a "sacred space" for that special language. Now words like "abomination," "curse," and "lower vibration" or whatever unique vocabulary the group uses holds that almighty power all the time.

In American culture, religious language (particularly Protestant language) is everywhere, informing secular choices we make without us even explicitly noticing. I recently came across a frozen low-fat mac 'n' cheese meal with the word "sinless" printed on the packaging. Conjuring the devil to talk about microwavable noodles felt a touch melodramatic, but that's how deep religious talk runs in American culture: There are sinners and saints, and the latter choose 2 percent dairy.

The permeable membrane between religion and culture is also what allows so many corners of the capitalist marketplace to call upon God to promote their products . . . including and especially the multilevel marketing industry (a cult category we'll discuss in depth in part 4). Christian-affiliated direct sales companies like Mary Kay Cosmetics and Thirty-One Gifts encourage recruits by saying that God is actively "providing" them with the "opportunity" to sell makeup and tchotchkes . . . and to convert others to do so, as well. Billion-dollar businesswoman Mary Kay Ash was once confronted in an interview about her famous tagline: "God first, family second, Mary Kay third." When asked if she thought she was using Jesus as a marketing ploy, she responded, "No, he's using me instead."

iv.

You could fill a book longer than this one with a list of all the thought-terminating clichés, loaded language, and us-versus-them labels cultish religions around the world use to convert, condition, and coerce their followers.

To start, take a look at Shambhala, where thought-terminating clichés were disguised as wise Buddhist truisms. In 2016, ex-Shambhalan Abbie Shaw moved to the group's idyllic Vermont commune to work the front desk and study meditation for what was only supposed to be a casual summer. A recent college graduate from California who'd relocated to New York City for a job in PR, Abbie missed the co-ops she'd lived in as a student at UC Santa Cruz. By her mid-twenties, Abbie was looking to press a spiritual reset button. That's when she dropped into a Tibetan mindfulness class and quickly fell in love with its teachings of "basic goodness"—the idea that all beings are born whole and worthy, but become lost along the way. That's why we meditate: to get our basic goodness back.

Abbie was hungry to learn more, but extended meditation retreats were expensive. So when an instructor told her about the opportunity to spend three months with Shambhala for free, working and living in a small pastoral town, it seemed like just the "journey" she was looking for.

Shambhala had dozens of meditation centers and retreats all over the world; Vermont was one of their largest. Abbie couldn't wait to get out of the city. She booked her ticket.

Right away, there was a lot to love about Shambhala—the camaraderie, the teachings of generosity and acceptance, even the trees seemed too good to be true. "I remember when I first landed in Vermont, I had never seen so many shades of green," Abbie told me over coffee, two years after defecting.

Shambhala was founded in the 1970s by Tibetan monk and meditation guru Chögyam Trungpa. Largely responsible for bringing Tibetan Buddhism to the West, Trungpa had studied comparative religion at Oxford and earned a reputation, even among many non-Shambhalans, as an enlightened genius. He counted among his pupils the poet Allen Ginsberg, author John Steinbeck, David Bowie, and Joni Mitchell. "I'm confused now how to feel about him because his books are amazing," Abbie confessed. "He was a master of language. A poet."

But Trungpa also had a raging alcohol problem, which everyone knew and quietly accepted. Complications from alcohol abuse are what ultimately led to his death in 1987 at the age of forty-eight, after which his son, known as the Sakyong, took his place. Trungpa didn't try to hide his addiction; in fact, he found ways to work it into his teachings. Notoriously, Shambhala celebrations overflowed with booze and debauchery. "In the Buddhism world, the Shambhalas are known as the party Buddhists," Abbie recounted with ambivalence. Trungpa also famously slept with many of his students, some of whom became Abbie's teachers. "There was no way that stuff was all consensual," she winced. "But everyone was just like, 'Oh, it was the seventies.'"

Trungpa was the nucleus of the Shambhala "mandala." This was the organization's chain of command: a sea of plebeian practitioners and a pecking order of teachers above them. Trungpa was obsessed with militaries and hierarchies, especially after his stint in England, so he infused his rhetoric with war metaphors; followers learned to call themselves "warriors of Shambhala." A pyramid of power is very anti-Buddhist, however, so Trungpa disguised it as a circle, a mandala, with no "top" but a cozy center instead.

If members had a question or concern, there was no skipping rank. Abbie remembers an acharya (a high-ranking teacher) toward the mandala's center, a wealthy white man whose wife was, in Abbie's words, "a total asshole." Milking the limited authority available to her, the wife would revel in making worker bees like Abbie perform menial tasks, like handwashing napkins or repeating tedious rituals in front of her. But whenever Abbie tried to bring up the wife's actions to a shastri (a low-ranking teacher), she was delivered the same thought-terminating cliché: "Why don't you sit with that?"

This was a bastardization of a key Buddhist teaching, which says to "drive all blames into one." Essentially, it means that if you're experiencing something negative, you can't change the outside world, so you have to look inward to solve the conflict. (So many shady New Age gurus—ranging from NXIVM's Keith Raniere to Teal Swan–type self-help guides—warp similar teachings to fault followers for their own mistreatment under the guise of "internal work" and "overcoming fears.") "What people struggle with," Abbie continued, "and it's a huge philosophy question in Buddhism, is how do you challenge social injustice?" How do you address external problems that are so clearly not rooted in your own baggage, while still following Buddhism's principles? "There are a lot of really interesting answers," said Abbie, "but in Shambhala, we didn't get any." In Vermont, the presented "solution" was always the same: Why don't you sit with that?

Shambhala's use of cultish language was manipulative in an eerily passive way . . . totally unlike Scientology, whose founder wasn't one for subtlety. L. Ron Hubbard got his start less as a spiritual leader and more as a sci-fi buff who took his fandom way too far. Hubbard was obsessed with space fantasy and George Orwell, and he authored hundreds of science fiction stories, which served as precursors to Scientology's texts. In the style of conlangs (constructed languages) like J. R. R. Tolkien's Middle-earth tongues, Hubbard published not one but two unique Scientology dictionaries: the Technical Dictionary and the Admin Dictionary. Together, these volumes contain over three thousand entries. As of this writing, you can look up portions of the Technical Dictionary online and go absolutely cross-eyed combing through entries from A through X. Hubbard filled these books with existing English words ("dynamic," "audit," "clear," etc.) charged with new Scientology-specific meanings, as well as made-up neologisms—Dianetics and thetans are among the most recognizable.

Hubbard liked the technical sound of jargon from fields like psychology and software engineering, so he co-opted and redefined dozens of technical terms to create the impression that Scientology's belief system was rooted in real science. The word "valence," for example, has several definitions across linguistics, chemistry, and math, and generally refers to the value of something. But in Scientology, "valence" signifies possession by an evil spirit or personality, as in the sentence, "You sure mock up a good SP valence." To a neuropsychologist, an "engram" is a hypothetical change in the brain related to memory storage, but to a Scientologist, it's a mental image recorded after a painful unconscious episode from a PC's past. Engrams are stored in the reactive mind and require auditing if the PC has any hopes of going clear (and if you can understand that sentence, mazel tov, you're on your way to speaking fluent Scientology).

The linguistic world Hubbard created was so legit-sounding—so inspired and comprehensive—that it sparked a host of copycat "cult leaders." NXIVM founder Keith Raniere lifted all kinds of terms straight from Scientology, like "suppressives," "tech," and "courses," as well as illusory, pseudo-academic acronyms, like EM (exploration of meaning, NXIVM's version of auditing) and DOS (Dominus Obsequious Sororium, Latin for "Dominant Submissive Sorority," a secret all-female club within NXIVM composed of so-called "masters" and sex-trafficked "slaves"). Like in

Scientology, Raniere knew his followers were motivated by a desire for exclusive, erudite wisdom; his knockoff Hubbardese helped him exploit that.*

In the style of Newspeak, Hubbard took dozens of common words that boast a range of colorful English meanings and reduced them to one incontestable Scientology definition. "Clear" means at least thirty different things in everyday English (easy to understand, empty or unobstructed, acquitted of guilt, free of pimples, etc.). But in Scientology, it has but one solitary definition: "a person who has completed the Clearing Course." Using it any other way would be to demonstrate a lack of understanding of Hubbard's texts. That would be considered PTS, a threat to the church, which you'd want to avoid at all costs.

Scientology knows it has no power without its cultish language, but that the language is also what implicates the group as dangerously cultish. So, to stay as clandestine and protected as possible, the church holds a slew of copyrights on its writings, terminology, names, even symbols. Infamously litigious, Scientology frequently buries outsiders and defectors who comment on or satirize its language too

---

* Raniere, however, lacked Hubbard's vision, and was caught and charged for racketeering and sex trafficking, long before building a Scientology-level empire. In 2018, lawyer and religion scholar Jeff Trexler commented in *Vanity Fair*, "Not all [aspiring 'cult leaders'] have the same talent level [as] L. Ron Hubbard. . . . [He] was a master." Less a "movement" and more a failed pyramid scheme, NXIVM, joked Trexler, was like "the Amway of sex." (Though I'd actually argue that the multilevel marketing giant Amway is more of a threat to society than NXIVM ever was. We'll talk about that in part 4.)

publicly (oops) under groundless lawsuits and metaphysical threats that exposing untrained ears to mere talk of Xenu and other high-level Scientology concepts will bring on "devastating, cataclysmic spiritual harm."

On the phone with Cathy, I told her I hadn't remembered Mr. Blue Suit talking about evil galactic monarchs or thetans during my experience at Scientology HQ that summer in LA. "Well, of course not," she replied. "They don't start you out with that stuff. They'd lose you. If they told me about aliens when I first got there, I would have been out, and it would have saved me a lot of money." For this reason, Scientology's intro courses—Overcoming Ups and Downs in Life, Communication—are all quite broad, and delivered in plain English. To ease you into the ideology, the vernacular is introduced bit by bit.

"They start just by shortening a lot of words," Cathy told me. Indeed, Scientology's lexicon is replete with insider-y acronyms and abbreviations. If a word can be shortened, they do it: ack (acknowledgment), cog (cognition), inval (invalidation), eval (evaluation), sup (supervisor), R-factor (reality factor), tech (technology), sec (security), E-Meter (electropsychometer), OSA and RFP (parts of the organization), TR-L and TR-1 (training routines), PC, SP, PTS, and so on ad nauseam.

Spend ten or twenty years committed to the church, and your vocabulary will be replaced wholesale by Hubbardese. Take a look at this dialogue, an example of an entirely plausible conversation between Scientologists that Margery Wakefield composed for her 1991 book *Understanding Scientology*. Translations (by yours truly) are in brackets.

Two Scientologists meet on the street.

"How're you doing?" one asks the other.

"Well, to tell you the truth, I've been a bit out ruds [rudiments; tired, hungry, or upset] because of a PTP [present time problem] with my second dynamic [romantic partner] because of some bypassed charge [old negative energy that's resurfaced] having to do with my MEST [Matter, Energy, Space, and Time, something in the physical universe] at her apartment. When I moved in I gave her an R-Factor [reality factor, a harsh talking-to] and I thought we were in ARC [affinity, reality, and communication; a good state] about it, but lately she seems to have gone a bit PTS so I recommended she see the MAA [an officer in the SEA-Org] at the AO [Advanced Organization] to blow some charge [get rid of engram energy] and get her ethics in [getting your Scientology shit together]. He gave her a review [auditing assessment] to F/N [floating needle, sign of a completed audit] and VGIs [very good indicators] but she did a roller coaster [a case that improves and worsens], so I think there's an SP somewhere on her lines [auditing and training measures]. I tried to audit her myself but she had a dirty needle [an irregular E-Meter reading] . . . and was acting really 1.1 [covertly hostile] so I finally sent her to Qual [Qualifications Division] to spot the entheta on her lines [something that happens if you've recently consumed black PR]. Other than that, everything's fine . . .

In the beginning, learning this private terminology makes speakers feel, well, cool. "In the early days, it was really fun . . . or 'theta,' as we'd say," Cathy told me, referencing Scientology's slang term for "awesome." Who doesn't love a secret language? "It made you feel superior, because you had these words that other people didn't, and you did the work to understand them."

It's not just religious cult leaders who use language to imbue followers with a false sense of elitism; I've noticed similar us-versus-them rhetoric in cultier areas of my own life. For a few years, I was employed as a writer at a cliquey online fashion magazine, and one of the first things I noticed about my chic new colleagues was how they spoke almost entirely in inscrutable abbreviations (or "abbrevs"). They even made up abbreviations that took exactly as long to say as the full-length words (for instance, they always referred to this one website called "The Ritual" as "T. Ritual"), simply because it sounded more exclusive—harder for "uncool people" to understand. To me, it was clear that this language served as a detection system to identify insiders and outsiders. And it was a way of gaining control, of coaxing underlings to learn the lingo, to conform, which they did eagerly, in hopes of being "chosen" for special opportunities and promotions.

In Scientology, it was hard to see how a few fun acronyms could cause much harm. But under the surface, these word shortenings were deliberately working to obscure understanding. In any given professional field, specialized jargon is often necessary in order to exchange information more succinctly and specifically; it makes communication clearer. But in a cultish atmosphere, jargon does just the opposite: Instead, it causes speakers to feel confused and intellectually deficient. That way, they'll comply.

This confusion is part of the big trick. Feeling so disoriented that you doubt the very language you've been speaking your whole life can make you commit even more strongly to a charismatic leader who promises to show you the way. "We want to make sense of reality, and we use words to explain to ourselves what's happening," Steven Hassan explained. When your means of narration are threatened, it's distressing. By nature, people are averse to such high levels of internal conflict. In states of bamboozlement, we defer to authority figures to tell us what's true and what we need to do to feel safe.

When language works to make you question your own perceptions, whether at work or at church, that's a form of gaslighting. I first came across the term "gaslighting" in the context of abusive romantic partners, but it shows up in larger-scale relationships, too, like those between bosses and their employees, politicians and their supporters, spiritual leaders and their devotees. Across the board, gaslighting is a way of psychologically manipulating someone (or many people) such that they doubt their own reality, as a way to gain and maintain control. Psychologists agree that while gaslighters appear self-assured, they are typically motivated by extreme insecurity—an inability to self-regulate their own thoughts and emotions. Sometimes gaslighters aren't even 100% aware that what they're doing is manipulative. In cultish scenarios, however, it's often a deliberate method of undermining the fundamentals of truth so followers will come to depend wholly on the leader for what to believe.

The term "gaslight" originates from a 1938 British play of the same name, in which an abusive husband convinces his wife she's gone mad. He does this in part by dimming the gaslights in their house and insisting that she's delusional every time she points out the change. Since the 1960s, "gaslighting" has been used in everyday conversation to describe one person's attempts at tricking another into mistrusting their entirely valid experiences.† "Gaslighting sometimes happens when words are used so people can't quite understand," explains sociologist Eileen Barker. "They become confused, made to feel fools. Words can sometimes mean the exact opposite of what you think they mean. Satanic groups do this, where evil means good and good means evil." Loaded language and thought-terminating clichés (like Shambhala's "why don't you sit with that") can prompt followers to disregard their own instincts. "Words," says Barker, "can make it so you don't quite know where you are."

In Scientology, by far the most exotic form of gaslighting shows up in a process called Word Clearing. I could not believe my eyes the first time I read about this dizzying ex-

---

† Although, I have found that on social media in particular, "gaslighting" is sometimes tossed around willy-nilly (say, to over-dramatize simple miscommunications, where no manipulation took place), which is a shame, since the word's intended meaning is both specific and very useful.

ercise, through which a follower strips their vocabulary of what the church calls misunderstood words, or MUs. "According to church doctrine, the reason all of you reading this essay aren't sitting in a Scientology course room right this minute is because you have MUs," wrote ex-Scientologist Mike Rinder for his blog. "LRH's tech is flawless and not to be questioned—everything he wrote is easy to understand and makes perfect sense. If something can't be grasped, it's simply because a person bypassed an MU."

While reading Scientology literature during a course or auditing session, a member must demonstrate that they've fully understood every word in the text by the church's standards. You do this by grabbing a Scientology-approved dictionary (they endorse a select few publishers) and looking up each MU you cross. If any new MUs appear in the original MU's entry, you have to look those up, too—a dreaded process called a word chain—before you can continue reading. From the most obscure polysyllabic term down to the tiniest preposition,‡ every MU must be word-cleared. If you look up an MU and still can't word-clear it, you must track down its derivation, use it in a sentence, then sculpt a physical demo of the sentence using Play-Doh. These wearisome

---

‡ Scientology actually offers a whole upper-level course extravagantly titled Key to Life where you word-clear all the grammatical basics—conjunctions, determiners, single-letter words. "Can you imagine having to look up the word 'of'?" Cathy asked me. (As a linguist, I actually could, yes, though certainly not on Scientology's terms.) Graduating from Key to Life is considered extremely prestigious just because you've invested so many hours of tedium into the church.

steps are all part of Hubbard's teaching methodology, Study Tech.

How does an auditor decide you've misunderstood a word? Telltale signs might include displaying disinterest or fatigue (yawning, perhaps), and certainly disputing something you've read. Once, Cathy descended into a Word Clearing nightmare while reading a book called *Science of Survival*. In it, there was a chapter condemning homosexuality. "I was like, 'I don't get this,' so they made me word-clear everything, until I finally was sent to Ethics because I disagreed," she recalled. The whole process was expensive and defeating. "Can you imagine?" Cathy continued. "You're in a course, and you have one or two evenings a week to be in there, and you get stuck on one word, which takes you the whole three hours to clear? At a certain point, you don't want to question stuff. You're like, 'Just go through it. Just agree with it.'"

V.

Personally, when I think of cultish religious language, I don't think of kooky acronyms or mantras or Word Clearing. I think of one thing and one thing only: speaking in tongues.

I've been haunted by this practice, desperately curious to understand it, ever since I was fourteen and first watched the documentary *Jesus Camp*. Filmed in North Dakota, *Jesus Camp* profiles a Pentecostal summer camp where little kids learn how to "take back America for Christ." My parents rented the DVD in late 2006 and I watched it twice, back to back, rubbernecking like mad, just to make sure I hadn't hallucinated these adults preaching the evils of evolution, public school, Harry Potter, homosexuality, and abortion to kids barely old enough to read. In one scene, a perspiring male preacher in his fifties repeats a quote from Doctor Seuss's *Horton Hears a Who*—"A person's a person, no matter how small"—delivering a pro-birth sermon with such emotional gravity that it brings the young campers to tears. The preacher beckons the children to join him in a roaring chant—"Jesus, I plead your blood over my sins and the sins of my nation. God, end abortion and send revival to America." He rouses them to demand that God raise up righteous judges to overturn *Roe v. Wade*. The children crowd around the preacher bellowing, "Righteous judges! Righteous judges!" He places red tape over their mouths, scrawled with the word "Life," and they suspend their little palms in the air, pleading.

While that was all wildly engrossing to my fourteen-year-old self, by far my favorite part of the movie was when the kids spoke in tongues. Scholars tend to use the term "glossolalia" to describe this practice, in which a person utters unintelligible sounds that seem to approximate words from some perceived foreign language during states of religious intensity. Glossolalia is commonly found in certain Christian sects like Pentecostalism, in addition to fringier, more controversial religious groups like The Way International.

Among believers, glossolalia is typically thought to be a heavenly gift. Their belief is that the "words" pouring from the speaker's mouth are from an angelic or ancient holy language, which is then "translated" by someone else, as interpretation is a separate gift. "What's interesting is the reaction of the person speaking glossolalia to the translation, because sometimes you can tell they don't like what the translator is saying, but they go ahead anyway," commented Paul de Lacy, a Rutgers University linguist and one of the world's only modern glossolalia scholars.

What researchers like de Lacy have found is that the words a glossolalia speaker produces aren't actually all that foreign. They're not words you'd find in a dictionary, but they do tend to follow the same phonetic and phonological rules as the orator's native tongue. So you wouldn't be likely to hear an English-speaking glossolalist start a word with the consonant cluster /dl/, since this sound doesn't exist in English (though it can be found in other languages, like Hebrew). You'd also never hear, say, a Bulgarian glossolalia speaker use a rhotic American /r/. And a glossolalist from Yorkshire wouldn't suddenly drop every last feature of their North English lilt while speaking in tongues.

Glossolalia is a faith-based practice, so one can't say in any scientific way what it really is. But it is clear what glossolalia does. "The primary function of glossolalia is group solidarity," explains de Lacy. "The person's demonstrating they are part of the group." Other science shows that speaking in tongues just plain feels good—it's the linguistic equivalent of shaking your body around as a way to let loose. A 2011 report from the *American Journal of Human Biology* found that glossolalia was associated with reduced cortisol and elevated alpha-amylase enzyme activity, two typical signs of stress reduction. It has also been found to lower inhibitions and increase self-confidence, which is a side effect of religious chanting, too. (A small 2019 study out of Hong Kong found that when compared to non-religious chanting and resting states, Buddhist chanting generated brain and heart activity associated with a lack of self-consciousness and feelings of transcendent bliss.)

In a vacuum, there is technically nothing dangerous about glossolalia, but in practice, it has a sinister side. In the mid-1970s, John P. Kildahl, a psychologist and author of *The Psychology of Speaking in Tongues*, observed that glossolalia seemed to provoke greater intensity of faith. This was especially true when a person's first time speaking in tongues occurred right after a period of intense personal trauma (which Kildahl found to quite often be the case). When someone's debut glossolalia episode followed an earth-shattering life change, they frequently formed a sense of dependence on the experience. "Almost as a reason for one's being," said Kildahl. That is to say, glossolalia can provoke a potent conversion event.

For multiple reasons, speaking in tongues can make a person quite suggestible. Christopher Lynn, an author of that *American Journal of Human Biology* study, determined that glossolalia is basically a form of dissociation, a psychological state in which areas of conscious awareness are separated. With dissociation, a person's behaviors or experiences seem to just happen all by themselves, outside of their control, as if in a trance. There's a wide spectrum of what scholars might classify as dissociation, from severe cases of dissociative identity disorder all the way down to common feelings of detachment, like searching all over for your phone when it's right in your hand, or zoning out while staring at a bonfire. But dissociation can also present as self-deception, where appearances in consciousness seem real despite evidence to the contrary. Under the pressures of an ill-intentioned leader, glossolalia can compromise a speaker's ability to unsnarl the overwhelming metaphysical experience they seem to be having from the guru's influence.

In the end, glossolalia is a powerful emotional instrument—the ultimate form of loaded language—and some religious higher-ups absolutely take advantage. The Way International, a violent and controlling evangelical Christian group, is famous for teaching its members that every true believer can and should speak in tongues, as it is the "only visible and audible proof that a man has been born again." One anonymous ex-Way member recalled a traumatic glossolalia experience from her childhood for the blog *Yes and Yes*: "When I was 12, I was . . . required to speak in tongues in front of everyone, and I was so shy I couldn't do it," she said. "The man hosting the class . . . put his face very close to mine and essentially bullied me into speaking in tongues." The girl's parents watched the interaction unfold from across the room, benumbed by cognitive dissonance. "I was crying," she continued. "The man was inches from my face . . . using the language of love in the most terrifying, bullying way."

Say you're a child like this Way International survivor was or one of the *Jesus Camp* kids, who grew up in an oppressive religious environment and only ever knew its language. You'd think these young folks would be doomed; if "brainwashing" were real for anyone, it would have to be impressionable kids. But the truth is that it's still quite possible to develop a sense of doubt, even when you're very small and lack the access or permission to describe it.

Just look at Flor Edwards. Now a writer in her thirties, Flor was raised in one of the most notorious Christian doomsday cults in modern history, the Children of God, which she documents in her memoir, *Apocalypse Child*. Later renamed the Family International (for "branding" reasons), the group was founded in California in 1968. Its leader, David Berg, known as Father David, later ordered his followers to move to developing countries, believing Western nations would be "first to burn in the fires of hell."

Along with her parents and eleven siblings, Flor spent most of her '80s-era childhood in Thailand.

The Children of God is perhaps best known for its troubling convolution of Christianity, love, and sex. As part of his dogma, Berg decreed that an adult male follower was welcome to have sex with anyone, even underage girls, a rule he euphemistically christened the "Law of Love." The Children of God was also infamous for its signature practice of flirty fishing. Alliterative and innocent-sounding, "flirty fishing" could be the name of an iPhone game. Instead, it was a mandate that female members recruit men into the fold by seducing them with sex. "The media now refers to it as 'prostitution for Jesus,'" Flor told me in an interview, a mild irritation in her voice. "There's a verse in the Bible that says, 'Follow me and I'll make you fishers of men.' It's when Jesus is calling his disciples to, I guess, drop their nets and follow him." But Berg, who considered himself a prophetic interpreter, decided the verse meant women had to go out and use their bodies to "fish for men." In the Children of God, "God is love, love is sex" was a tagline everyone knew.

This juxtaposition of salaciousness and religion felt radical to Berg's hippie-minded flock. "He would cuss and swear. He was very informal. It wasn't like, 'My dear followers, I'd like to take a moment to address blah, blah, blah,'" Flor described. Berg's adamant anticapitalism, anti-church stance resonated with many '70s-era seekers, who admired his philosophy that Christianity needed a makeover—that the new church needed to replace the old church. "Just like an old wife needed to be replaced with a new wife," relayed

Flor. "He would literally say we were the young sexy new bride for Jesus."

This was the linguistic atmosphere in which Flor came of age, yet she was still able to resist it, at least in her head. "I was born into the Children of God, but there was definitely a part of me that always felt suspicious, though I wasn't allowed to voice that," she said. Where did her suspicions come from? "My gut," she told me. "Sometimes it was just logic, like, 'Wait, you're saying this but then we're doing that? Why do we have to hide all the time? Why do we have to pretend like we're in school?' But the bigger ones were really this protective instinct over my siblings. When I'd see them treated a certain way, I knew it wasn't right. You shouldn't be getting disciplined when you're six months old. You shouldn't be being trained to be God's 'prostitutes for Jesus' when you're so young. No matter what you call it."

So even though it's true that not everyone who joins and stays in an abusive religion is troubled or unintelligent, it's equally true that finding yourself ears-deep in that kind of cultish quandry couldn't happen to "just anyone." We'll learn more about why some people have instincts like Flor's, and others don't, in part 4.

vi.

I've heard the phrase "sexual nerds" used to describe people who are into kink—feet, whips, that sort of thing. These folks can be thought of as "nerds" because what they're really doing is experimenting in corners of sexual culture that might not be considered conventionally cool or glamorous. Analogously, I like to think of certain cultish religious types as "spiritual nerds." They're the people who geek out on niche theological theories that others might not come across, who find themselves on a lifelong journey of reckoning with their life purpose and are willing to look outside the box to find it. "I've always been curious about the outskirts of society," Abbie Shaw, the ex-Shambhalan, told me. "I grew up in a privileged family, a traditional synagogue, a big city. Now I'm a Buddhist and work on Skid Row."

There is nothing inherently wrong with spiritual nerdiness. Exploring different belief systems, taking nothing you've learned in Sunday school for granted, and coming to your own decisions is what so many twenty-first-century young people are already doing, to varying degrees. As Abbie said, "I'd been searching for a long time before Shambhala. I showed up and thought, 'Let's just see where this goes.'" But Abbie still struggles with how much unquestioned faith she had to put into her teachers. Sometimes she flashes back to a chant she had to recite daily called "the supplication for the Sakyong." The chant reinforced members' unending devotion to their leader, Trungpa's successor, asking the Buddha to prolong his life. Abbie always had uneasy feelings about the Sakyong, and she bristled against this obligation to ritualistically exalt him. At the same time, she loved her community enough to assume the best and roll with it. Looking back, she's disturbed by how long her trust was drawn out: "It was never supposed to be two years of my life," she confessed.

Sticking with the kink metaphor, there's only one way to have a constructive, nontraumatizing experience using whips and bondage, and it's by having a key component down pat: consent. You have to have a safe word so that your partner knows exactly when you want out. Kink fundamentally doesn't work without this. Metaphorically, you need a safe word with religion, too. When you're experimenting with faith and belief, there has to be room to ask questions, express your misgivings, and seek outside information, both early on and deep into your membership. "The most important thing to remember is that if something is legitimate, it will stand up to scrutiny," Steven Hassan told me.

In 2018, Abbie had already decided to leave Shambhala when a bombshell news story surfaced. That summer, the *New York Times* published a series of grievous reports accusing the Sakyong of sexual assault. A group of ex-Shambhala women united to bring forward their testimonies about not just the Sakyong, but also some high-ranking teachers.

Abbie released a pensive exhale: "It was surreal to watch this whole community crumble."

Soon after the controversy, Abbie quietly slipped out of Vermont. Not quite at the Scientology point along the influence continuum, Shambala's exit costs didn't threaten her physical safety or all-out decimate her life; in a way, her departure felt anticlimactic, like a balloon idly trickling to the floor. She moved to Los Angeles to pursue a master's in social work, and now she practices a less hierarchical form of Buddhism. Abbie attends a variety of meditation groups and then goes home to her own apartment, which she shares with three roommates ("so I still get the communal aspect," she laughs). She has a mini altar in her room, and sometimes privately draws on teachings she learned in Vermont. "I try to take what I liked and leave the rest," she said. "I'm still figuring out what to make of everything that happened."

Cathy Schenkelberg, too, dabbles in alternative spirituality, keeping a healthy distance from Scientology and all her old relationships from that time. After leaving the organization, she had to replace everyone in her life—her friends, her agent, her manager, her accountant, her dentist, her chiropractor—because they were all in the church. But sometimes, when she least expects it, Cathy will overhear a Scientology term out in the world, and those pangs of paranoia she felt for so many years suddenly crackle through her nervous system. "I have a visceral reaction when fellow ex-Scientologists use the terminology. It's PTSD to me," Cathy confessed. "I say, 'Out of respect, could you please not use

Scientology language? It upsets me.' Here, I'll use a word: It *enturbulates* me."

My old Scientology confrère Mani and I haven't seen each other much since our personality test "kidnapping" nearly ten years ago, but I reached out to her as soon as I began writing this chapter. She's still in LA, doing the acting thing. I realized I'd never gotten her take on that day's events. I started to fear that maybe my amygdala had caricatured the memory and she'd long ago forgotten it. "Do you ever think about that experience?" I texted her. Her response arrived quickly, in all caps: "I DO ALL THE TIME."

My most crystallized recollection from the ordeal was Mani's inexplicable calm and endurance. She just cheerfully went along with the whole thing for hours, like fully committing to a hammy acting bit—with me, the wet blanket foil, begging to bail. But Mani recalls being far more distressed. "I remember how they kept us separated," she messaged back. "I remember a woman telling me (sternly) that it would be very quick (it wasn't), not to be afraid to be truthful with myself as this was the only way they could properly assess what I would need, and that 'me and my friend would be back together before we knew it.'" Mani revealed that over the past decade, she's had other, more frightening Scientology encounters. But our personality test was "the real introduction."

I suppose for aspiring actors in Los Angeles, or dreamers anywhere, really, it's something of an occupational hazard: Whether you're on a quest for spiritual enlightenment, eternal salvation, or a Tom Cruise level of renown so powerful that you essentially become a god on Earth, devoting your life to something so behemoth that heaven itself is on the line requires big risks, tough commitments, and a pretty intense suspension of reality to believe it's possible. The stakes are just that high. In some cases, you get out within a few hours, a little bit shaken; in others, you lose everything. But there is always a story.

As soon as you get your language back, you can tell it.

Part 4

Do You Wanna Be a #BossBabe?

i.

Roses are red
Money is green
The American Dream
Is a pyramid scheme

Hey girl! I LOVE your posts. You have SUCH a fun energy!! Have you ever thought about turning that energy into a side hustle? Let me ask you a question ;) If there were a business where you could work part-time from home but make a full-time living, would that interest you at all? Because that's what I've been up to. Some people are super closed-minded to stuff like this which limits their opportunities, but you seem open to new things, which is exactly what it takes to be successful!! Would you be down to hear more? I could call you sometime this week? It's way too much to type out lol. My number is xxx-xxx-xxxx, what's yours? I look forward to hearing back, boss babe! xoxo

I'm ears-deep into one of those miserable Facebook benders—
a stalkerish wormhole where all of a sudden, I've found myself terribly invested in what someone I don't even know
wore to prom in 2008—when a few rogue clicks lead me
to a post I never thought I'd see: Becca Manners from middle school is trying to sell a weight loss scam to her 3,416
"friends."

I first met Becca, the most self-possessed tween girl in all
of Baltimore County to my knowledge, in rehearsals for our
seventh-grade musical. Becca and I bonded over some dirty
joke and were tight all the way through twelfth grade. We
ignored the school dress code together, scream-sang Ala-
nis Morissette in the car together, had a million sleepovers,
and now here we are, age twenty-seven and 2,700 miles
apart, judging each other's lives on social media. Becca and
I haven't spoken in almost a decade, but my periodic internet lurkings tell me that she's married, sober, living up the
road from her parents, and wants all her Facebook friends,
including me—currently in LA, inhaling an overpriced cocktail and a gust of car exhaust—to ask her about her new
#wellness business opportunity.

It's early summer when photos of my old pal sorority-
squatting next to bags of sugar to represent the pounds she's
quickly shed start spamming my newsfeed. All the photos
are accompanied by vague captions like "Feeling amazing
and my journey is just getting started! #sugarshotresults."
She never says exactly what the product is or who she's
working for, but I can tell just by her hazily inspirational
status updates, forced exclamation points, and nebulous

hashtags that it could be nothing but the perky dialect of direct sales. "Welp, another one bites the dust," I text my current best friend, Esther, who grew up in Florida and can name a dozen ex–high school classmates of her own who've been sucked into the same "cult" as Becca: the cult of Multilevel Marketing.

Multilevel marketing, network marketing, relationship marketing, direct sales . . . there are at least half a dozen synonyms for MLMs, the legally looopholed sibling of pyramid schemes. At once a pillar of Western capitalism but relegated to the fringes of our workforce, MLMs are pay-and-recruit organizations powered not by salaried employees but "affiliates." These are largely white-male-founded, white-female-operated beauty and "wellness" brands whose recruits peddle overpriced products (from face cream to essential oils to diet supplements) to their friends and family, while also trying to enlist those customers to become sellers themselves. MLM pitches always follow a similar script: They feature talk of this "once-in-a-lifetime opportunity" to be the "boss babe" you really are, "start your own business," and "make a full-time income working part-time from home" to gain the "financial independence" you've always wanted. American MLMs number in the hundreds: Amway, Avon, and Mary Kay are among the best recognized, alongside Herbalife, Young Living Essential Oils, LuLaRoe, LipSense, dōTERRA, Pampered Chef, Rodan + Fields, Scentsy, Arbonne, Younique, and the iconic Tupperware.

When I think of the typical MLM recruit, I think of women like Becca—middle-class shiksas from my high school who stayed in our hometown (or moved to Florida . . . always Florida), got married young, had babies shortly thereafter, and spend an impressive sum of hours on Facebook. A year or several into stay-at-home motherhood, they get roped into hawking the slimy serums of Rodan + Fields, paper-thin leggings of LuLaRoe, or something similar (you name it, I've seen it in my newsfeed). Most MLMs target non-working wives and moms, and they have since the dawn of the modern direct sales industry in the 1940s. Direct sales advertising has always riffed on whatever "female empowerment" buzzwords were trendy at the time. While midcentury MLM recruitment language promised that Tupperware was "the best thing that's happened to women since they got the vote!" in the age of social media, it plays on the faux-spirational lingo of commodified fourth-wave feminism.

Modern MLM language is defined by the sort of snappy, uplifting quotes you might find printed in flouncy brides-maid cursive on Pinterest: "You got this, boss babe"; "Channel your inner #girlboss"; "Build a fempire"; "Be a mompreneur"; "#WFH so you can make money like the SHE-E-O you are without having to leave your kids!!" These phrases work initially to love-bomb potential sellers; then, over time, they become loaded with the weight of the American Dream itself, conditioning followers to believe that "giving up" on the business would mean giving up on your very life's purpose. In the early days, direct sellers introduced their overpriced, chemical-smelling trinkets in person, host-ing at-home product demonstrations called "parties." But these days, many women choose to kick it new school and parade their goods across social media, as their snarky former classmates cringe-scroll past. My best friend Esther is a twenty-six-year-old Hodgkin's lymphoma survivor who posts a lot about cancer-free living and radiates just the breed of health-conscious positivity many MLMs enjoy exploiting. She gets one or two Instagram DMs a week from different direct sales recruiters trying to seduce her into the flock. "Hey girlboss!!! Love your content!!! You're such a badass!!! Have you ever thought about turning your cancer journey into a business?!?!" She screenshots them all, sends them to me, and deletes.*

As far as I'm concerned, an MLM is to a pyramid scheme as a Starbucks Vanilla Bean Crème Frappuccino is to a straight-up milkshake: One is just a glorified version of the other—an assertion that would scandalize any devoted MLMer. "I would NEVER be involved with a pyramid scheme. Pyramid schemes are ILLEGAL," they tend to say as their stock defense. This phrase is a thought-terminating

---

* MLMers are willing to turn any tragedy—from a cancer diagnosis to a worldwide pandemic—into an opportunity to sell and recruit. It didn't take long after COVID-19 ravaged the US in early 2020 for MLM recruits to start making public claims that their products could protect against both the virus and financial insecurity. The Federal Trade Commission sent warnings to over fifteen direct sales companies, including Arbonne, dōTERRA, and Rodan + Fields, after their affiliates blew up social media with images of "immunity-boosting" essential oils, captioned with the hashtags "#covid #prevention," and verbiage like "RODAN and FIELDS is always open for business even during quarantine! I've been working from home for over 3 years now and still making money when other people aren't! Isn't it about time you found out what it is I do and how this company really works? . . . #workfromhome #financialfreedom."

cliché, and it's an amusing one, because if you take the logic even one step further, it becomes obvious that simply saying something is illegal doesn't mean it's not real or that you're not involved. You can't rob a bank and then, when accused, just say, "I didn't do it, robbing banks is illegal," to prove your innocence. In the city of Mobile, Alabama, it's against the law to throw plastic confetti, but that doesn't mean plastic confetti doesn't exist or that people don't use it. Sometimes citizens of Mobile throw plastic confetti without knowing it's illegal, and sometimes they know plastic confetti is illegal but use it anyway because they don't realize the confetti they're using is made of plastic. Either way, it's still a thing, and it's still not cool.

Pyramid schemes are indeed outlawed, and for good reason. They have the capacity to cheat people out of a couple hundred dollars or drive them all the way to bankruptcy and despair. They can shatter entire communities, even national economies, like those of Albania and Zimbabwe, which have been decimated by schemes both pyramid and Ponzi. It's no surprise, then, that pyramid schemes don't announce themselves as such. Instead, these companies hide in plain sight behind all sorts of euphemistic labels: gifting circles (also called looms, lotuses, or fractal mandalas), investment clubs, and, most commonly, multilevel marketing companies—MLMs for short.

Like the challenge of distinguishing between a religion and a cult, there are few objective distinctions between pyramid schemes and "legit" MLMs. In theory, the difference seems to be that members of MLMs like Avon and Amway chiefly earn compensation from selling a particular good or service, while pyramid schemes primarily compensate members for recruiting new sellers as quickly as possible. But in practice, a pyramid scheme is essentially just an MLM that was run poorly and got caught (more on that shortly).

Both organizations are set up like this: A company's charismatic founder starts by love-bombing a small group of people into accepting an invitation to start their own business. Unlike typical entrepreneurship, there's no education or work experience necessary to get involved; the offer is open to anybody who really wants to "change their life."

There is no base salary—that would make this a job and you an employee. The MLM makes sure to charge these words so they trigger images of bureaucratic indentured servitude and misery. Instead, you earn a small commission for whatever product you personally manage to unload. That makes this a "business opportunity" and you an "entrepreneur." Much better.

Only two steps are required to get you started on this simple path to financial freedom: First, purchase a starter kit containing samples and marketing materials, which will cost you anywhere from $50 to $10,000 or more. Pennies, either way, for a new business owner's initial start-up cost. Opening up a store or launching an e-commerce brand is so expensive, but getting in on this movement? Practically free when you think about it.

Next step: Each month, recruit ten new members (sometimes it's less, but often it's not) to join your team, which you'll want to give a jaunty nickname like the Diamond

Squad or the Good Vibe Tribe, or maybe something cheeky like You Win Some, You Booze Some. This will help everyone feel bonded. Then, encourage each of those members to recruit ten monthly sellers of their own. You'll take a small cut of all the earnings underneath you (from the starter kits and inventory your recruits purchase, and also from their product sales). The generation of sellers below you is called your "downline," while the person who recruited you is your "upline." Meanwhile, the MLM founder, sitting pretty at the very top of this tetrahedron, takes a cut of everything.

In order to move product and grow a downline, you'll need to spread the word about your amazing new business to everyone you know. To do this, you'll be encouraged to host lots of parties, both IRL and online. You'll want to buy snacks and wine, or spend hours concocting cute virtual activities to incentivize attendance. You'll beseech guests to thumb through the brochures and lotions or whatever in hopes that they'll buy something, or—better yet—want to sign up to sell the stuff themselves. It doesn't matter if the company's products are any good or fill a market demand, and neither does the fact that zero sales experience is required to come aboard. The typical rules of economics do not apply here. The system is promised to work no matter what. As long as you pay the buy-in fee, follow the company's path precisely, and don't ask too many questions, the American Dream itself will be yours.

This pay-and-recruit pattern continues for each new group of recruits, affiliates, consultants, distributors, guides, ambassadors, presenters, coaches, or whichever entrepreneurial-sounding title the company chooses for its enrollees, who are made to feel special and chosen, even though literally anyone who ponies up can join. Money from recent joinees siphons to their upline, helping those above meet their monthly or quarterly sales quotas, which are disguised with friendlier-sounding labels like "goals" and "targets." Fail to reach these periodic minimums? Expect to be demoted or kicked out of the company. That can't happen. You'd let everyone down, especially yourself. So, you might end up just buying all the inventory personally and eating the cost, with your eyes fixed firmly on the prize: to ascend the company's structure, a geometric shape that would certainly never be described as a pyramid with levels, but instead maybe a "ladder" with "rungs." Surely, next month you'll find tons of recruits, achieve your goals, and finally be awarded a ritzier title: Senior Consultant, Head Coach, Sales Director.

"There's a lot of discussion around what I would describe as the purchase of hope," analyzed Stacie Bosley, an economics professor at Hamline University in Minnesota. Bosley is one of the only financial researchers in the world who formally studies MLMs. Evidently, the male-dominated field of economics doesn't seem to think an industry dominated by #girlbosses would be a hotbed of academic intrigue. (How wrong they are.) "Sometimes the MLM industry will even acknowledge that really what people are buying is a form of hope," Bosley says. It's part of why most MLM recruitment language is so grandiose and indirect—they avoid technical terms like "investment" and "employment," favoring aspirational phrases like "amazing opportunity" and "empowering activity."

But these sugarcoated code words are hiding some really sketchy numbers. As these generations of downlines all grow, the market rapidly becomes overcrowded with everyone and their mother (literally) mining the same saturated communities, trying and failing to enlist newbies underneath them. The number of hopefuls expands exponentially from a small profitable few at the peak to a screwed-over mass at the base. If the MLM's model, which your upline and founder endorsed over and over at all their business opportunity presentations and millionaire workshops, goes perfectly to plan, then yes, you will become rich within a year . . . but according to basic math, guess how many people will be in your downline by the end of those twelve months? Over a trillion. That's 142 times the world population, and a whole lot of diet pills.

Study after study shows that 99 percent of MLM recruits never make a dime, and the lucky 1 percent at the top only profits at everyone else's expense. The calculations speak for themselves, but even if you're totally in the red, with an empty bank account and a storage locker full of eye cream nobody wants, at least you get to stay a part of your team—your "family"—whose fellow recruits you might call your sisters and whose leaders you might even refer to as Mom and Dad. By this point, you've developed a deeply emotional, codependent bond with these people. You text with them all day. You're in secret Facebook groups together. You have weekly meetings via video chat, where you all drink pink wine ("because you earned it!") and spill your souls to each other. You save up all year to attend the company's costly conferences so you can see your fellow boss babes in person.

So, you'll likely choose to ignore your damages, forget the math, and hold out, especially since you were emphatically promised a big payday at the end of all this. Plus, everyone above and beneath you is counting on you to make money. If you give up now, you'll disappoint your Diamond Squad. You'll disappoint your family and your "family." You'll disappoint God. You won't be a #girlboss anymore. You'll be nothing. Under that kind of pressure, things can get undeniably cultish.

MLMs are scammy, but they aren't just your average scams. They're complex, life-consuming organizations with a language and culture all their own. MLMs have strong and pervasive ideologies that are missionary in character, and members revere their founding leaders, who share a desire not just to run a successful company but to rule the free world, on the level of religious worship. The famous University of Chicago sociologist Edward Shils defined "cult charisma" as "whenever an individual is understood to be connected with crucial questions of human existence." To this degree, MLM leaders are as influential as 3HO's Yogi Bhajan and Shambhala's Chögyam Trungpa. They convert you with compliments and exclamation points and fauxspiration. They condition and coerce you with loaded buzzwords (often invoking God), and they use thought-terminating clichés to silence dissent. They train you to employ these same techniques with everyone you know, at every turn.

MLMs wield us-versus-them verbiage to tightly bond their followers and frame them as better than traditionally employed Americans. At Amway, the world's biggest MLM, anyone who works for an "employer" as opposed to an upline mentor is said, with disdain, to have a J.O.B., a "jackass of a boss." "When you work for someone else, you will never get paid what you're worth," Amway's recruits are all taught to say. To MLMers, the word "entrepreneur" represents not just a career but a "morally superior way of being in the economy," comments Nicole Woolsey Biggart, a UC Davis sociologist and author of *Charismatic Capitalism: Direct Selling Organizations in America*.

MLMs gaslight you into believing that if you follow their flawless system and don't succeed, there is simply something wrong with you. "Every willing and hardworking person can be successful in this business . . . *a good system always works!*" is a thought-terminating cliché pulled directly from Amway's handbook. Known for its extreme juxtaposition of motivational buzzwords with dark threats of failure, MLM language conditions you to think that if you're not swimming in cash, it's not the company's fault— it's yours. You didn't have enough faith or perseverance to unlock your potential and earn what should've been a guarantee. There are countless MLM vision boards all across the web, featuring emotionally manipulative platitudes like "People often fail in MLMs before they ever begin because the approach is from the head, not the heart," and "I really hate when broke people who don't work complain about being broke. #billionairemindset." In an article titled "Top 50 MLM Quotes of All Time," the website OnlineMLMCommunity.com showcases a litany of misattributed inspirational quotes, including this axiom, falsely associated with Winston Churchill: "The pessimist sees difficulty in every opportunity. The optimist sees opportunity in every difficulty"—as if the British statesman's successes had anything to do with direct sales, even if the quote really were his.

"It was like mental warfare," reflects Hannah, a former "presenter" at the Christian makeup MLM Younique, on her experience being gaslit by the company. As a college student, Hannah blew $500 on inventory before getting kicked out of the company for failing to meet her sales quota. "If I was in a situation where I didn't have [my] university, a partner, and other community groups . . . I would have felt so awful about myself. . . . Being told you're not good enough multiple times a day could ruin some people."

In the end, MLMs aren't in the business of selling start-up ventures to entrepreneurs. Like most destructive "cults," they're in the business of selling the transcendent promise of something that doesn't actually exist. And their commodity isn't merchandise, it's rhetoric. For many recruits who never sell a single product, the entire MLM experience consists of committing to a community, proudly calling yourself a consultant, conferencing into team pump-up calls, and attending expensive conventions. The numbers don't make sense, but the words keep you there anyway.

Several months after Becca Manners's weight loss posts suddenly disappeared from my Facebook feed, I decided to send her a cautiously worded message. I knew I had to tread lightly. Had Becca lost everything and was too embarrassed to admit publicly that she'd been duped? Had the MLM forced her into silence with veiled or explicit threats? Had she secretly made out like a bandit and didn't want to reveal herself as a scammer? "Terribly sorry if this seems random, but am I remembering correctly that you've been involved with direct sales endeavors in the past?" I wrote. "I'm writing about the language of multilevel marketing and would love to hear about your experience."

In all of Becca's "after" photos, she exuded health and happiness, but combine the rules of MLM membership with the universal desire to look flawless on social media, and it could have easily been a lie. To my delight, she responded within the hour:

> Omg of course I'll talk about it! I did a diet program last year called Optavia. And that shit was legit a crazy cult.

"Oh, goodie," I replied.

ii.

Heyyyyy boss babe! Thank you soooooo much for responding!! I really think you'll be a perfect fit for this! I don't have much info to send via DM, the only website I have is for my current clients, but we have several different plans available depending on what you're looking to accomplish. We treat our clients like family, so it's really important I have the right information before moving forward, and I won't know what's best until we chat. The call will only take about 20 minutes :) I'm so excited to share more!! xoxo

To me, MLMs' ra-ra speech style—the excessive exclamation points and "Just believe in yourself, and you can become rich"—reeks of toxic positivity . . . or forcing a silver lining around an experience that is actually quite complex, upsetting, and deserving of more careful attention.

In the messaging of every single MLM I looked into, from Amway to Optavia, there was this startling hybrid of love-bomb-y talk about the power of a positive mind-set and ominous warnings about the danger of a negative one.

On its face, promoting a chin-up attitude to your business associates might sound good and fine, but MLMs condition their recruits to fear "negativity" so viscerally that they avoid breathing a word of criticism about the company or anyone in it. "You don't gossip. You don't say bad things about other people. If they hear you doing it, or hear about you doing it, you will hear from your director," cautioned one ex-Amway distributor. Amway labels any attitudes or utterances they don't like "stinkin' thinkin'." Using this deceptively cute catchphrase, they're able to isolate followers from any stinkin' thinkers on the outside, who will pose a threat to their success. If a friend or family member expresses doubt in the company, you're instructed to "snip them out of your life."

Followers become conditioned to speak in the MLM's unnaturally cheerful register everywhere they go—with friends, family, strangers, and especially on social media. On Instagram and Facebook, you can clock a boss babe instantly, whether they explicitly mention a product or not. All it takes is that robotically chirpy syntax to give them away. It's as if someone is standing behind them as they type, cracking a symbolic whip to make sure they're always selling and recruiting, even if they're just posting about their dog. Like followers of an oppressive religion, MLM recruits wind up trapped in ritual time.

Whenever I hear this too-good-to-be-true-type rhetoric, my gut tells me to run like hell. And yet as good as it might feel to write off anyone who buys the grandiloquent poppycock of direct sales as a hopeless dunce, the truth is that this toxically positive rhetoric is fundamentally baked into American society. The cult of multilevel marketing is a direct product of the "cult" that is Western capitalism itself.

In the United States, networking marketing as we know it got its start in the 1930s, post–Great Depression, as a reaction to employment regulations introduced by the New Deal. Although it wasn't until a few years later, after World War II, that the direct sales industry really exploded. That's when it became a women's game.

During WWII, women entered the workforce in unprecedented droves while men fought abroad. But after the fighting ended, those women were sent back into the home to care for their children and veteran husbands. In the 1950s, twenty million Americans migrated to suburbia, where there were few job opportunities for women, many of whom missed the excitement, independence, fulfillment, and cash that came with professional life.

It was around this time when a businessman named Earl Tupper invented a type of sturdy polyethylene food storage container. He named it Tupperware. The product hadn't exactly been flying off shelves until a single mother from Detroit with a knack for direct sales named Brownie Wise (real name) got ahold of Tupper's wares and decided not only would suburban moms make the perfect consumers for this stuff, they could make a powerful sales force, too. Wise and Tupper joined forces, and the at-home "Tupperware party" was born.

Long before the invention of the hashtag, Wise used pseudo-female-empowerment verbiage to recruit women into her network of dealers, managers, and distributors. This set the stage for a long future of faux-feminist MLM claptrap. "A Tupperware career is so rewarding!" reads one vintage ad in cherry-red cursive. The illustrated poster depicts a high-society woman with corn-colored hair, pearl earrings, and a cashmere sweater. Holding a book (though not reading it), she smiles deliriously while gazing up out of frame at what I can only assume are her dreams. "Earnings begin immediately when you become a Tupperware dealer!" cheeps another '40s-era sketch of a different jolly white lady. "You can earn as much as you want. You earn while you learn. You are an independent business owner. Your own boss. . . . There is nothing quite like the opportunity you have for earnings as a Tupperware dealer—NOW!"

Over the following decades, direct sales kingpins followed in Wise's footsteps, angling their products and language toward white stay-at-home moms. They filled women's ears with promises of financial independence, the sort that wouldn't threaten their traditionally feminine, wifely image. To this day, unemployed women, especially those living in blue-collar towns, continue to make up the majority of MLM recruits.

Quickly, the direct selling industry figured out how to target other communities locked out of the dignified labor market. Immigrant Spanish speakers, inexperienced college students, and economically marginalized Black folks became additional targets. The industry takes advantage of the trust that already exists within tight-knit groups like churches, military bases, and college campuses. Their ideal recruit is one who is striving for financial stability and has a proven track record of faith and optimism, whether it's hope for a fresh start in a new country, youthful enthusiasm for the future, or belief in a higher power. The typical MLM joinee isn't some greedy jerk looking to get rich quick; they're an everyday person looking to pay their basic bills. A blend of monetary struggle, close community, and idealism is the jackpot for any upline.

Christian communities wind up being a hotbed for MLMs, many of which actively identify themselves as "faith-based": Mary & Martha, Christian Bling, Younique, Thirty-One Gifts, and Mary Kay are just a few of the many MLMs that lead with an explicitly religious credo. In dozens of American neighborhoods, you'll find salt-of-the-earth people holding the Bible in one hand and pricey lotion samples in the other. It's why the state of Utah is home to more MLM headquarters than anywhere else in the world—Mormons, as direct sales leaders have discovered, are an ideal sales force. "Latter-day Saints are born and bred to be missionaries . . . so preaching the gospel to friends often naturally flows with selling MLM products to their friends," a source told the investigative podcast *The Dream.* "When your uncle comes to you and says, 'I have this great life-changing opportunity,' sometimes it sounds a lot like a message you would hear at church."

Religion has been intertwined with MLMs—and with American labor culture in general—since before the United States even existed. The marriage of godly blessings and monetary "blessings" goes back half a millennium to the

Protestant Reformation. Sociologists attribute the dawn of modern capitalism to this sixteenth-century movement, which gave birth to so many of our contemporary American workplace values, like the basic idea of "a good day's work," "keeping your nose to the grindstone,"* and "the good paymaster is lord of another man's purse." Protestant Reformers, especially French theologian John Calvin, conceived of the idea that God plays a role not just in human beings' spiritual successes and failures but also in our financial ones. This idea helped create the "Protestant ethic," marked by diligent work, individual effort, and accumulation of wealth, which aligned perfectly with Europe's emerging capitalist economy.

Soon, everyone began aspiring to the new ideal of a pious, self-reliant entrepreneur. As professional labor became central to Christian life, the ability to call yourself a skilled, hardworking breadwinner indicated that you were a member of God's elect. So the "spirit of capitalism," with all its high highs and low lows, embedded in most Westerners' value systems. So much capitalist vernacular—from the "sacred" stock market bell to the "almighty dollar"—continues to have religious overtones . . . a ghost of the Protestant Reformation.

---

* The full quote from which this idiom purportedly derives reads, "This Text holdeth their noses so hard to the grindstone, that it clean disfigureth their faces," a reference to working hard to avoid punishment. It was written in 1532 by John Frith, a Protestant priest who was burned at the stake a few months later for publicly questioning the English Catholic Church. Isn't blending church and state fun?

By the 1800s, the Protestant ethic had spread to America, but it had evolved a touch. Now riches weren't perceived so much as a gift from God, but as a reward for independent achievement and a sign of good character. This revised Protestant ethic stressed ambition, tenacity, and competition, which jibed with the rise of industrial capitalism (defined by mass manufacturing and a clearer division of labor). The nineteenth century also saw the rise of a philosophical movement called New Thought, which gave us popular self-improvement ideas like the law of attraction. During this time, rags-to-riches stories like Mark Twain's *The Prince and the Pauper* and Charles Dickens's *Great Expectations* emerged as best-sellers. The first "self-help" book—aptly titled *Self-Help*—was published in 1859 to blockbuster success. It opened with the line "Heaven helps those who help themselves" and claimed poverty to be a result of personal irresponsibility. This new mind-over-matter attitude that you could control your own destiny, that you could govern everything from your career to your physical health just by believing in yourself, contributed to what we now think of as the American Dream.

Over the course of the next century, the Protestant ideal changed once more with the rise of big American business: Carnegie Steel, the Rockefellers' Standard Oil, Chicago's Union Stock Yards meatpacking district. In the twentieth century, independent success and competitiveness were downplayed as it became admirable to get along with your coworkers, hobnob with them, and work your way up the corporate ladder. At this stage, New Thought could be found in books and courses on how to become a great company man: *How to Win Friends and Influence People, Think and Grow Rich*, and *The Power of Positive Thinking* were all published between 1935 and 1955.

Throughout the mid-twentieth century, the message that happy thoughts and a healthy ego could make you rich swept America's churches. *The Power of Positive Thinking* was written by the famous minister Norman Vincent Peale, who ran a conservative Protestant church in New York City called Marble Collegiate. There, Peale preached the "prosperity gospel" to a congregation of mostly wealthy, influential Manhattanites—including, and especially, a young Donald Trump. (By no coincidence, Trump grew up to become a hard-core MLM enthusiast.) Known for his inspiring self-help oratory, Peale evangelized sentiments like "Empty pockets never held anyone back. Only empty heads and empty hearts can do that," and "Believe in yourself! Have faith in your abilities! Without a humble but reasonable confidence in your own powers you cannot be successful or happy."

You can hear Peale's influence in Donald Trump's speeches and social media posts half a century later. "Success tip: See yourself as victorious. This will focus you in the right direction. Apply your skills and talent—and be tenacious," Trump tweeted in 2013. Upon launching his presidential campaign in 2016, Trump's rants about self-reliance took a more paranoid turn. Early that year, when asked who he consults on foreign policy, he replied, "I'm speaking with myself, number one, because I have a very good brain and

I've said a lot of things. I know what I'm doing. . . . My primary consultant is myself."

From this complex history, the MLM—the uncanny love-child of Protestantism, capitalism, and corporatization—was conceived. The Protestant ethic remains very much a part of professional culture as a whole in the United States, and we all grow up internalizing its rhetoric—work hard, play hard; another day, another dollar. My partner and I have an extensive collection of coffee mugs embellished with little sayings, and the other day, I looked up and noticed for the first time that they all just shamelessly evangelize toxic productivity dogma: One mug says "Sleep is for the weak"; another reads "A yawn is just a silent scream for coffee." A silent scream? Are we all so conditioned to believe it's romantic to be overworked and exhausted, so terrified of leisure and "laziness," that we print cute jokes about it on drinkware? In twenty-first-century America, apparently so.

The language of Protestant capitalism is everywhere—all the way down to our coffee mugs—but it plays a starring role in the MLM industry, which at once indulges Americans' most quixotic aspirations and their gravest fears. It's especially pronounced in the way MLMs stress meritocracy, the idea that money and status are individually earned. Meritocracy is founded on the tenet that people can control their lives in big ways, that as long as they really try, they can pull themselves up by their proverbial bootstraps. Americans love the mythology that successful people deserve their success while struggling people are simply less worthy. MLM recruits, whose "success" is entirely based on commission from selling and recruiting, relish this notion even more. Per MLM ideology, no win is unearned, regardless of what or who is sacrificed to achieve it. And no failure is undeserved, either.

The majority of direct sales propaganda I've read emphasizes the "blood, sweat, tears, heart, and soul" necessary to build a sales team, urging sellers to view their efforts as a badge of patriotic honor and to wear it with a smile. Countless MLMs invoke nationalistic slogans to reinforce the idea that enlisting to be a #bossbabe means signing up to serve your country. One diet supplement MLM is literally named American Dream Nutrition; another is called United Sciences of America, Inc. Amway, which sells home goods and personal hygiene products like soap and toothpaste, is a portmanteau of "American Way."

Plenty of modern companies try to sell goods by associating them with larger identity benefits, like by buying this trendy lip gloss or that beach towel made out of recycled plastic, you will establish yourself as a hip, healthy, sexy, ecofriendly person in general. Sociologists call these "organizational ideologies," and they're not necessarily all bad. Most successful brand founders agree that having a "cultlike company culture" with intense values and rituals is simply necessary to secure repeat customers and loyal employees in today's dubious, transient market. These organizational ideologies should be taken with a grain of salt, of course, since basing one's politics, healthcare decisions, and very identity on what profit-driven brands have to say, even (and especially) ones that self-identify as "ethical," "sustainable," etc., is risky business. "Woke capitalism" does not equal social justice, just as hawking diet pills to your Facebook friends does not make you heavenly blessed.

By nature, MLMs take their organizational ideologies way further than most other companies, linking themselves not just to everyday earthly benefits but to the very meaning of life. Direct sales slogans boast spiritually charged promises like "Being Younique is better than being perfect" and "Existing and living are not the same thing. Choose one." A Pinterest graphic created by the essential oils MLM dōTERRA lists the recipe for a "forgiveness" blend that will allow consumers to "become empathetic, forgiving, freeing, light, loving, tolerant, understanding." Before his death, one of Amway's billionaire cofounders, Jay Van Andel, vowed that involvement with his company "gets people into a new life of excitement, promise, profit, and hope."

You might think that an industry as unhip and retro-seeming as direct sales might have gone out of style already. It's hard to believe it's survived the internet, where so many ex-MLMers put these companies on blast, spilling their stories of psychological abuse and money loss. Search "MLM scam" on YouTube, and endless pages of videos like "The MLM 'Girl Boss' Narrative Is a Lie," "I Filed for Bankruptcy After LuLaRoe and Now Work 2 Jobs," and "AMWAY: The Final Straw (with Audio EVIDENCE!)—How I Quit My MLM Cult" accumulate millions of views. Anti-MLMers occupy passionate nooks of Instagram and TikTok. In 2020,

TikTok banned MLM recruiters from the platform altogether. There is no shortage of incriminating evidence against the #bossbabe industrial complex.

And yet MLM rhetoric is such a successful assault on the human spirit, so consistently compelling and adaptable, that these companies only continue to thrive. In the 2010s, as ingredient-conscious millennials began overtaking the consumer market and demand for "all-natural" "nontoxic" personal care products increased, the shrewdest MLM founders accommodated. Direct sales wasn't just for old-school Suzy Homemakers anymore, it was for the savvy youth. "Clean beauty" MLMs with chicer, updated packaging pivoted to populating their seller bases with "micro-influencers"—women with small blogs and a few thousand social media followers who could be tempted by an unctuous DM about how their feed is *amazinggg* and would they like to add a second stream of income while becoming part of the clean beauty "movement"?! Pairing deliciously with the glamorous image of a self-employed influencer, this hipper generation of MLMs pitched itself as the perfect side hustle. The nimble direct sales industry always finds a way to reinvent itself—the capitalist cockroach that just won't stop reincarnating.

iii.

Hey lady! Just wanted to send a reminder that we're in the business of changing lives here!! Yes, we're making money, but it's so much bigger than that . . . it's a MOVEMENT. People deserve to be a part of it, they just don't know it yet, so it's up to you to show them the light!! You need to be reaching out to EVERYBODY . . . family, friends, Insta followers, the person behind you in line at Starbucks. Start up a conversation, and meet them where they're at. Our products basically sell themselves, so if you're not meeting your goals, you need to work HARDER and SMARTER like the boss babe you are. You have such potential. Don't let me down, but more importantly, don't let YOURSELF down!! xoxo

When my middle school friend Becca and I finally got on a call to talk about her MLM experience, it had been a decade since I'd last heard her voice. Becca, now twenty-eight, lives in a little white country house in Maryland with her husband, two dogs, and four cats. She works a nine-to-five

and still plays the same local singing gig she did in high school—Friday nights at Backstage BBQ Cafe. She goes to AA several times a week and spends most evenings playing with her baby niece. "I know, look what's become of me," she quipped, sporting that old Becca sarcasm and the cozy fronted vowels of our hometown's accent, which I never get to hear anymore.

Becca knew from the jump that Optavia (formerly called Medifast) was a shifty venture. She could hear it. "All that marketing mumbo-jumbo? It was so cringe," she affirmed. I guess I could have predicted Becca wouldn't be one of those wide-eyed hopefuls who accidentally finds themselves at the bottom of a pyramid scheme. Becca was well aware of Optavia's tricky setup, but she was also confident she could game it by tapping into her massive network of Facebook friends. "I one hundred percent knew it was a cult," she said. "But I was like, 'Whatever, I'll jump on that wagon.' Like, let's scam, you know?"

"Sure, sure." I gulped.

Optavia is a weight loss program that delivers prepackaged meals to consumers' homes, like Nutrisystem or BistroMD. "They definitely try to reel you in by saying all that 'Be your own boss. Work from home' shit." Becca eye-rolled through the phone. Several of Becca's friends were involved with the controversial MLM LuLaRoe, a billion-dollar leggings company that the Washington State attorney general sued for pyramid scheme activity in 2019. (As of the time of this writing, the case is pending trial.) Becca saw how wolfishly it consumed their lives, how much money they were hemorrhaging. But when her mother-in-law asked her to do Optavia, whose buy-in fees and quotas were relatively low, it seemed like the right MLM at the right time.

About a year prior, Becca's fiancé had been diagnosed with a rare blood cancer before the age of thirty. When he finally finished chemo and entered remission, Becca was spent: "I had put on a fuck-ton of weight because I was taking care of him. I was depressed, recently sober. And I'd just quit smoking cigs, which will make you fat in and of itself." Her husband's mom was an Optavia seller and had lost a bunch of weight following the program, but because it was so expensive, about $400 a month, Becca never considered doing it herself. Then her mother-in-law floated an idea by her: If Becca signed up to be a "coach," posted about her weight loss journey on Facebook a couple of times a week, and got a few other people to sign up, that would pay for her food. "She didn't try any of that boss babe shit on me, she just told me what was up," said Becca. "I was like, 'Cool, yeah, I can get some other people to sign up, give them the spiel.'"

Becca enrolled as a coach, paid the $100 start-up fee, and commenced the diet: "The way it works, you lose weight quick. I lost fifty pounds in four months," she confessed. "I mean, the second I stopped eating their food, I looked at a pizza and gained five pounds. It's not realistic to keep up with. But you get those 'before and after' pictures, post them with the mumbo-jumbo and the hashtags, and people want to know what you're doing."

MLM enrollment strategy requires secrecy up front, so

they enforce strict rules about what their "coaches" (recruits) are allowed to reveal to outsiders. Becca never posted Optavia's name on Facebook, because the company explicitly forbids it. Instead, she was provided scripts to post verbatim that made the program sound like this exclusive mystery, all to keep people from searching it and finding what a Scientologist would call "black PR."

Back in the '70s, the Moonies referred to their guileful recruiting and fund-raising tactics with the genteelism "heavenly deception." Similarly, MLMers sweet-talk their friends and family into deceiving others along with them. At Mary Kay, a policy euphemistically termed the "Husband Unawareness Plan" encourages wives to get involved without their husbands' "permission" and then teaches them how to keep their costs a secret. One Mary Kay Executive Senior Cadillac Sales Director laid out her version of the Husband Unawareness Plan in an instruction manual for her consultants: "If you do wish to shop for things today I want you to know that I accept CASH, Check, VISA, Mastercard, Discover, American Express. I also do interest free payment plans and the husband unawareness program or otherwise known as very creative financing; a little cash, a little on a check and a little on a card. No one will know the total."

Becca was told to withhold all specifics until she got a potential downline on the phone. That's when she'd conduct her "health intake"—a twenty-point survey featuring intimate questions like: "If you could not fail, how much weight would you like to lose? When was the last time you were there? What has changed between now and then? Do you remember what that felt like? What would it be like if you were there again? Are there any family members you also want to help? Thank you so much for telling me . . . I really believe I have something that can help you reach your health goals; I'm so excited to share it with you."

These intakes weren't medical examinations conducted by registered dietitians. They were trauma-bonding tactics carried out by regular people, like Becca and her mother-in-law. The company knows what it's doing by bestowing recruits with titles like coach, senior coach, Presidential Director, and Global Health Ambassador—it fills them with a sense of authority. "I think a lot of these women convince themselves that they really are a health coach," Becca asserted. "They say you are giving people an amazing gift of life. If your coach gives you a shout-out in our secret Facebook group, people are like, 'Incredible job! Saving lives!'" Everyone knows deep down that the difference between a coach and a senior coach has nothing to do with nutrition expertise; it's how many people they were able to add to their downline that month. Yet when the company is love-bombing you with a fancy title and adulating you as a lifesaver, you become conditioned to interpret it that way, if you want to.

Nothing gets Optavia's coaches hyped like its annual leadership retreats and conventions. Recruits save up all year to attend these events, skipping best friends' weddings and grandchildren's births if they must, for the chance to meet Optavia's charismatic leader and cofounder, Dr. Wayne Andersen. "They called him Dr. A and he's, like, their ruler," Becca winced, referencing the anesthesiologist turned self-described "leader of the movement to better health." "Dr. A comes out and spits culty inspiration about how we are saving people's lives one person at a time, how we are making America healthy. Of course they charge a fortune for tickets to see him."

All MLMs throw similar Tony Robbins–esque self-help bashes, which cost thousands of dollars to attend. Tupperware hosts an annual Jubilee. Mary Kay's Career Conferences are known for their masterfully orchestrated recognition ceremonies. Recruits don't just go for fun; these conventions are advertised as compulsory if a recruit really wants to "succeed." Though rest assured the point isn't to provide serviceable selling advice. It's to paint the most extravagantly flattering portrait of the company possible, to lure already-committed recruits deeper in. The average Amway event reads like a cross between a Christian tent revival, a political rally, a football game, and a supersized family reunion. Some Amway conferences are literally called family reunions.

More than any other MLM family, Amway wields unbelievable power—not just over people directly involved with the company, but over the entire American political system. Founded in 1959, Amway operates in a hundred countries and rakes in $9 billion a year, thanks to its network of four million distributors, called International Business Owners (IBOs). Amway is a Christian company whose fundamental message is that Americans have lost touch with the qualities that once made us great: individual freedom to achieve, traditional "American family values," and unswerving devotion to God's blessed America.* "I'm going to tell you what's wrong with this country," bellowed Dave Severn, one of the company's unicorn-rare Executive Diamonds, at a 1991 rally. (Amway's top titles are all named after precious gems and other treasures: Ruby, Pearl, Emerald, Diamond, Double Diamond, Triple Diamond, Crown, Crown Ambassador.) "They have allowed everything we stand for . . . to simply go down the tubes by hiring UN-CHRISTIAN PEOPLE to try and run a Christian-based society. . . . The Amway business is built on God's laws."

Amway's two deeply conservative founders were Jay Van Andel and Rich DeVos, who died in 2004 and 2018, respectively. That second name should sound familiar: The DeVoses are a Michigan-based family of politically influential billionaires; Rich was the father-in-law of Donald Trump's secretary of education, Betsy. With a personal net worth of over $5 billion, Rich DeVos served as the finance chair of the Republican National Committee, was BFFs with Gerald Ford, secured special Amway tax breaks for hundreds of millions of dollars, and funneled prodigious sums into Republican presidential candidates' coffers. Amway funded the campaigns of Ronald Reagan, both George Bushes, and, naturally, the most direct-sales-friendly president of all time, Donald Trump. Throughout the 2010s, Trump made

---

* "American family values" is a classic piece of loaded language weaponized by the political right to condemn abortion, gay marriage, and feminist politics as inherently anti-American.

a killing from his endorsements of several MLMs. These included a vitamin company and a seminar company, both of which paid him seven figures for permission to use his likeness as a mascot and to rebrand as the Trump Network and Trump Institute. (In 2019, a federal judge ruled that Trump and his three children could be sued for fraud in connection with these organizations.) To return DeVos's favors, these presidents all publicly lauded Amway and the Direct Selling Association in general as a commendable, profoundly patriotic enterprise.†

Rich DeVos's seventeenth-century interpretation of prosperity theology suggests that if you are not rich, then God does not love you. As he declared, "The free-enterprise system . . . is a gift of God to us, and we should understand it, embrace it, and believe in it." According to DeVos, if you feel as though you've been shut out of the system your whole life, then you'd be an imbecile not to give up on bureaucracy and turn to an MLM.

This is the rhetoric that permeates Amway's legendary rallies, where the run of show might go something like this: Delivered with the anthemic cadence of a Pentecostal preacher, an emcee kicks off with some anecdote about one or two of Amway's most successful IBOs. Then they introduce the featured speaker. Soundtracked by the *Rocky* theme song, the orator emerges while attendees go berserk.

---

† Even Democrats have accepted DeVos money in exchange for public praise—Bill Clinton took home $700,000 in 2013 after speaking at an Amway conference in Osaka, Japan.

189

The speaker—typically a white, male, gem-level IBO pocketing tens of thousands of dollars for the appearance—narrates his emotional success story while clicking through a PowerPoint of the homes, yachts, cars, and vacations he's acquired thanks to Amway. Shouts of "Ain't it great?" and "I believe!" echo throughout the venue. Diamonds and Pearls call out "How sweet it is!" An award presentation follows, and in closing, the audience joins in a tearful performance of "God Bless America." At the end, uplines look their downlines in the eye and literally say, "I love you."

It doesn't take a sociologist to see how deceptive it is to drop the "love" bomb on one's business subordinates—especially knowing they will never make a dime from the relationship, much less buy a yacht. Most recruits don't even want a yacht. They'd have no use for a yacht. Again, the reason they struck up with the company in the first place and then attended this overblown conference was because they're a stay-at-home mom or an immigrant attempting to build a decent life.

Say you're an MLMer who's been in business for a while, even attended a conference or two, and have finally started feeling like you want to get out. Mention these inklings to anyone inside, and you can expect your upline to spam your inbox with messages guilt-tripping and gaslighting you into staying. Becca was fortunate that her mother-in-law was a fairly chill upline, so when she decided to quit while she was ahead, a year into Optavia, she only had a handful of calls to ignore. But for other MLMers, the exit cost feels enormous. While there probably won't be Scientology-esque threats of alien body-snatching, you very well might experience agonizing guilt and anxiety that you're giving up on your dreams and losing a surrogate family. One former Amway IBO lamented how terrible it felt to have people who once told her they loved her suddenly ghost her with no remorse: "Right at the beginning you're confronted with love . . . [and] attention by Amwayians. You get the impression that people are really interested in you as a person. That's simply not true. It is only a means to bind you to the group."

iv.

Hey babe, I saw your message in the group Facebook chat. I know you're thinking about leaving. You're feeling frustrated and uninspired. I get it. BELIEVE ME. But the most successful people in this business are the ones who push through. Think of this as a test. Will you prove yourself to be a total boss babe and turn things around, or will you give up? Think of how much time and work you've already put in! Do you really want to throw it all away? Think of all the money you'll make if you keep going a couple months more. Think of those medical bills, think of your kids. Don't be SELFISH. Be STRONG!! You know we're all family here, so please: help ME help YOU. Let's hop on a call to talk this through before you do something you'll regret, okay? xoxo

There's another portion of the answer to what makes MLM language sound scammy and cringe to some people but inviting and believable to others. Whether we associate statements like "Do you want to swim in cash?" and "You could be a millionaire within a year!" with fraud has to do not

with the words themselves (which, all on their own and without any context, do sound enticing). Instead, it has to do with the different ways humans have evolved to process information. It has to do with the social science of gullibility.

According to Nobel Prize–winning psychologist Daniel Kahneman, gullibility exists because of two opposing data-processing systems that have developed in humans' brains: System 1 and System 2 thinking. System 1 thinking is quick, intuitive, and automatic. When someone tells us something, this system relies on personal experience and anecdotal knowledge to make a snap judgment. Among ancient humans who lived in small groups, where trust was built on life-long face-to-face relationships, this method was pretty much all you needed. Back then, you didn't have to be too skeptical when someone told you something, because that someone was probably your mom or cousin or another person you'd known forever. Nowadays, whenever we have a heuristic response to some piece of news, causing us to make an instant decision about it, that's System 1 thinking.

Then we have System 2, which involves slower, more deliberative, rational judgment. This is a much newer development. In the "information age," where billions of people interact with each other anonymously online, spreading questionable claims and deleterious conspiracy theories, System 2 thinking becomes useful, because when something sounds fishy, we don't have to lean on instinct to make decisions about it. We can take our time, ask questions, thoroughly investigate, and then decide how we want to react. Unfortunately, because this process is so much newer than System 1, it doesn't always work. In part, we have those deeply embedded human-reasoning flaws, like confirmation bias and hazy cognitive labor divisions, to thank for our System 2 dysfunction. Long story short, human beings are evolving to be able to handle lots of information about lots of different things; but we're not AI robots, and we're not doing it perfectly.

In contemporary life, when an MLM is pitched with all the bombastic fixings, many people have a gut reaction. They don't need to write out a pros-and-cons list or think about it critically (after all, the pitch likely came from someone they know and can judge easily). They're able to tell right away that either A) this indeed sounds like a great opportunity, or B) this thing is trash and not for them. That's System 1 at work. But other people find themselves needing more time and careful thought. Luckily, we have System 2.

The economist Stacie Bosley once did an experiment to demonstrate how Systems 1 and 2 pan out in pyramid scheme recruitment. She set up shop at a state fair and handed willing passersby $5 in cash, telling them they could either keep the money or try her "Airplane Game" (which is like a condensed version of a pyramid scheme). Some people took one look at the offer and said, "No way, lady. I'm keeping my five bucks. That's a scam." Other people took time to process it, looked at all the rules, assessed, and finally told her, "No, this is a bad deal." They came to the same conclusion, but via System 2 instead of System 1. Then there were people who deliberated carefully, but lacked the tools to do that well—the cognition, the literacy—so they decided to play the Airplane Game after all. And then there were those who just impulsively played the game and got screwed that way. Impulsivity, says Bosley, is a common diagnostic indicator of people's vulnerability to fraud.

It's not totally clear why some people have a System 1 Spidey sense for pyramid schemes, quack health cures, and other too-good-to-be-true messaging while others don't. Some researchers say it might be related to differences in trust that stem from early childhood—the theory being that when you develop trust as a little kid, it sets a lifelong expectation that the world will be honest and nice to you. All sorts of childhood exposures could cause a person to become more or less trusting. Some people, like my dad, might have had their trust damaged by an absent parent, or another kind of trauma. Certainly, when you add factors like stress and financial hardship, some people choose to ignore their skeptical instincts and find themselves neck-deep in a shakedown anyway. As much as I'd like to take full intellectual credit for my exquisitely sensitive scam nose, I know that my disdain for pyramid schemes likely correlates to the fact that I am privileged enough to have no urgent need for their promises.

Sociologists also say that higher education and training in the scientific method generally make people less gullible. And for better or for worse, so does being in a bad mood. In several experiments, researchers found that when someone is in a good mood, they become more innocent and unsuspecting, while feeling grumpy makes one better at sensing deception. Which has to be the most curmudgeonly superpower I've ever heard.

V.

My favorite line I've heard MLMers use to defend their business is "This isn't a pyramid scheme. Corporate jobs are the REAL pyramid scheme." It's both a nonsense thought-terminating cliché and a flashing neon sign of us-versus-them conditioning. But while MLMs talk a lot of smack about corporate America and corporate America thinks of MLMs as a scammy joke, they are ultimately both derived from the same Protestant capitalist history. And the toxically positive fable that our society is a true meritocracy—that you can climb the ladder from the bottom to the top if you just work hard and have faith— imbues the rhetoric of our "normal" workforce, too.

Many modern companies actively aim to gain a cult following in the image of companies like Trader Joe's, Starbucks, and Ikea—brands that succeeded in cultivating extreme solidarity and loyalty among both employees and patrons. To learn more about the language of cultlike corporations, I hit up a Dutch business scholar and management consultant named Manfred F. R. Kets de Vries. Having studied workplace leadership styles since the 1970s, Kets de Vries confirmed that language is a critical clue when determining if a company has become too cultish for comfort. Red flags should rise when there are too many pep talks, slogans, singsongs, code words, and too much meaningless corporate jargon, he said.

Most of us have encountered some dialect of hollow workplace gibberish. Corporate BS generators are easy to find on the web (and fun to play with), churning out phrases like "rapidiously orchestrating market-driven deliverables" and "progressively cloudifying world-class human capital." At my old fashion magazine job, employees were always throwing around woo-woo metaphors like "synergy" (the state of being on the same page), "move the needle" (make noticeable progress), and "mindshare" (something having to do with a brand's popularity? I'm still not sure). My old boss especially loved when everyone needlessly transformed nouns into transitive verbs and vice versa—"whiteboard" to "whiteboarding," "sunset" to "sunsetting," the verb "ask" to the noun "ask." People did it even when it was obvious they didn't know quite what they were saying or why. Naturally, I was always creeped out by this conformism and enjoyed parodying it in my free time.

In her memoir *Uncanny Valley*, tech reporter Anna Wiener christened all forms of corporate vernacular "garbage language." Garbage language has been around since long before Silicon Valley, though its themes have changed with the times. In the 1980s, it reeked of the stock exchange: "buy-in," "leverage," "volatility." The '90s brought computer imagery: "bandwidth," "ping me," "let's take this offline." In the twenty-first century, with start-up culture and the dissolution of work-life separation (the Google ball pits and in-office massage therapists) in combination with movements toward "transparency" and "inclusion," we got mystical, politically correct, self-empowerment language: "holistic," "actualize," "alignment."

This jargon isn't damaging in and of itself. As always, words need context. And when used in competitive start-up environments, those in power can easily take advantage of staffers' eagerness to achieve (and basic need for employment). Excessive "garbage language" may signal that upper management is suppressing individuality, putting employees in a headspace where their entire reality is governed by the company's rules, which likely weren't created with much compassion or fairness in mind. (Research consistently shows that something like one in five CEOs has psychopathic tendencies.) "All companies have special terms, and sometimes they make sense, but sometimes they're nonsense," said Kets de Vries. "As a consultant, sometimes I enter an organization where people use code names and acronyms, but they don't actually know what they're talking about. They're just imitating what top management says."

At Amazon, for instance, Jeff Bezos's ideals are strikingly similar to those of MLM leaders: disdain for bureaucracy, fixation on hierarchies, incentives to rise to the top no matter who gets thrown under the bus, and a juxtaposition of lofty motivational-speak with metaphors of defeat. Bezos created his own version of the Ten Commandments called the Leadership Principles. It's a code for how Amazonians should think, behave, and speak. There are fourteen of these principles—all vague platitudes, like "think big," "dive deep," "have backbone," and "deliver results." Employees recite them like mantras. According to an explosive 2015 *New York Times* Amazon exposé, these rules are part of the company's "daily language . . . used in hiring, cited at meetings, and quoted in food-truck lines at lunchtime. Some Amazonians say they teach them to their children."

After an Amazon employee is hired, they are assigned to commit all 511 words of the Leadership Principles to memory. They are quizzed a few days later, and those who recite the principles perfectly receive a symbolic award: permission to proclaim "I'm Peculiar," Amazon's catchphrase for those who admirably push workplace boundaries. From then on, employees are expected to tear each other's ideas apart in meetings (similar to the vicious confrontations of the Synanon Game), "even when doing so is uncomfortable or exhausting" (that's according to Leadership Principle #13). If an underling gives an opinion or responds to a question in a way their manager doesn't like, they can expect to be called stupid or interrupted midsentence and told to stop speaking. According to ex-Amazonians, maxims often repeated around the office include: "When you hit the wall, climb the wall" and "Work comes first, life comes second, and trying to find the balance comes last." As Bezos himself wrote in a 1999 shareholder letter, "I constantly remind our employees to be afraid, to wake up every morning terrified."

Though petrifying your staff into obedience might help a company meet its goals faster in the short term, Kets de Vries says that rigidity stifles innovation, which in the long term is bad for both the business and its employees. (And that's to say nothing of ethics or empathy.) During his management consultations, Kets de Vries advises senior execs to ask themselves: Does the company foster individuality and nonconformism to drive breakthroughs? Does it encourage employees to have a life and language of their own? Or does everyone speak in the exact same tone using the exact same verbiage, which sounds suspiciously like that of the person in charge? "Being in a top management position, if you're not careful, you go into an echo chamber," Kets de Vries explained. "People are going to tell you what you want to hear, so you start to get away with your madness. And that madness becomes institutionalized very quickly."

I interviewed a former employee of a "sustainable fashion" start-up, initially about her involvement with The Class by Taryn Toomey (a "cult fitness" studio we'll discuss a bit in part 5), and she told me the only reason she got involved with the workout "cult" in the first place was in response to finally quitting her hellish job. For the three years she worked at the fashion company, its physically stunning, psychologically sadistic leader prevented her from sleeping, earning a living wage, or maintaining outside relationships. Eventually the role sent her into a self-described nervous breakdown, and she left to do some soul-searching—that's when she found The Class, which wound up being a wholly positive experience for her. "The workout group is nothing like my old job, which took over my entire existence," she told me. "My boss expected us to treat her company as our religion. It actually kind of ruined my life for a while."

Millions of Americans have worked for a cultlike company at some point, and some of us have even suffered through an atmosphere as tyrannous as Amazon's. On the illusive ladder of American capitalism, it's just a few rungs up from a corporation that pays you not in money, but in lies . . . the star-spangled MLM.

vi.

I said before that an MLM is just a pyramid scheme that hasn't gotten caught. So how do you catch one?

To find the answer, let's look back at the story of how the Federal Trade Commission (FTC) shut down its very first MLM. In the early 1970s, a shoddy cosmetics company perplexingly named Holiday Magic (it had nothing to do with annual festivities) began fielding a stampede of lawsuits. The business had been founded about a decade earlier by William Penn Patrick, the single most snake-oil-y gasbag of all the direct sales guys I've come across. Based in Northern California, this dude was a tightass wannabe Republican senator in his thirties whom the *Los Angeles Times* once called the state's "strangest politician."

Like most other MLM founders, Patrick was big on prosperity theology and New Thought, and he was famous for turning inspirational mottoes minacious: "Tell [recruits] they're going to be happier, healthier, wealthier, and receive what they want out of life with the Holiday Magic program," he wrote, adding in the same pen stroke, "Any person who fails in the Holiday Magic program must fall into one of the following categories: lazy, stupid, greedy, or dead." Patrick was also known for throwing the uttermost bizarre MLM conference in history. Called Leadership Dynamics, it took place in a crappy Bay Area motel and cost a thousand bucks to attend. For two days straight, Patrick had recruits engage in a series of freaky power games: He made them climb inside coffins and strung them up on gigantic wooden crosses, where they'd dangle all afternoon. Like Jim Jones, Chuck Dietrich, and (to a lesser degree) Jeff Bezos, he also forced them into "group therapy" sessions where they verbally tormented each other for hours on end.

Patrick's behavior was unhinged from all angles, but when the FTC brought him to court, their most compelling argument against him, and what eventually allowed them to shut down Holiday Magic, was their points about his speech. Ultimately, the court ruled that Patrick's deceptive hyperbole, loaded buzzwords, and gaslighting disguised as inspiration were what defined him as a pyramid schemer. This makes sense, because in every corner of life, business and otherwise, when you can tell deep down that something is ethically wrong but are having trouble pinpointing why, language is a good place to look for evidence. This is where the FTC turned to squash Holiday Magic, and over the next few years, its attorneys cited the same type of outlandish, fraudulent messaging as they prosecuted a litany of MLMs—including the biggest one they ever went after, Amway.

In 1979, the FTC finally accused Jay Van Andel and Rich DeVos of pyramid scheme activity, which led to a massive drawn-out case. But, as we know, Amway never closed up shop. (Again, this was a company whose founders golfed with heads of state—there was no chance the government was going to take them down.) The judge fined the company $100,000 (chump change for the corporate heavyweight) and sent them on their merry way.

Ultimately, the FTC losing its case against Amway offered the whole direct sales industry a measure of protection from there on out. Since 1979, the FTC has only canned a handful of MLMs, and never any of the giants. Now, every time an MLM comes under fire, they can say, "No, no, no, you have us all wrong. We're not a pyramid scheme. We're not a cult. We're just like Amway. We're a meritocracy. We're the chance to be an entrepreneur, a business owner, a #bossbabe. We're not a scam—we're the American Dream."

And as far as the courts are concerned, these sentiments are just true enough to believe there's nothing cultish about them at all.

Hey girl. I hate that I have to do this. But I just got word from the top, and unfortunately we're going to have to let you go. When you first joined my team, I was so excited about your potential. But despite all the time and effort we put into growing you, it doesn't seem like you really wanted it. Some people aren't the right fit for this opportunity, and trust me, as your upline, that's harder for me than it is for you. I'm going to have to remove you from the Facebook group and deactivate your account. I guess you weren't a boss babe after all. x

Part 5

This Hour Is Going to Change Your Life . . . and Make You LOOK AWESOME

i.

I'm vigorously power marching in place, like a toy soldier. It feels dopey, and I want to half-ass it, but I told myself I'd either do this with everything I've got or not at all. Rolling my forearms and fists in front of me with as much gusto as my muscles will allow, I'm squeezing my eyes shut while repeating the phrase "I am powerful beyond measure."

My parents are on either side of me, staggered slightly so there's enough room, performing the same move and joining me in the affirmation: "I am powerful beyond measure." "Embody it, awaken it!" cries our glowing leader, Patricia Moreno, projecting equal parts tenderness and ferocity. She calls this move WILLPOWER.

A few eight-counts later, we're punching the air in front of us, twisting our torsos with each hook. This move is called STRONG. "It's the reminder to stop talking about what you can't do, and call up your strength," Moreno narrates. "YOU decide that TODAY you are strong enough to make any change you want to make. Say, 'I am stronger than I seem.'" Still punching and twisting, we repeat: "I am stronger than I seem." "Beautiful! Feel like a warrior!" croons Moreno.

Two more movements complete our four-step routine: The next one is called BRAVE. Jumping up on one foot, kicking the opposite leg back behind us, we curl our hands into clenched spheres and rocket-launch them into the sky, one at a time. "Whenever you're stressed, just do that move, and it'll help interrupt worries, and doubts, and fears!" impels Moreno. "And then you change your language and you say, 'I am braver than I think!'" My parents and I echo the line, exploding our bodies into the air: "I am braver than I think!"

Last move: ABUNDANCE. We touch our palms to our hearts, zestfully shoot them open in a wide V above our heads, touch our hearts again, then extend our arms down by our hips to mirror the previous posture. Meanwhile, we repeat: "I am blessed with all I need." "Gratitude is the attitude that will CHANGE. YOUR. LIFE!" roars Moreno. "You have to think about, talk about, focus on the blessings you already have." Now we're breaking into a jumping jack, arms wide at the top and a deep toe touch at the bottom, shouting, "I am blessed with all I need!"

"Let's do them all!" invites Moreno, and we repeat the four movements in a row: WILLPOWER, STRONG, BRAVE, ABUNDANCE.

And then, out of nowhere, tears. I'm no more than five minutes into Moreno's movement affirmations when my voice breaks into a warble. My mom turns and smiles uncomfortably. "Amanda, are you . . . crying?" I hear her attempt not to sound judgmental. My parents haven't seen me cry in two years. "Everyone said this would happen!" I shriek in self-defense, at once laughing and blubbering, betrayed by this liquidy reflex.

With that, the spell is broken. "All right, that's enough," my dad grumbles, shaking off the routine like a costume he just noticed was ridiculous. "I'm going to the garage to get on the Lifecycle. I exercise BY MYSELF!"

"We know, Craig. Take the recycling with you," my mother retorts, still marching in place, rolling her hands.

It's high jinks here at the Montell household: My science professor parents and I, the most cynical trio ever to shout the phrase "I'm blessed with all I need" mid–jumping jack, are taking a free online intenSati class. This media-proclaimed cult-favorite workout was created in the early 2000s by former aerobics champion and today's virtual instructor, fifty-five-year-old Patricia Moreno, whose shiny black ponytail and radiant grin are broadcasting from an iPad in my parents' sunroom. Baptized by Cosmopolitan .com as "a super fit Mexican Oprah" meets a "jock version of J.Lo," Moreno makes athletics and enlightenment seem like an effortless combo. Her high-energy technique pairs elements of dance, kickboxing, and yoga with spoken affirmations, so each move has a mantra that goes with it. In the lingo of intenSati, these move-affirmation pairings are called "incantations"—a concept Moreno learned at a Tony Robbins conference at the turn of the millennium. intenSati (a play on "intensity") is a portmanteau of "intention" and "sati," the Pali word for "mindfulness." It could definitely be classified as "woo-woo."

At fifty-eight and sixty-four, my mom and dad are in fantastic shape, way better than I am, thanks to all the biking and swimming they do in Santa Barbara, where they moved from Baltimore seven years ago. They're not "group workout people," they love to remind me, but while I'm visiting for the weekend, I've convinced them to try out one of the cult fitness classes I've been researching for this book. "I know all about at-home workouts." My mother beams, gathering her hair into a neat bun. "I signed up for Peloton, you know."

intenSati was recommended to me by Natalia Petrzela, a student turned instructor who started following Moreno (both physically and ideologically) in 2005. I was inclined to listen to Natalia, who seemed more down-to-earth than the "cult workout" stereotype I'm used to seeing in Los Angeles: the Equinox-subscribed wellness crusader who goes to SoulCycle three times a week and CorePower Yoga the other four days, lives in Lululemon leggings, and hasn't ingested a simple carbohydrate since season twelve of *The Bachelor*. Natalia is a fitness historian at the New School in New York City with a PhD from Stanford, who relatably identifies as "not athletic" and "alienated by sports." She promised that if I, a feminist killjoy who's intimidated by exercise, were going to fall in love with any cult workout, she's pretty sure intenSati would be the one. "I was just as skeptical of this culty workout stuff as you," Natalia swears. "I remember intenSati was first described to me as 'using voices and visualizations to transform your body and your outlook,' and I was like, 'Hell no, this is so woo-woo.'"

"All right, all right," I respond. "I'll give it a whirl."

The marriage of mystical self-help messaging with a hardcore exercise class might not seem remarkable now, but when Natalia found intenSati in the mid-aughts, the two concepts had only just become acquainted. Moreno didn't know it when she created the workout in 2002, but its launch was perfectly timed: At the turn of the twenty-first century, boutique fitness was just beginning to erupt as a major industry. In the 1980s and '90s, most Americans got their exercise in big-box gyms or community centers like the YMCA; small, pricier workout classes with charismatic instructors, strong branding, and transcendent benefits were not yet the norm.

As recently as the 1950s, the medical community didn't even universally recommend exercise for women (much less that they sweat their asses off while shouting empowering things about themselves in public multiple times a week). In the 1920s and '30s, one of the only successful American fitness salons was a chain called Slenderella, whose philosophy was entirely built on slimming women's bodies daintily, without sweat, and purely for cosmetic purposes. Classes offered rhythmics (light stretching and dance), promising to trim female clients "in all the right places" minus the "toil and suffering" of real exertion, which was ruled to be contemptuously unfeminine, leading to big "manly" muscles and reproductive risks. American women instead developed a fixation with "reducing" (and ever since, weight loss has remained a dismal "cult" of its own).

It wasn't until the late 1960s when everyday Americans fully came around to the idea that working out to the point of perspiration was good for everyone. In 1968, the blockbuster fitness book *Aerobics* helped convince the public that exercise was indeed beneficial for both men and women.

Over the following decade or two, women embraced exercise with gusto and soon figured out what cognitive anthropology studies would later reveal: that it was more fun to do it in groups. (Endorphins surge even more powerfully when we exercise together).

In the 1970s and '80s, with the women's liberation movement well under way, the passage of Title IX, and the invention of the sports bra, women were poised to gather together and get fit. This is right around when Jazzercise took off (and by 1984, it would become one of the country's fastest-growing franchises, second only to Domino's Pizza). Invented by professional dancer Judi Sheppard Missett, Jazzercise turned millions of women on to the concept of community fitness. Celebrity instructors like Jane Fonda and Raquel Welch, with their signature bright spandex and sprightly delivery, became some of the first "fitness influencers."

Big-box gyms and health clubs like 24 Hour Fitness and Crunch took over the workout market for a while throughout the late '80s and '90s—around the same time yoga found its way to everyday Americans. Of course, yoga had already existed for millennia; references to the practice can be found in Indian texts dating back 2,500 years. But for much of yoga's history, its only practitioners were religious ascetics. For these Eastern yogis, there were no acrobatic sun salutations or cranked thermostats. Yoga was more like meditation, and it was entirely centered on stillness. (To this day, some monks in India continue to perform feats of marathon motionlessness, posed without a twitch for days on end.) Almost all of the West's popular assumptions about yoga theory come from after the 1800s. That's when developments in photography allowed pictures of yoga poses to make their way overseas. Europeans were transfixed by these images and merged the Indian postures with their existing notions of bodybuilding and gymnastics. Yoga historians say much of what modern Americans recognize as yoga today is partly a result of this mash-up.

Toward the end of the twentieth century, yoga planted the seed that fitness studios could be more than just places to change your body; they could also be intimate temples of emotional well-being, even spiritual enlightenment. But the rituals needed to create that sense of mysticism—rituals like affirmations, mantras, and chanting, whose roots are in religion—weren't yet overlapping with intense exercise. The idea to mix the physical and the metaphysical was still about as far from people's minds as crossing a doughnut with a croissant. Which is to say, it was coming, and it was going to be huge, but the recipe hadn't come together quite yet.

But then . . . the twenty-first century happened. Not long after the stroke of midnight on Y2K, every piece of American fitness history seemed to fuse and detonate, kicking off the "cult fitness" industry as we know it. In 2000, we got the Bar Method, the studio that catalyzed America's fixation with the ballet-inspired fitness craze. The same year we got CrossFit, which catered to a very different demographic than barre, but whose "boxes" had an equally boutique-y, anti-gym vibe. (At its peak in early 2020, CrossFit flaunted over ten thousand boxes, generating $4 billion annually.

That was before many locations disaffiliated with the brand name due to Greg Glassman outing himself as a shameless racist. More on that in a bit.) With 2001 came Pure Barre, which scaled to over five hundred North American studios. The following year brought CorePower Yoga, which grew into two hundred-plus locations. SoulCycle, with its nightclub-esque lighting, loud music, and zippy instructors, arrived in 2006, just a few months before LA fitness instructor Tracy Anderson helped Gwyneth Paltrow lose her baby weight, boosting Hollywood personal trainers to a celebrity station of their own.

Over the following fifteen years or so, boutique fitness studios multiplied and spun off of each other, making them a fixture in American society. According to the International Health, Racquet & Sportsclub Association, the US health and fitness industry was worth over $32 billion in 2018. Soon, there was a workout class for any interest. Whether you were into cycling, circuit training, running, yoga, dancing, pole dancing, boxing, jiujitsu, Pilates on a land-bound mechanical surfboard,* or literally anything else, you could find a devoted fitness community. In addition to SoulCycle, CrossFit, and countless barre, Pilates, and yoga shops, we

---

* This is a real workout that exists in LA at a studio called Sandbox Fitness. In a room covered in actual sand, clients mount stationary surfboards and perform a variety of nearly impossible strength exercises aided by resistance bands dangling from the ceiling. I learned of this unusual torture from a modelesque action film star whom I interviewed for a magazine article in 2017. "You get so ripped," she gushed, her pupils dilating. "I do it every morning. You *have* to try it."

got Barry's Bootcamp (high-intensity interval training—aka HIIT—with a sassy twist), Orangetheory (like Barry's but more competitive), November Project (free outdoor boot camps held at six a.m.), The Class by Taryn Toomey (like boot camp meets yoga . . . with screaming), modelFIT (what all the models do), Platefit (like modelFIT but on a giant vibrating apparatus), intenSati (you're familiar), Rise Nation (the SoulCycle of stair climbing), LIT Method (the SoulCycle of rowing), LEKFIT (the SoulCycle of trampolining), Peloton (like SoulCycle via Zoom), and dozens upon dozens more.

Unlike the YMCAs and Jazzercise classes of the past, these intimate studios positioned themselves as sacred spaces—as *movements*—offering a potent ideological, deeply personal experience. Within these hallowed, inspirational-quote-bedecked halls, you'll not only perfect your squat and decrease your resting heart rate, you'll also find a personal mentor, meet your best friends, get over your ex, summon the confidence to ask for a raise, manifest your soul mate, get sober, get through chemo, and prove to yourself once and for all that you're powerful beyond measure and blessed with all you need.

"SoulCycle talks about how people 'come for the body but stay for the breakthrough,'" said Casper ter Kuile, a researcher at Harvard Divinity School and author of *The Power of Ritual*. "It's a good workout, but that's only the beginning." In these classes, fitness devotees find a sense of release, insight on what's important to them, and a sanctuary away from the pressures of their everyday existence. "It is more safe and more powerful than even church," a deep-dyed Soul-Cycler who rides in San Francisco's Castro neighborhood told Harvard Divinity School. At SoulCycle, he said, "I feel like I'm at home."

It is no accident that the studio fitness industry blew up so suddenly and powerfully in the early 2010s—a time when adults' trust in both traditional religion and the medical establishment took a sharp decline. An unshocking 2018 poll by the Multiple Chronic Conditions Resource Center found that 81 percent of American millennials are unsatisfied with their healthcare experience, due to everything from high insurance costs to institutional race and gender bias. Not to mention the US's lack of public fitness programs (like, say, Japan's "radio calisthenics" broadcasts, which folks are free to follow at home or together in community parks each morning at no cost). Younger Americans feel like they have no choice but to take their health into their own hands.

Combine this withdrawal from mainstream medicine with young people's disillusionment with traditional faith, and cult fitness exploded to fill these corporeal and spiritual voids. In a 2015 study called "How We Gather," ter Kuile explored the ways millennials find community and transcendence beyond conventional religious communities, and found that studio workout classes were among the ten most profound and formative spaces. At least for a certain demographic . . . because as soon as people began coveting fitness so intensely, they started to crave more exclusivity, too.

In high school, I paid $99 a year for my Planet Fitness

membership (which, granted, I almost never used), but ten years later, exercising might cost up to half that much just for one class. (And that doesn't count the designer uniform implicitly required—the $100 Lulus, the $80 rose quartz–infused glass water bottle, which is a real product I found on Net-A-Porter.) A home Peloton bike costs $2,000 and the app an additional monthly fee. Certainly, there are less overtly elitist fitness movements happening all over the US—some right up the street from the Goop-obsessed Malibu stereotype: A 2014 ethnography of LA's El Monte "Zumba Ladies" documents a tight-knit community of Latina women of all ages and shapes whose $4 banda-meets-*Flashdance*-style exercise classes, complete with kitschy neon Spandex, are nothing short of divinely feminine sanctuaries. But those aren't the trendy workout spaces that make *Cosmopolitan* headlines.

The audience to which "cult fitness" primarily caters—urban-dwelling millennials with income to spare—overlaps quite precisely with the contingency that has renounced traditional religion. For this population, "wellness" start-ups and influencers started doing the work of spiritual and community leaders. It's always chancy to put such trust in the hands of someone whose bottom line is their own brand, but for consumers who felt like they had nowhere else to turn, the risk seemed worth it.

Starting in the 2010s, America's fastest-growing companies in general became the ones that offered not only desirable products and services, but also personal transformation, belonging, and answers to big life questions like:

Who am I in this increasingly isolated world? How do I connect with people around me? How do I find my most authentic self and take the steps to become that person? In so many pockets of American culture, folks turn to workout studios for these answers. "Meaning-making is a growth industry," said ter Kuile. Like church, fitness brands became both a social identity and a code by which to lead your life. The fitness "movement" encompasses customs and rituals, social expectations, and consequences for failing to show up. People meet their closest friends and spouses in the studio; true diehards quit their jobs to become instructors themselves. "I don't want to ride. I don't ever want to ride. A good-hair day is a good-enough excuse for me not to ride. Now I'm riding five or six times a week because we have built such a supportive community," effused one devout Peloton user in a 2019 *New York* magazine interview. "It goes so beyond the bike."

Workout studios wound up feeling, to some degree, holy. After all, they became some of the only physical spaces where the young and religiously ambivalent could put down their devices and find in-the-flesh community and connection. "We're living in dark times," remarked Sam Rypinski, owner of a "radically inclusive" Los Angeles gym called Everybody. "We're very segregated and separated. . . . We're cut off by technology. We don't connect with our bodies . . . [or] each other. So if there's a space that encourages that on any level, people are so happy to be there."

On top of cerebral notions of "meaning-making" and existential loneliness add the rise of social media fitness influencers (and the so-called aspirational body standards they promote), plus innovations in workout technology (high-performance athleticwear, fitness trackers, streaming classes), and it's no wonder the business of exercise boomed in a godlike way.

At some point during the mid-2010s, the phrase "cult workout" entered our vocabularies—a succinct label to describe the fitness industry's intensified societal role. Participants in Casper ter Kuile's Harvard Divinity School study sincerely told him things like "SoulCycle is like my cult," and they meant it in a good way. The cult comparisons were something brands didn't know how to handle at first. In 2015, I interviewed SoulCycle's senior vice president of "Brand Strategy and PR" about the company's status as a cult workout. Cautiously, she told me, "We don't use that word. We say 'community.'" It was very clear that she didn't want to leave people any room to conflate her employer with the likes of Scientology.

But over the years, fitness studios have really leaned into the churchly role they play in members' lives. SoulCycle's website explicitly reads: "SoulCycle is more than just a workout. It's a sanctuary." Publicly crying, eulogizing lost loved ones, confessing wrongdoings, and testifying to how the group changed one's life are customs regularly found and embraced within studio walls. "I want the next breath to be an exorcism," is among the supernatural catchphrases SoulCycle instructors preach in class.

A few years ago, I spoke with Taylor and Justin Norris, the founders of LIT Method, an up-and-coming indoor rowing brand. The peppy husband-and-wife duo cut the ribbon on their West Hollywood studio in 2014, aiming to replicate SoulCycle's success. (They're still working on it.) When I asked how they felt about the association between their business and the word "cult," they said, in unison, "We love it." "They call us the Bolt Cult on Instagram because our logo is a lightning bolt." Taylor beamed, flashing a telegenic grin. "I know there's a negative connotation to 'cult,' but we see it in a very positive way."

ii.

When I first began investigating workout cults, it was their aggressively worshipful language—the chanting and screaming, the woo-woo jargon and pump-up monologues—that triggered my System 1 impulses. *A cult is like porn: You know it when you hear it.* SoulCycle's theatrically uplifting maxims ("You can climb this mountain! You're a boss!" "Change your body, change your mind, change your life!") seemed like the bogus waffling of a self-help blowhard. Like something out of *Midsommar*, The Class by Taryn Toomey is known for encouraging students to scream at the top of their lungs as they perform burpees and pike push-ups and instructors coo New Age–y encouragement: "Notice how you're feeling," "Release what's stagnant and ignite a new fire." intenSati's blend of zingy rhyming affirmations with metaphysical yoga vocabulary sounds like occultists casting spells.

To folks with low cringe thresholds who have a hard time suspending their disbelief (the Montells, for example), the fanatical chanting and cheering trigger tableaus of religious extremism and pyramid scheme rallies. To outsiders, just knowing their friends and family are capable of conforming to such behaviors can feel unsettling.

Across the board, "cult workout language" tends to be ritualistic and rarefied because it's good for business. The loaded mantras and monologues are designed to create an experience so stirring that people can't resist coming back and spreading the word. Certainly, exercise brands have always capitalized on peer pressure to generate return customers—group weigh-ins, fitness trackers. When my parents got Apple Watches, I beheld them ruthlessly vie for the highest number of steps every day for a summer. But competition alone, research suggests, is not enough to keep folks committed. Exercisers driven only by numbers tend to quit within twelve months. It's when elements of belonging, self-worth, and empowerment enter the picture that members are moved to renew their fitness memberships year after year. Language is the glue that binds that "addictive" combo of community and motivation.

With this in mind, it's important not to overdramatize; and as a whole, woo-woo workout mantras are very different from the deceptive, reality-warping dogma of leaders like Marshall Applewhite or Rich DeVos. I can safely say that most "cult fitness" rhetoric I came across wasn't camouflaging evil motives, and importantly, there tended to be boundaries separating it from the rest of members' lives. By and large, it obeyed the rules of ritual time. At the end of a "cult workout" class, you're allowed to clock out and start talking like yourself again. And most people do, because when participants engage with the language of "cult fitness," it's usually with open eyes. Unlike in Amway or Heaven's Gate, most followers know they're participating in a fantasy—that they're not really "entrepreneurs" or "in craft" (or "champions" and "warriors," as it were). Whether instructors are using the language of ancient monks, motivational speakers, Olympic coaches, the army, or some mishmash, it's all a means of creating an illusion. The words and intonation put exercisers in a transcendent headspace, but just for the length of a class. If it gets to be too much, followers are free to tap out at any time without life-ruining exit costs. To go back to the kink analogy, fitness studios have their followers' consent. At least they're supposed to.

However, as we've learned, wherever there are magnetic leaders charging money for meaning, there's the chance for things to go awry. There's a reason cult fitness language feels so otherworldly—it's to make these classes feel essential not only to followers' health but to their lives as a whole. Just as much as it's there to provide the follower a stimulating experience, it's to psychologically attach them to the instructor, as if this fitness class, this guru, holds the ultimate answers to their happiness. When language blurs the lines separating fitness teacher, celebrity, therapist, spiritual leader, sex symbol, and friend, it starts to mess with ritual time. When that happens, the power instructors wield can tread into exploitative territory. And of course, no fitness company thinks, "You know what, maybe our brand is becoming *too* influential. Maybe we should cool it on the chanting." After all, they're actively trying to gain a "cult following." It's the whole point. Brands know that language is the key to accomplishing this—and they don't hold back.

Like the studio's own version of the Ten Commandments,

SoulCycle's studio walls are emblazoned with mantras that envelop riders into a unified "we." "We aspire to inspire," reads the two-foot-tall print. "We inhale intention and exhale expectation. . . . The rhythm pushes us harder than we ever thought possible. Our own strength surprises us every time. Addicted, obsessed, unnaturally attached to our bikes." All you're objectively doing is riding a stationary bicycle in a big loud room that smells good, but when the narrative surrounding you—literally written on the walls—is one of tapping into a strength you didn't know you had, alongside other people who are just as "addicted, obsessed," you feel like you're a part of something more. Add a blast of mood-boosting endorphins to the mix, and you find yourself in a state of uncanny euphoria that you'll want to spread like a missionary to all your friends and coworkers.

"I'm an educated, skeptical person, but it just feels so fucking good to let go of all of that for forty-five minutes in a dark room where no one can see you cry because someone told you you're worthy," said Chani, a friend of mine from college, in defense of her SoulCycle obsession. Chani does not identify as "religious"; in fact, when I asked, she scoffed at the insinuation. "SoulCycle is just a place where you can escape being what you have to be as a discerning, self-possessed woman trying to succeed," she qualified. "You can just give yourself over to the culty lady telling you what to do. It's like womb regression in there. You get to be like, 'I'm a tiny scared baby,' and then you come out and you're like, 'Yeah I bought hundred-and-twenty-dollar Lululemons, and fuck you.'"

To be fair, like sexual nerdiness, the grunting and chanting can seem freaky to outsiders in part for the same reason they feel so damn good to insiders: It's that aspect of surrender, of letting down your guard as a poised individual in order to enmesh yourself in the vulnerable, amorphous, feel-good blob of the experience. Naturally, that's going to look weird to someone just peering in. ("No one looks 'cool' at SoulCycle," Chani laughed.) And even with the potential to go wrong, the language of "cult fitness" can be incredibly healing.

Changing the language of the fitness industry from talk of patriarchal body hatred to talk of goddesslike power was the whole reason Patricia Moreno founded intenSati in the first place. In the late 1990s, group fitness class rhetoric was largely about working off the sins of the food you'd consumed, about sculpting your tummy and thighs to conform to some normative vision of a "bikini body." After a lifelong personal struggle with eating disorders and diet drug misuse, Moreno was driven to alter this damning narrative. She decided she was going to take her athletic expertise and combine it with positive affirmations so her students could become "spiritually fit as well as physically fit."

Moreno created a new vocabulary of sixty metaphorical names for workout moves, so instead of saying "punch," or "squat," or "lunge," the movements would be called "strong," and "gratitude," and "commitment." Each month, she'd choose a theme for her classes and come up with incantations to reflect it. She took inspiration from yoga's dharma talk and began each class with a story about a personal struggle from her life. "So if we were talking about strength that month, I'd tell a story about a time I had to be strong, like through my miscarriage," she explained to me in an interview. "Then the incantations would say, 'I can do hard things. I am better than before. I am born to drive. I'm glad I'm alive!'" She spits a sequence of rhyming mantras like spoken word poetry.

At first, Moreno's students rolled their eyes at the idea of "incantations." The tough-as-nails Manhattanites weren't interested in a talk therapy session; they wanted their asses kicked. Wasn't getting shouted at about their muffin tops the only way to achieve that? Natalia was one of those world-weary New York trainees—that is, until a few weeks in, when she found herself earnestly shouting "My body is my temple. I am the keeper of my health. I am love in action. All is well" at every intenSati class she could make time for. By then, she was a convert.

SoulCycle, too, concocts specific movement-language pairings to metaphorically catapult riders toward their dreams. Every SoulCycle "journey" follows a similar course, its climax falling on a strenuous "hills" odyssey narrated by a hair-raising sermon. Riders turn up their bikes' resistance and climb with all their might to the symbolic finish line as their instructor douses them in verbal inspiration. SoulCycle instructors are trained to wait for these moments, when students are so physically beat that they'll be more receptive to kernels of spirituality, to deliver their best lines.

One SoulCycle star known far and wide for her "hills" monologues was Los Angeles-based Angela Manuel-Davis, Beyoncé and Oprah's Spin instructor of choice. A proud evangelical Christian, Manuel-Davis wielded explicitly religious verbiage on the bike—talk of genesis, angels, and miracles. "'Enthusiasm' comes from the Greek word *enthous*, which means 'in God,'" she'd preach, thrusting her arms toward the heavens. "Divine inspiration. Divine inspiration. I want you to be enthusiastic and excited . . . about this opportunity to close the gap between where you are in your life and where you were called, created, and intended to be. . . . Every single one of you was created in purpose, on purpose, for a purpose." With a deep understanding of religious speech's performative power, Manuel-Davis told audiences, "Life and death is in the power of the tongue. You have the ability to unlock somebody's greatness by your words . . . not only to the people in your life, but to yourself. You are who you say you are."

These are some hard-core evangelical buzzwords, but Manuel-Davis attested she wasn't using them to create insiders and outsiders, or to make others conform to her ideology. "I give people room to make it about what they need," she told Harvard Divinity School. "This is about individual faith and spirituality." Those who weren't feeling it didn't have to take Manuel-Davis's credo with them outside the studio, or even come back at all—but a whole lot of people did. Manuel-Davis's classes were known to sell out within minutes.* "I

* Then in 2016, an attendee got injured in Manuel-Davis's class and filed a lawsuit. To the devastation of her many acolytes, Manuel-Davis resigned from SoulCycle in 2019 to launch a boutique fitness cult of her own called AARMY, in partnership with another former SoulCycle idol named Akin Akman, whose loyal gaggle of fiendish riders were known as "Akin's Army."

don't go to Angela to get a workout; I go to hear a message," one rider professed. "Angela sees you. . . . She speaks to your soul."

Even with more agnostic instructors, the language rituals of boutique fitness classes mimic those of religious services. Whether it surrounds God or crushing your goals, rituals help people feel like they're a part of something greater. As Casper ter Kuile put it, they're a "connective tissue tool." Ritual also temporarily removes a person from the center of their own little universe—their anxieties, their everyday priorities. It helps mentally transition followers from worldly, self-focused humans to one piece of a holy group. And then, theoretically, it should allow them to transition back into real life.

Just as Christian congregates will say the Lord's Prayer at the same point in church every week, intenSati instructors and attendees open each class by joining in what Moreno calls the Warrior Declaration: "Every day in a very true way, I co-create my reality. As above, so is below, this is what I know." Like ministers inviting parishioners to mingle before a service, SoulCycle instructors encourage students to hobnob with the riders next to them. "At the beginning of class, everyone has to turn and say hello, exchange a name, and chat," explained Sparkie, a "master instructor" in Los Angeles who's been with SoulCycle since 2012. "'You're going to be sweating next to them. Get to know them.' It gives people an opportunity to connect, because connection is the key."

November Project's boot camp–style workouts all start out the same way, whether you're in Baltimore or Amsterdam or Hong Kong: Come six thirty a.m., participants kick off a rallying ritual called "the bounce." Gathered in a tight circle, everyone joins in the same script, their voices crescendoing into a Spartan bellow:

"Good morning!"

"Good morning!!!"

"Y'all good?"

"Fuck yeah!"

"Y'all good?!"

"Fuck yeah!!!"

Then everyone chants, "Let's go!!!!!" At the end of the session, participants always take a group photo, turn to someone they don't know, introduce themselves, and close out with the same final line: "Have a great day."

Ideally, my parents and I would've tried out intenSati in person, but in April 2020, that wasn't exactly possible. Two weeks into California's COVID-19 quarantine, we were forced to exercise at home. I figure, though, if my thesis about language and power is correct, then Patricia's incantations should compel me even through a screen. I didn't actually think they'd work, of course. On paper, the workout coalesces two things I gravely detest: cardio (blegh) and group activities that require you to awkwardly shout things out loud. In Los Angeles, where I live, a new cult workout brand pops up every day, and I've rolled my eyes at them all.

But there I was, four incantations into an intenSati class, jumping around and laugh-crying like the suckers I've always scorned. After our mini workout, my mom went off to perform a few solo sun salutations, while I immediately looked up Patricia Moreno's virtual class schedule, thinking, *Shit, is this what conversion feels like?*

iii.

Fitness may be the new religion, but instructors are the new clergy. The "cult workout" empire would be nothing without its Patricia Morenos and Angela Manuel-Davises, who do so much more than guide classes. Instructors learn followers' names, Instagram handles, and personal life details. They hand out their cell phone numbers and counsel followers on matters as grave as whether they should divorce their spouse or quit their job. They share intimate stories and hardships from their own lives and invite followers to reciprocate. Followers form deep-rooted loyalties to their favorite teachers and start referring to classes not by brand name but by instructor name. It's not "I'm going to SoulCycle at four p.m. today and six p.m. tomorrow," but "I'm going to Angela's class today and Sparkie's class tomorrow."

A workout brand is "not so much a 'cult' as it is a collection of 'cults,'" remarked Crystal O'Keefe, a project manager by day and Peloton apostle by night. Crystal runs a Peloton-themed podcast and blog called *The Clip Out* and is known to her few thousand followers as Clip-Out Crystal. "July 15, 2016, is the day I received my Peloton. I remember it so well," she wrote to me sentimentally, like the beginning to her memoir. "I now have completed almost 700 rides."

Launched on Kickstarter in 2013, Peloton is a subscription-based fitness app offering all kinds of online workout classes (termed "shows" in corporate Peloton-speak). There's dance aerobics, yoga, Pilates, and, by far its most popular offering, Spin. Thousands of participants log on from their garages and basements to ride their $2,000 Peloton-brand stationary bikes, which stream the shows from built-in touchscreen monitors. Because Peloton classes are hosted online, as opposed to in limited studio spaces, thousands of riders can take the same class at once. In 2018, the app streamed a Thanksgiving "Turkey Burn," which 19,700 users attended at the exact same time.

Five years after their initial crowdfunding campaign, Peloton had raised almost a billion dollars and was deemed the first-ever "fitness unicorn." A wellness editor I used to work with assured me that Peloton's virtual model, which is simple and nonproprietary, is without question the future of boutique fitness (a prediction that seems even likelier post-COVID-19, when workout studios were forced to digitize overnight or die).

On the Peloton app, each rider chooses a username (the cheekier, the better; there are entire subreddits dedicated to cute Peloton handle ideas: @ridesforchocolate, @will_spin_for_zin, @clever_username) and has access to everyone's speeds, resistance levels, and ranks. These stats appear on a leaderboard on one side of the screen, which adds a gamified edge to the experience. After class, riders exchange digital shout-outs, take virtual selfies with their beloved instructors, and post their numbers on social media—hashtagged in bulk with #pelofam, #pelotonmom, #onepeloton, etc.—so their internet pals can like, share, and comment: "Keep up the energy!!!!!" "Which instructor is your fave?!?!"

Clip-Out Crystal has several faves. She rotates between five or six Peloton instructors and described them each with adoration and specificity. She spoke of "gritty, no-nonsense" Robin, who says things like "You can't buy hustle at the dollar store" and "I only ride with royalty, straighten that crown." Then there are the softies who narrate with easygoing sentiments like "It's not that deep," "Just do your best," and "If you can't smile, you're going too hard." She also told me about Peloton's crown jewel instructor, Jenn Sherman, known as JSS to her thousands of diehards. JSS is the subject of a robust Facebook fan page called the "JSS Tribe," populated by groupies who would follow her anywhere—a "cult" within a "cult" within a "cult."

Boasting an upbeat BFF charisma, Sherman sings on the bike (always endearingly off-key) to her greatest-hits playlists and curses during difficult climbs. "Each F-word pushes me harder," rhapsodized Clip-Out Crystal, who acknowledges that without a strong oratory style, a Peloton instructor couldn't build a cult following. Speech is what constructs that little world inside the screen, making each "relationship" between guru and follower feel intimate, like Joaquin Phoenix and Scarlett Johansson's voice in the movie *Her*.

Companies like Peloton and SoulCycle know that the cultish mystique of hotshots like JSS is everything. So higher-ups put immense effort into recruiting magnetic instructors and training them to develop a unique vibe and vocabulary—a mini cult of their own. Naturally, not just any LA fitness hottie can teach Spin. You need star power; you need duende. And brands have devised formidable recruitment strategies to find it. SoulCycle doesn't scout fitness trainers—they seek performers: dancers, actors, influencers. Savvy social butterfly types who know how to captivate an audience. Who thrive on that dynamic. Instructors need to cultivate a social media persona, to "live and breathe" the brand even off the clock. Even to strangers on the phone. When SoulCycle vet Sparkie and I first got on our call, I began with a customary "Hi, how are you?," expecting your average "good" or "fine." Silly me. Sparkie, as her name suggests, never shuts off. "I'm FABULOUS, BABE!" she exploded with such speed and buoyancy, I felt winded just listening. "Better than ever, busier than ever. I'm so busy I don't even remember what this interview is about! Nice to meet you!! Who are you again?!"

SoulCycle's talent team holds intense, Broadway theater–esque auditions where the first round of aspiring principals is allotted thirty seconds to hop on a bike, blast a song, and show they've got what it takes. Finalists enter a rigorous ten-week instructor training program, where they learn to talk the talk. They pick up all the exclusive terminology—"party hills" (warm-up exercises), "tapbacks" (a signature move involving zesty backward butt thrusting), "Roosters" (5 a.m. classes and the "Type A" riders who take them), "noon on

Monday" (a slogan referencing when class bookings open up each week), and how to make everything sound "soulful" with a capital S.

Peloton's exclusive recruitment process is arguably even more intense, since their online model allows them to maintain a tight roster of only twenty or so top-tier instructors. To earn initiation into the elite Peloton fam, aspirants are put through hours of interviews and callbacks with everyone from marketing experts to producers, and then months of training to guarantee they've got the magnetism to attract thousands to every show.

Sparkie, a born-and-bred LA vegan with lilac hair and sleeves of rainbow tattoos, gained her passionate SoulCycle following with a repertoire of kitschy, old-school mottos inspired by her grandfather ("Anything worth doing is worth doing well!" "It's not how you start, it's how you fucking finish!"). She spent several years heading SoulCycle's training program, helping newbies "find their voice" as instructors. "The key to creating the following is to sound authentic. When you sound like popcorn, people can hear it," Sparkie told me. She recalled one nineteen-year-old trainee who was worried about what words of wisdom she could possibly offer riders: "And I was like, you're not going to stand in front of the woman surviving cancer or the dad supporting a whole family and give them life wisdom. If you're like, 'I know times are hard! You're going to get through this!' they're going to look at you and be like, 'What do you know, child?' Instead, be the joyous, young, fun being that you are. If you're like, 'Do you guys want to party and have a good time?' they're gonna be like, 'Yeah! My life sucks right now, and I just want to fucking party.'"

This combination of optics—from followers' melodramatic message T-shirts ("Weightlifting is my religion," "All I care about is my Peloton, and like 2 people") to the liturgical rituals to the super-intimate instructor-student relationships—seems like overkill. Most of the fitness buffs I spoke to copped to this. But they also professed that the benefits vastly outweigh the negatives. Once you get hooked on a workout community, not only are you going to continue, you're also going to evangelize it to all your friends to prove this thing is actually incredible and that you're not *really* in a "cult." Or at least not a cult any worse than the culture that created you . . .

iv.

In the US, we are taught to fetishize self-improvement. Fitness is a particularly compelling form of self-improvement because it demonstrates classic American values like productivity, individualism, and a commitment to meeting normative beauty standards. The language of cult fitness ("Be your best self," "Change your body, change your mind, change your life") helps connect aspects of religion—like devotion, submission, and transformation—to secular ideals like perseverance and physical attractiveness. Earnestly seeking out a fringe religious community would be a stretch for many modern citizens, but following that shot of woo-woo with a chaser of capitalistic ambition makes it go down a little smoother. With groups from intenSati to CrossFit, we've created the secular "cults" we deserve.

There was a period in history when exercise and American Protestantism overlapped more explicitly. In the nineteenth century, long before it was customary for everyday people to work out at all, some of the only groups that devoutly exercised were Christian Pentecostals, who promoted fitness as an overtly religious purification process. To them, idleness and gluttony were offenses punishable by God, while disciplining the flesh through grueling strength training and fasting was a sign of virtue. For them, lazing around the house while eating junk food was not a metaphorical sin, but a literal one. By contrast, some churches nowadays actively condemn modern gym culture as an overcelebration of the self as opposed to God. "CrossFit is not like church; it is more like the hospital, or even the morgue," critiqued a Virginia-based Episcopal priest in a 2018 blog post. "It is not a place where bad people go to be made good, but a place where bad people are loved in their badness. The grace of God is the only salvation plan that does not lead to burnout."

It's hard to conduct a productive conversation with someone who's arguing that their understanding of spirituality is "the only" valid one. It's also undeniable that American workout culture carries a strong Protestant charge of its own.

Just look at the general vocabulary we use to talk about fitness: cleanse, detox, purify, obedience, discipline, perfection. These terms have unquestionably Biblical undertones, and when repeated day after day, the language of cleansing and purification can condition listeners to believe that achieving "perfect fitness" is possible, if you try hard enough, and that it will in turn "perfect" their whole life. This mentality can feel like a soothing Epsom salt bath in a society that leaves so many citizens feeling existentially high and dry. At the same time, it can make participants more vulnerable to getting involved (and staying involved) with a potentially power abusive guru.

I'm not the first to notice that the conflation of the work we do on our bodies and the value of our humanity can sound eerily Amwayian. You can hear it in statements like "You can get inner peace and flat abs in an hour"—a promise Tess Roering, former CMO of CorePower Yoga, made of the brand in 2016. The fitness industry's maximalist ethos that throwing yourself wholeheartedly into a program—that working harder and faster, never quitting, and intensely believing in yourself—will give you flat abs and inner peace is uncannily reminiscent of the prosperity gospel. This Amway-esque ambiance is subtler in some studios than it is in others, but across platforms, a single promise resonates: Your body fat percentage will drop and your gluteus will elevate, and so will your life's value, but only through sweaty, high-priced labor.

You can hear swells of New Thought in CrossFit's unswerving more-is-more rhetoric. Capitalizing on the athletic vernacular and warlike delivery of a drill sergeant, CrossFit trainers (or "coaches," as they're called on the inside) bellow slogans like "Beast mode," "No guts, no glory," "Sweating or crying?," "The burden of failure is far heavier than that barbell," and "Puking is acceptable. . . . Blood is acceptable. Quitting is not." Invoking rituals like Hero WoDs ("hero workouts of the day," move sequences named after fallen members of the military and law enforcement), they manufacture the atmosphere of soldiers in training.

CrossFit boasts a staunchly libertarian atmosphere, derived from the personal politics of its founder, Greg Glassman, who has famously uttered quotes like "Routine is the enemy" and "I don't mind being told what to do. I just won't do it." It's no coincidence, then, that the CrossFit climate is one of lawlessness, where within the anarchical universe of the box, followers are not only allowed but encouraged to work out so hard they vomit, urinate, or end up in the hospital.

Jason, a cancer survivor and ex-CrossFitter who joined his local box on a quest of self-empowerment after finishing chemotherapy, was forced to quit after developing chronic shoulder pain and a knee injury so severe, it required surgery. In a 2013 Medium post about his experience, he wrote, "The first year was exhilarating. . . . I began bragging about my lifting numbers, and quickly amped up the frequency of my visits from three to four, then five days per week. Without even realizing it, I became that evangelizing asshole." But eventually, CrossFit's ungovernable rhetoric, which conditions members to believe that pushing their bodies to injury is inevitable and even admirable, caught up to Jason. "The messed-up part is that injuries in CrossFit are seen as badges of honor, the price of getting righteously ripped, bro," he revealed.* So when he complained to his

---

* In some cases, getting "seriously ripped" can cost you your vital organs. Experts have noted a strong association between Cross-Fit and rhabdomyolysis, a rare medical condition that results from working your muscles so hard that they break down and release toxic proteins into the bloodstream, which can cause kidney damage or failure. CrossFit coaches are so familiar with the condition that they've given it a nickname: Uncle Rhabdo. In some boxes, you'll find depictions of Uncle Rhabdo as a sickly clown hooked up to a dialysis machine, his kidneys spilling onto the floor. ("Pukie," a different ghoulish clown, is a more prominent mascot.) Online, I found a handful of T-shirts for sale featuring the slogan "Go Until You Rhabdo."

coaches about the shoulder and knee pain he was experiencing, they gaslit him into thinking it was all his fault. "You're supposed to push yourself to the limit," Jason wrote, "but when you hit the limit and pay the price, you're the idiot who went too far." "No guts, no glory" may be a tagline, but it's also among the thought-terminating clichés CrossFit might use to silence your grievances.

Many of the fitness fiends I spoke to argued that their group couldn't possibly be a real cult because "everybody is welcome." And while I agree that you can't really compare SoulCycle and CrossFit to the likes of Heaven's Gate and Scientology, inclusivity isn't the reason. Why would they have dedicated so much energy to creating a whole exclusive code language, if it were? Needless to say, most Americans can't afford to spend thousands (if not tens of thousands) a year on exercise. Not to mention the millions of folks who are BIPOC, disabled, and/or above a size 4, whom the messaging of these studios often subtly or overtly ostracizes. Many high-end workout studios adopt a very similar version of the white feminist #girlboss messaging that can be found in MLMs. (I probably shouldn't have been surprised when, a few months after our interview, Sparkie the SoulCycle instructor became a distributor for "nontoxic" skincare MLM Arbonne, #bossbabe Instagram posts and all.)

The prosperity gospel says that if you don't succeed in becoming the picture of flawless fitness—if you don't acquire the six-pack and the inner peace (like if you are poor, marginalized, and can't clear the structural hurdles keeping you from those things)—then you deserve to be unhappy and die early. You didn't "manifest." It's Rich DeVos's same message, just delivered in a slightly different dialect.

It might sound cloyingly heartfelt to roar "I am powerful beyond measure" while punching the air as hard as you can, but it's nowhere near as spooky as yoga studios full of rich white women wearing the same overpriced athleisure, possibly embellished with a bastardized Sanskrit pun—"Om is where the heart is," "Namaslay," "My chakras are aligned AF"—and calling themselves a "tribe." Commodifying the language of Eastern and Indigenous spiritual practices for an elitist white audience while erasing and shutting out their originators might not seem "culty"—it might just seem commonplace, which is exactly the problem.

For years, CrossFit HQ denied any suggestion that its culture was unwelcoming to Black members. But during the Black Lives Matter protests in June 2020, Greg Glassman shot off a series of racist emails and tweets (in one, he responded to a post about racism as a public health crisis with "It's FLOYD-19"), prompting white CrossFitters to finally start coming around to what many Black folks had known for decades: The place was not really "for everyone." And the linguistic red flags had always been there: By glorifying the police in the names of its Hero WoDs, CrossFit had been telling on itself all along. Hundreds of gyms disaffiliated with the brand, big activewear companies pulled their contracts, and Glassman stepped down as CEO.

A few months after Glassman's fall from grace, it was SoulCycle's turn for a scandal. In late 2020, things were already going south for the company due to COVID-19 lockdowns forcing location closures left and right, when multiple damning exposés surfaced online: According to reporting from Vox, underneath all the motivational Soul-speak, studios across the country harbored long track records of toxicity. Cults of personality formed around certain "Master" instructors, who took advantage by creating hierarchies of favorite and least favorite clients, giving private "off-the-clock" rides, and allegedly sleeping with some students. ("Your riders should want to be you or fuck you" was a mantra instructors reportedly learned and internalized. One all-star openly referred to her riders as "little sluts.") Some top instructors were known for verbally bullying riders and "lesser" employees, as well as stoking all the studio drama that surrounded them, relishing in their deification, like high school Queen Bees.

Purportedly, SoulCycle HQ knew of and condoned the bad behavior, covering up complaints about its most prized instructors making bigoted side comments to riders and staff. (Let's just say they involved the words "Aunt Jemima" and "twinks" and calling curvy staffers "not on brand.") Reports of sexual harassment had allegedly been ignored, as well. The company "treated [instructors] like Hollywood stars anyway," read one headline, which Natalia Petrzela DMed me the hour it broke. Insiders reported that higher-ups threw complaints in the trash, while bankrolling one implicated instructor's $2,400 Soho House membership and rental Mercedes-Benz, like nothing happened. This news didn't exactly come as a shock. "When you elevate instructors as godlike, abuses of power *will* follow," Natalia tweeted. "It makes sense that we saw this kind of reckoning first in yoga, where leaders have long been revered as 'gurus'; it was only a matter of time for instructors [with] a 'cult following.'"

I read a 2020 study from the *European Journal of Social Psychology* revealing that folks who received "spiritual training" in certain supernatural crafts like energy healing and lightwork were more prone to narcissistic tendencies (bloated confidence in their abilities, increased hunger for success and social approval, denigration of anyone lacking their self-evaluated superpowers, etc.). This was compared to people who hadn't gone through any spiritual training at all, as well as students studying less performative disciplines, like meditation and mindfulness. The study showed that even as these gurus encouraged compassion and self-acceptance in others, their own egos swelled. "Master" SoulCycle instructors seem to display a similar response: existing pride in their natural charisma combined with the company's extreme training is the recipe for a god complex closer to that of a 3HO Swami than an ordinary mortal employed to teach stationary cycling.

As of this writing, SoulCycle hasn't commented on the specific accusations or fired any alleged abusers. And Cross-Fit loyalists have ensured that their beloved culture—Hero WoDs, beast mode, and all—lives on, no matter the brand name. Some say the mark of a truly "successful cult" is the power to outlast the death or cancellation of its founder.

In that case, CrossFit and SoulCycle, alongside Scientology and Amway, have prevailed—at least so far.

Certainly the whitewashed, Protestant capitalism-fueled language of "namaslay," "detoxing," and "harder faster more" reflects (and perpetuates) oppressive standards that go beyond fitness. We can find talk of tribes and "push to your max" in so many American industries, from Wall Street to Hollywood to Silicon Valley. This language is pervasive and troublesome, no doubt, but its motives and impact are also importantly different from those of figures like Jim Jones, L. Ron Hubbard, and Rich DeVos. In the case of these leaders, the goal was not so much to reinforce the problematic power structures of our larger society, but more to exploit followers in a way that directly benefited the guru and only the guru. One type of leader uses language (perhaps even unwittingly) to support frameworks that already exist; the other uses language, always deliberately, not to uphold the current order of things but instead to swoop in and create something tyrannically new. In the end, some problematic leaders are really just followers of the larger system. But a truly, destructively *cultish* leader is one who wishes to overthrow the system and replace it with something that grants them ultimate power.

V.

If a fitness brand or leader falls closer to the Scientology end of the cultish spectrum, you'll hear it. Tune in to the loaded language, us-versus-them verbiage, thought-terminators, and verbal abuse that make up the language of cultish influence, and the leaders' motives will ring loud and clear. Examine, for instance, the speech of ill-famed hot yoga guru Bikram Choudhury . . .

Long before he was sued for sexual assault and fled the United States, Bikram Yoga's eponymous founder was a well-known egomaniac and bully. In the early 1970s, Choudhury moved from Calcutta to Los Angeles, where he created his hot yoga empire, which boasted 1,650 studios worldwide at its peak in 2006. During his glory days, Choudhury enjoyed a litany of nicknames that reflected his bellicose cult of personality—the Anti-Yogi, the Walter White of yoga, the crowned head of McYoga. He shattered visions of the peaceful, meditative yoga master by screaming, cursing, and name-calling in class. The content of his profanity-filled caterwauling wasn't Peloton-style inspirational, but instead shamelessly misogynist, racist, and fat-shaming.

"Suck that fat fucking stomach in. I don't like to see the jiggle jiggle."

"Black bitch."

"Chickenshit."

These are direct quotes, loudly proclaimed in public.

In his famous teacher trainings, Choudhury preached to sweltering halls of five-hundred-plus aspiring Bikram instructors, who'd each paid between $10,000 and $15,000 for the opportunity to follow him. Poised on a high throne (always equipped with a personal air conditioner), he would bellow call-and-responses, making no attempt to hide his megalomania. Choudhury would exclaim, "It's my way or the . . . ," and the group would call back in unison, "Highway!"

"The best food is . . . ?"

"NO FOOD!"

Of course, no one would ever stick around if all Choudhury did was insult people; like most toxic figures, the slurs and screaming were juxtaposed with the seductive language of love-bombing. Inside of a minute, Choudhury might decree your potential to become a brilliant teacher, call you a bitch, and then serenade you with his mellifluous singing voice, all while you contorted your body into near-impossible poses in blistering heat.

But devotees of Choudhury swore he was like "a big kid." His lullabies and moodiness, even his tantrums, gave him an "innocent adorable" factor, they attested. Confirmation bias allowed fans to interpret Choudhury's blatant lies (he gloated about winning yoga competitions that never even took place) and statements of grandeur ("I don't even sleep thirty hours a month," "I'm the smartest man in the world you ever met," "I'm the only friend you've had in your life") as "childlike" rather than disturbed. The sunk cost fallacy told them he'd make their careers if they just attended one more training.

During his hot yoga workshops, Choudhury's pupils were known to pass out, suffer dehydration, and develop upper respiratory infections. Because they were conditioned to trust their beloved guru as all-knowing, they learned to disregard their own pain and gut instincts. Choudhury was also accused of grooming and sexually assaulting at least half a dozen female trainees. In 2016, the man responded to rape allegations with more us-versus-them name-calling, hyperbole, and gaslighting: A parody of himself, Choudhury denounced his accusers as "psychopaths" and "trash," adding, "Why would I have to harass women? People spend one million dollars for a drop of my sperm." In 2016, Choudhury fled the US without paying the nearly $7 million he owed survivors in punitive damages, and a year later, a Los Angeles judge issued a warrant for his arrest. (As of this writing, he has not been brought to justice and continues to lead teacher trainings outside the US.)

As soon as Choudhury's American empire crumbled, another controversial yoga "cult" took its place: CorePower. After the fall of Bikram, Denver-based CorePower Yoga swept in and rapidly became the largest yoga chain in America. While Bikram proudly claimed to be the "McDonald's of yoga," CorePower's cofounder, the (now deceased) tech mogul Trevor Tice, self-branded as the "Starbucks of yoga."

Over the following decade, CorePower faced five federal lawsuits for the financial exploitation of its instructors and clients, having to forfeit over $3 million in settlements. Not dissimilar to a pyramid scheme, the studio pays instructors an unlivable hourly wage, promising raises and promotions only to those who recruit students to its $1,500 teacher training program. CorePower instructors are told to deliver their teacher training pitches at the end of class, after Savasana, the final resting pose. While practitioners lie in a relaxed, loosey-goosey puddle, teachers offer what CorePower calls a "personal share" (an intimate disclosure from their lives)—and they're told to make it "soul-rocking."

Soul-rocking is a benchmark piece of CorePower loaded language. Instructors' performance is, in fact, judged on how many "souls" they're able to "rock" (aka how many students they can get to sign up for teacher training). After the personal share, instructors are urged to target individual students, love-bomb them with compliments about their skills and dedication, and offer to buy them a Starbucks to tell them about becoming a teacher themselves.

"It was like they saw something special in me," Kalli, a CorePower student from Minnesota, told the *New York Times* in 2019. Kalli had just finished class one day and was feeling all mellow when her favorite instructor approached her with a wide smile and told her she thought Kalli had the chops to do her job. She didn't disclose the cost of teacher training (they tell instructors to keep that part "open-ended"); she just showered Kalli with praise and followed up repeatedly both in and out of the studio. "It felt like we had a friendship that was really actually not real," Kalli reflected.

When Kalli finally found out about the $1,500 price tag, she'd already been fantasizing for weeks about her dreamy future yoga career. She couldn't decline now. Kalli wrote the check and went through the eight-week program. Only at the end did she find out it didn't actually qualify her to teach. Like Scientology's levels, CorePower waited until they knew she wouldn't back out before they mentioned she had to complete an additional $500 "extensions" course. Kalli ponied up once more. But even after that, CorePower never offered her a job. That's because their training program produces a glut of certified teachers who saturate the market, just like an MLM. A 2016 survey reported that there are two hopefuls in some form of teacher training for every employed instructor. "You're being taught to be calm and breathe, but at the same time, being taken advantage of," Kalli told the press.

One of the phrases CorePower weaponized most successfully was "return the karma"—an emotionally charged euphemism and thought-terminating cliché wrapped into one. In Hinduism, karma yoga is one of three paths to spiritual liberation: It's learning to lead a life of selfless service, expecting nothing in return. But at CorePower, "return the karma" was invoked to coerce teachers into substituting for each other's classes and performing hours of mandatory work outside the studio—class prep, email customer service, marketing for the brand—all without pay. By calling on such a profound spiritual phrase with eternal implications, the company could succinctly trigger guilt and loyalty in its employees. If someone wanted to question an unfair policy, CorePower could just point to "karma" to smother their claim.

Court documents reveal that CorePower's own lawyers discredit karma as a vacant "metaphysical precept" in the same nonsense language category as "soul-rocking." But for followers, it was loaded enough to retain their allegiance even when they knew the company was screwing them. Kalli left her CorePower career dreams behind to become a registered nurse but continues to take yoga classes at a local CorePower studio. In order to afford her $120 monthly membership (she receives no discount for having gone through teacher training), she works as a cleaner at a different CorePower location once a week. On the side, she teaches "goat yoga" (they really do have everything now) at a small farm in the Minneapolis suburbs. Her bio proudly reads "CorePower Trained Instructor."

vi.

Upon finding yourself in a cultish fitness community that may or may not be entirely healthy, here are a few questions worth asking: Is this group genuinely welcoming of all different people? Or do you feel excessive pressure to dress and talk like everyone else (even outside of class)? Are you allowed to participate casually, to dabble in this activity? Or do you find yourself putting all your time and faith in this group alone, basing all your decisions on theirs? Do you trust the instructor to tell you to slow down, maybe even take a few weeks off or try a whole different exercise, if your body needs it? Or will they only tell you harder, faster, more? If you miss a class or quit, what is the exit cost? Pride? Money? Relationships? Your whole world? Is it a price you're willing to pay?

For me, it's become easier to spot the difference between a warehouse full of five hundred yoga trainees war-crying that it's their leader's way or the highway (or a Spin instructor debasing their students as "little sluts") and a studio of sixteen women, who are dressed how they like and free to cancel their memberships without the threat of shame or worse, joining in a mantra like "I am stronger than I seem." Both businesses are profiting from the language, but they're also literally naming whom they want to empower: In one case, it's the guru, and in the other, it's the people.

"I feel like what 'cult fitness' really means is that people are so moved by something that helps them grow and change," intenSati's Patricia Moreno concluded. Because Moreno's aim is so transparently to teach her students to reclaim their own personal power, as opposed to asserting her power over them, she's never felt the need to defend intenSati as not a "real cult." To me, that lack of defensiveness speaks volumes.

By and large, new religion experts are not terribly concerned that the drawbacks of cult fitness stack up to the likes of Scientology, either. "I definitely think some of these workouts are 'culty,' but I say that with scare quotes," commented Stanford anthropologist Tanya Luhrmann. The main "cult" symptom Luhrmann finds in fitness buffs is the belief that if they attend classes regularly, their lives will dramatically improve overall. As long as they attend class five times a week and say the mantras, then that will change the way the world unfolds for them. It's that sense of excess idealism again—that conviction that this group, this instructor, these rituals, have the power to accomplish more than they probably can.

It is entirely possible to exploit that faith. However, what keeps me from roasting the cult fitness industry too dramatically is that ultimately, you're in charge of your own experience. At Spin class, you control the resistance on your bike; if you want to ignore the "culty lady" at the front of the room (or onscreen) and slow down, you can. If you pray to a higher power, you can do that while chanting about divine inspiration. But if you just want to jump around and party, you can do that, too. And after six months, if things start to get toxic or you just want to try something else, you're free to. If the bonds you built on the leaderboard are really that strong, they'll last even after you decide to switch to surfboard Pilates.

After all, the studio is not what singularly gives your life meaning. It very well might bring you fulfillment and connection for forty-five minutes at a time, but you'd still be you without it. You're already blessed with all you need.

Part 6

Follow for Follow

i.

It's June 2020, one of the most contentious months in contemporary American history, and my Instagram algorithm is on the fritz. Amid posting about the global COVID-19 pandemic and Black Lives Matter, while keeping up with all the New Age swamis, MLM recruiters, and conspiracy theorists I've followed over the past year, my Explore page can't seem to tell whether I'm a social justice warrior, a *Plandemic* truther, an antivaxxer, a witch, an Amway distributor, or just really obsessed with essential oils. There's a smug satisfaction that comes with briefly allowing myself to believe I've confused the Instagram Eye, whose presence is so omniscient and mysterious (and indispensable to me), sometimes it feels like the only God I've ever known.

I suppose I get what I deserve, then, when in the midst of a two-hour social media binge, I come across the profile of a spiritual guru named Bentinho Massaro. With an Instagram bio that reads "Synthesizer of Paths," "True Scientist," "Philosopher," and "Mirror," Massaro is a thirtysomething white dude who claims to vibrate at a higher frequency than other humans, higher even than Jesus Christ. Sporting forty thousand Insta followers, icy-blue eyes, a robust wardrobe of tight black T-shirts, and a confident voice cloaked in some indeterminate European accent, he reads like a cross between Teal Swan and Tony Robbins. A Hemsworth would definitely play him in the movie. About a dozen proverbial red flags erect in my frontal cortex. I click Follow.

A deeper dive soon reveals that Bentinho Massaro was born in Amsterdam but relocated to Boulder, Colorado, and later to the occult mecca of Sedona, Arizona, to run pricey spiritual retreats. All the while, he puts spectacular effort into growing his web presence. Using a Silicon Valley–savvy social media strategy and a portfolio of snazzy websites, he aims to sell you . . . well, your soul.

Costing as little as an Instagram follow or as much as $600 per hour on Skype, you can gain access to doses of Massaro's sacred science—the answers to everything from how to cultivate profound personal relationships to how to become "a human god." In his YouTube videos, Massaro sits close to the camera, creating the cozy atmosphere of a home gathering or a one-on-one conversation, as he expounds upon subjects like "The Inner Black Hole," "Presence-Energy Vibration," and "Cutting Through the Illusion of Mind." Navigate over to his Instagram and you'll find minute-long clips where Massaro just stares intensely into the lens, grinning, barely blinking, intermittently murmuring, "I love you." He calls these parasocial gaze-offs his moments of "oneness—no separation between you or me." Hundreds of supporters flood his comments with praise: "You are infinite intelligence, love/light," "Thank you Ben for this wave of consciousness," "MASTER, teacher, . . . YOU have an amazing ability . . . Please lead us."

Massaro's ideology is, shall we say, eclectic. He believes

in ancient aliens, asserts he can change the weather with his mind, and has announced that he doesn't want children because he already has seven billion. It should sound familiar by now that Massaro insists he, and only he, possesses the "God's-eye view" required to guide humanity toward heaven's "absolute truth." His teachings, he proclaims, will lead to the "cessation of suffering and endless bliss." Massaro vows that over the course of any given earthling's lifetime, they won't access even "10 percent of what goes on in [his] consciousness in a single day." His ultimate vision? To bring his internet fellowship offline, buy a big slab of land in Sedona, and build an enlightened new city.

Amid lectures on paths, vibrations, and raising your frequency, some of Massaro's rhetoric takes a grim turn. His mystical vernacular is fraught with thought-terminating clichés, intended to gaslight followers into mistrusting science, as well as their own thoughts and emotions. In one lesson, he commands, "Thinking about something is the surest way to miss out on the beauty of that actual something. . . . See where you have these allegiances to logic, to reason, to linear description, and simply start destroying these." In another video, he shouts at a female student after she expresses feeling disrespected by the phrase "fuck you," saying, "If you weren't so high up in your own ass about this fucking concept of respect, you would actually see how much love there is behind me saying what I say."

Massaro always finds a twisted way to justify his use of verbal aggression: Once on Facebook, he posted, "Being friends with an awake being is nearly impossible, because:

A) his first priority is your purification and elevation into truth; not kindness . . . and B) he is not like an ordinary person and thus cannot be successfully compared with normal standards or related to as just another person (which the finite mind does not like)." His shouting and cursing, he says, are an expression of divine kindness. "I can scream at you all freely," he declaims, adding that verbal abuse is a necessary part of the spiritual path, and that questioning it simply reflects the lowly human's "limited and opinionated mind."

As with Teal Swan, Massaro's videos also promote unsafe messaging about suicide: "Don't fear death; be excited about it," he says in one clip. "Looking forward to death makes you truly come alive. . . . Wake up to something important. Otherwise, kill yourself."

These sentiments mostly flew under the radar until December 2017, when Massaro hosted a spiritual retreat in Sedona that went horribly wrong. The twelve-day New Age boot camp was promised to offer one hundred guests exclusive access to Massaro's most profound teachings. By then, "cult leader" accusations had already started trickling onto the web. The day before the retreat, a Sedona-based reporter named Be Scofield published an incriminating exposé characterizing Massaro as a "tech bro guru" using growth-hacker marketing to build a quack spiritual consortium: endangering followers' bodies with ridiculous health advice (like living on nothing but grape juice for weeks—Massaro called this "dry fasting"), manipulating them into cutting off friends and family ("Fuck your relationships.

They mean nothing," he'd say), and trusting him as an all-knowing deity.

On the sixth day of the Sedona retreat, an attendee named Brent Wilkins, who'd followed Massaro devotedly for years, broke away from the group. He got in his car, drove to a nearby bridge, and jumped, ending his life.

News of Wilkins's death circulated hastily, and a chorus of Jim Jones comparisons quickly followed. The internet dubbed Massaro an "Instagram douche meets cult leader" and "Steve Jobs meets Jim Jones." Massaro was quiet for months afterward, until he finally posted a response on Facebook, not addressing the death or any specific concerns but instead firing the "cult" label right back at Be Scofield. In the ultimate battle of thought-terminating clichés, he avowed that Scofield was "part of one of the biggest cults on our planet today: The Average American Cult—indoctrinated by media, scared of just about anything outside of their own family home, and ready to pull a gun out on anyone they do not understand."

The day after Wilkins's death, detectives showed up at Massaro's residence to confront him about his questionable suicide messaging. But in the end, no charges were brought against him. In a culture where malignant social media interactions contribute to depression, anxiety, and suicide in such complicated ways, it was ultimately too tricky to place singular, prosecutable blame, even on a figure as disreputable as Massaro.

In the end, the Brent Wilkins tragedy didn't shake the faith of (or even reach) most of Massaro's supporters, most of whom never considered "following" the guy beyond Instagram. Still, over the next few months, small waves of devotees quietly disconnected from him—clicked Unsubscribe, excised his lingo from their vocabularies, even joined a "Bentinho Massaro Recovery Group" on Facebook. Painfully, they came to the realization that their guru was just a man, poisoned by his own addiction to a cult much larger than his own—the cult of social media attention. While they once admired their "spiritual rock star" for using Instagram and YouTube to make infinite consciousness available to everyone, it became clear that Massaro's movement only existed to satisfy his own desire for adoration, which, thanks to the alternate universe he created for himself online, became more bottomless every day.

"But I guess this is what a lot of people do on the internet," commented Lynn Parry, an ex–Massaro loyalist who was close with Brent Wilkins before he died, in an interview with the *Guardian*. "They put out a perfect persona . . . [and] without meaning to, they make other people feel like they're not good enough . . . and for people like Brent, for many of us really, it's just too much for the spirit to handle."

ii.

Flashback two decades before Bentinho Massaro's retreat-gone-wrong to 1997, the same year the very first social media site was invented. In March, when Heaven's Gate's mass suicide sent seismic panic throughout the country, everyday Americans were prompted to wonder how, oh how, could a clearly deranged UFO-obsessed guy like Marshall Applewhite provoke such a disaster? When it was suggested that the Heaven's Gate website, a cacophony of bright fonts and extraterrestrial ramblings, might have played a role in recruiting and radicalizing followers, commentators scoffed. While one *New York Times* reporter called Heaven's Gate "an object lesson in the evils of the Internet," a journalist from *Time* incredulously rebutted, "Spiritual predators? Give me a break. . . . A Web page that has the power to suck people . . . into a suicide cult? . . . The whole idea would be laughable if 39 people weren't dead."

As far as the average 1990s imagination could stretch, cults required an in-the-flesh location to have real influence. Without a secluded commune or isolated mansion, how could anyone possibly become separated from their family and friends, have their individuality suppressed, and ideologically convert to a destructive dogma in a way that incited real-world harm?

In the years since Heaven's Gate, the virtual and physical worlds have merged. For better and for worse, social media has become the medium through which millions of us construct kinship and connection in an ever-transient society. In early 2020, reporter Alain Sylvain wrote that social media and pop culture have become "the modern-day campfire." It's something that '90s *Time* writer couldn't have predicted: a world where seekers satisfy their spiritual desires with a hodgepodge of nonreligious rituals practiced largely online. It's a world where our closest confidantes can be found on Beyoncé fan forums and private Peloton Facebook groups, and where one's ethics and identity are wrapped up in the influencers they follow, targeted ads they click through, and memes they repost.

Twenty years post–Heaven's Gate, most zealous fringe groups rarely convene IRL. Instead, they build an online system of morality, culture, and community—and sometimes radicalize—with no remote commune, no church, no "party," no gym. Just language. In lieu of a physical place to meet, cultish jargon gives followers something to assemble around.

When I first downloaded Instagram in the summer of 2012, I couldn't help but notice how curious it seemed that the app called its account holders "followers" instead of friends or connections. "It's like a cult platform," I remember saying to pals. "Is it not encouraging everyone to build their own little cult?"

I didn't even know the word "influencer" back then (the term didn't become popular until 2016, according to Google search data), so I couldn't have foreseen that "spiritual influencers" would soon become a whole category of new religious leader. Less than a decade after Instagram's launch, thousands of astrologers, self-help sages, and holistic wellness guides like Bentinho Massaro and Teal Swan, who might have never even developed an interest in metaphysics before the internet (much less monetized it), use apps and algorithms to spread their gospel. These digital gurus fulfill modern America's renewed demand for New Age ideas with images of tarot readings, updates on the cosmos, and abstract talk of frequency fields and galactic perspectives. Their high-octane feeds provide just as much eye candy as a beauty or "lifestyle" influencer, but the promises are far greater. The Instagram mystic doesn't operate on a business model but a spiritual mission; they aren't just selling spon con and merch, but transcendent wisdom. Double-tap and subscribe, and you'll obtain access to higher vibrations, alternate dimensions, even life beyond death.

"I've asked myself, if Buddha or Jesus lived today, would they have a Facebook page?" Bentinho Massaro posed in a 2019 interview, adding that he finds that Instagram lends itself particularly well to the divine. "The pictures have an energy," he told the reporter, his glacial eyes glittering.

Brent Wilkins's suicide was a rare and concretely tragic example of the fate that can befall a seeker who submerges too deeply in the warped "reality" of an online guru. But for most people, someone like Massaro is just another account to thumb past. Unlike the cults of the '70s, we don't even have to leave the house for a charismatic figure to take hold of us. With contemporary cults, the barrier to entry is the simple frisson of tapping Follow.

Not every spiritual influencer is hazardous; in fact, many provide what I'd classify as a largely positive experience, offering inspiration, validation, and solace, even if just for a moment mid-scroll. In 2018, I investigated the growing phenomenon of "Instagram witches" for Cosmopolitan.com, and what I found was a diverse coalition of millennial women and nonbinary people growing devoted digital followings with whom they attentively engaged over recipes for plant-based tinctures and astrological insights. This community of online witches seemed like a haven for many LGBTQ+ and BIPOC folks who felt unwelcome in so many old-school religious spaces. They'd be practicing their craft either way; Instagram simply gave them a platform to share it and make a real living out of it. Almost everyone I investigated seemed genuinely motivated by helping people above anything else, and no one used the thought-terminating clichés, circuitous euphemisms, or other intentionally deceptive tactics that we now know constitute the worst kind of cultish language.

But inevitably, the clout-hungry always find their way to social media—a machine that works to fuel our scammiest, most narcissistic tendencies. Reporter Oscar Schwartz wrote for the *Guardian* that as far as algorithms are concerned, "there is little difference between the genuine and pernicious guru." Spiritual influencers are sanctified by the apps for the same reason any other content creator is—because their posts are on-trend and hyper-engaging. They exchange regrammable quotegrams full of buzzy wellness vernacular for ego-boosting likes and ad dollars, profiting from Apple Pay–enabled seekers aiming to soothe the distress and ennui of contemporary existence.

Because their actual beliefs take a back seat to the success of their brand, these gurus are willing to fudge them according to whatever the zeitgeist seems to want. If CBD supplements are all the rage, they'll suddenly flood their feeds with affiliate posts and act like cannabis has been part of their ideology all along; if conspiracy theory–type content seems to be doing well, they'll head in that direction, even if they don't fully understand the volatile rhetoric they're trafficking in.

Spend a few minutes poking around the Bentinho Massaro borough of Instagram and you'll find dozens upon dozens of similar accounts. In one corner, you'll find "alternative healing" opportunists masquerading as benevolent medical professionals. Like . . . "Dr." Joe Dispenza, a generic-looking middle-aged white guy who well over a million Instagram followers somehow trust as their New Age sage. Dispenza's army of adoring acolytes claim he's helped them manifest everything from their dream job to their spouse to their cancer remission. Dispenza shrewdly exploits SEO and other web-marketing strategies to make millions selling an extravagant emporium of self-help workshops and retreats, public speaking engagements, corporate consultations, guided meditations, CDs, gifts, and books like *Becoming Supernatural* and *Evolve Your Brain*. Branding himself as the ultimate "scientific" spiritual authority, Dispenza's Instagram bio reads "Researcher of epigenetics, quantum physics & neuroscience," and he proudly flaunts his studies in biochemical sciences at Rutgers University, as well as his "postgraduate training and continuing education"—whatever that means—"in neurology, neuroscience, brain function and chemistry, cellular biology, memory formation, and aging and longevity." Taking a page out of L. Ron Hubbard's playbook, Dispenza marries academic-sounding language with the paranormal. Examine, for instance, his definition of a quantum field: "an invisible field of energy and information—or you could say a field of intelligence or consciousness—that exists beyond space and time. Nothing physical or material exists there. It is beyond anything you can perceive with your senses."

Needless to say, most followers don't have a background in neuroscience or quantum mechanics, so they hear the esoteric jargon and—using a System 1 thought process—they conclude that Dispenza must be legit. "He's mainly speaking to people who may have little to no academic understanding of these fields but the words are a literal inaccurate description of the quantum field," commented Azadeh Ghafari, a licensed psychotherapist and frequent exposer of digital wellness scammers on her Instagram account, @the.wellness.therapist. "To say that 'nothing physical or material exists there' is not only categorically false but shows that this person does not have a present-day understanding of what is called the vacuum state or the quantum vacuum." Ghafari suggests this litmus test: "Anytime any New Age guru making $$ from the stuff they're peddling utters the words 'quantum' anything, give them a basic physics equa-

tion (DM me for some). If they can't solve it, move along."
The internet scammeth, and the internet fact-checketh away.

Indeed, a quick probe reveals that Dispenza never graduated from Rutgers and has no PhD. His only diplomas include a general BS from Evergreen State College and a degree from a chiropractic school in Georgia called Life University. And yet google Dispenza's credentials, and his exceptionally well-optimized web presence will provide the top result: "Dr. Joe Dispenza is a well-known neuroscientist." As a white man in his fifties, just the kind of guy our culture wants a neuroscientist to look and sound like, he is largely trusted without question.*

In a nearby ZIP code of the guru-sphere, you'll find twentysomething women adding an antiestablishment flavor to aspirational Insta-baddie branding. Blond and blue-eyed, Heather Hoffman (@activationvibration) is typically found bralette-clad, sporting an ornate septum piercing alongside appropriative face jewels. Her ultra-produced, triple-filtered images feature rainbow lens flares and jewel-tone lotus blossoms that accompany daily affirmations just vague enough to sound profound (e.g., "Receive the succulence of

---

* Because the majority of Dispenza's followers get to know him through his carefully crafted internet persona, most never dig to find out he's connected to a controversial New Age circle called Ramtha. The group was founded in the late '80s by a self-proclaimed ESP master (and proud Trump supporter) named J. Z. Knight, who has been quoted spewing all kinds of QAnon-esque rhetoric and generally bigoted nonsense (like that all gay men used to be Catholic priests). But Ramtha devotees—which have included a handful of A-list celebrities—hear what they want to hear and ignore the rest.

your own source, and your external seeking shall cease"). Her long, convoluted captions feature a dialect of New Age–speak so cryptic that insiders want to like and comment, while outsiders can't help but keep scrolling through to find out what her beliefs actually are: "integrating potent codes," "quantum transformation," "multidimensional space of time," "divine alignment," "upgrading your DNA," "energy matrices, grids, and frequencies."

In one video, Heather squats on the floor in a green bikini, playing Tibetan sound bowls, undulating her torso. Using a honeyed soprano, she begins speaking a form of glossolalia she calls "Light Language." The comment section overflows with all kinds of "divine goddess," "hypnotizing," and "Heather you are next level light code!" In another clip, she sits before a mandala tapestry lecturing that COVID-19 was caused by government "fear propaganda" and that protecting yourself means "deactivating" your "matrix grid of fear" so as not to pollute the "divine order." Heather has been reincarnated precisely to cure humans of problems like these, she says, through her ability to access "Source" (God) and other spiritual "realms" available only to her, since everyone else has fallen victim to a "program." To access her wisdom, just sign up for one of her online courses, like the "Cellular Activation Course—Upgrade Your DNA" for $144.44, or, to tap into her most exclusive wisdom, pay $4,444 for eight one-on-one mentoring sessions.

Creeping along the influence continuum toward Scientology, these figures will cajole you into buying their e-book, then their meditation playlist, then their online hypnosis course, and by that point, your spiritual journey would be worthless if you didn't sign up for a workshop or retreat. For you, it might feel like the quest for self-actualization, but for them, it's a profitable, scalable, passive-income-generating cash cow.

Ghafari points out that when an online guru uses too much "absolutist language," that's New Age scammer red flag number one. "Anyone who talks about the concept of feeling our past, our inner trauma, in a universal, over-simplified way," she clarifies. "For example, statements like, 'All of us are traumatized as kids, which is why we need to x, y, z,' or, 'All of us are from the cosmos and we're just floating in a quantum field, *blah blah blah*.'" If simple quantifiers and qualifiers are absent from a guru's messaging, that's a sign they are likely unqualified to speak as a mental health authority, and are less interested in actually helping people than they are in convincing as many followers as possible to invest in their prophetic gifts.

"New Age holistic psychology and wellness is not about trauma-informed care. It's about pushing pseudoscience and marketing," Ghafari concludes. Alternative wellness gurus like Bentinho Massaro and Heather Hoffman fume about the evils of Big Pharma until they're blue in the face. "But they push a far more deceptive form of capitalism," says Ghafari. They don't want to sell you pills. They want to sell you a key to enlightenment they don't actually possess.

To some onlookers, mystical Insta scammers might not seem like that much of a threat; you'd have to be seriously out of touch to put real faith in these people, right? But researchers have found that the folks most attracted to New Age rhetoric are more with-it than one might think. Michael Shermer, a science writer and founder of the Skeptics Society, has written about the correlation between intelligence and belief in "weird ideas." According to Shermer, studies show that American test subjects with the lowest education levels have a higher probability of subscribing to certain paranormal beliefs, like haunted houses, Satanic possession, and UFO landings; but it's test subjects with the most education who are likeliest to believe in New Age ideas, like the power of the mind to heal disease. Psychologist Stuart Vyse has remarked that the New Age movement "has led to the increased popularity of [supernatural] ideas among groups previously thought to be immune to superstition: those with higher intelligence, higher socioeconomic status, and higher educational levels." Therefore, he remarks, the age-old view that people who believe in "weird" things are less intelligent than nonbelievers may not hold entirely true.

Objectively, made-up metaphysical interpretations of "quantum fields" and "upgrading your DNA" are just as irrational as ghosts and alien visitations; but the fact that they're associated with a demographic of social media–savvy young people with college degrees makes them seem more acceptable. It's not that smart people aren't capable of believing in cultish things; instead, says Shermer, it's that smart people are better at "defending beliefs they arrived at for non-smart reasons." Most people, even skeptics and scientists, don't come to the bulk of their beliefs for reasons having to do with empirical evidence. No one sits down and reads a bunch of scientific studies, then weighs the pros and cons before deciding to believe that, say, money equals happiness, or that cats are better than dogs, or that there's only one right way to clean a colander. "Rather," Shermer says, "such variables as genetic predispositions, parental predilections, sibling influences, peer pressures, educational experiences, and life impressions all shape the personality preferences and emotional inclinations that, in conjunction with numerous social and cultural influences, lead us to make certain belief choices."

This is all to say, being smart and hip to the zeitgeist is not enough to protect someone from cultish influence online. And even if shady social media characters like Joe Dispenza and Bentinho Massaro don't seem like that big a deal in the grand scheme of things, by contributing to a world that values "Light Language" and sci-fi physics over real science, as if facts are just opinions, they wind up making space for more urgently dangerous groups to take advantage.

It's exactly this paranoiac rejection of "mainstream" healthcare and leadership that gave such momentum to QAnon, whose rhetoric overlaps considerably with that of the "alternative wellness" sphere: "great awakening," "ascension," "5G." The diagram of QAnon and New Agers looks more circular every day. It appeared an unlikely crossover, at first: that of violent right-wing conspiracy theorists and seemingly progressive hippie types. But America's ever-escalating unrest has led a disarming number of citizens (mostly white, middle class ex-Christians—similar to the folks who joined Heaven's Gate back in the day) to a similarly anti-government, anti-media, anti-doctor place.

In the early 2010s, well before QAnon, the term "conspirituality" (a portmanteau of "conspiracy" and "spirituality") was introduced to describe this rapidly growing politico-spiritual movement defined by two core principles: "the first traditional to conspiracy theory, the second rooted in the New Age: 1) a secret group covertly controls, or is trying to control, the political and social order, and 2) humanity is undergoing a 'paradigm shift' in consciousness" (this definition comes from a 2011 paper from the *Journal of Contemporary Religion*).

When the COVID-19 pandemic hit the US in 2020, it was like rocket fuel feeding conspirituality's flame.

Antivaxxers and Plandemic truthers would fall squarely into the category of conspirituality, but so would plenty of less conspicuously QAnon-related wellness aficionados: the sorts who might sign up for an essential oils MLM, for example, or wear "Namaslay" T-shirts to their whitewashed yoga classes, or run a "holistic self-care" Instagram account. The sorts who maybe searched for "all-natural health remedies" on YouTube one night and ended up in "all doctors are brainwashed" conspirituality territory, unable to navigate their way out. Trickily, not every conspiritualist even knows or is willing to admit that their beliefs have anything to do with QAnon. In fact, some of these believers regard the terms "QAnon," "conspiracy theorist," and "antivaxxer" as offensive "slurs." And the more outsiders invoke these labels, the more firmly insiders dig in their heels. After all, both camps think the other is "brainwashed."

In broad strokes, QAnon started in 2017 as a fringe-y online conspiracy theory surrounding an alleged intelligence insider called Q. The ideology began as something like this: Q, a faceless figure, swore to have "proof" of corrupt left-wing leaders—"the deep state," or "global elite"—sexually abusing little kids around the world. (According to Q, Donald Trump was working tirelessly to thwart them before being "fraudulently" dethroned.) The only way to undo this evil cabal of high-powered liberal predators was with the support of Q's loyalists, known as "Q Patriots" or "bakers," who'd hunt for meaning in their anonymous leader's secret clues—"Q drops" or "crumbs"—which were sprinkled throughout the web. To trust in Q meant to reject mainstream government, vehemently scorn the press, and contest doubters at every turn. It's all a necessary part of the ongoing "paradigm shift." QAnon developed rallying cries, including "You are the news now" and "Enjoy the show," referencing the impending "awakening," or apocalypse.

In September 2020, a *Daily Kos*/Civiqs poll reported that over half of the Republicans surveyed believed either partially or mostly in QAnon's theories . . . at least the theories they were aware of. Because tumble further down the QAnon rabbit hole, and you'll find Satanic Panic–esque, flagrantly fascist beliefs that not every subscriber even knows about (at least not at first): theories about Jeffrey Epstein co-conspiring with Tom Hanks to molest hordes of minors,

Hillary Clinton drinking the blood of children in order to prolong her life, the Rothschilds running a centuries-old ring of Satan worshippers, and beyond.

But QAnon quickly grew to encapsulate much more than stereotypical far-right extremists. Take a soft turn to the left, and you'll find a more outwardly palatable denomination of conspiritualists whose paranoias might be slightly less focused on Hillary Clinton worshipping Satan and more on Big Pharma forcing evil Western medicine on them and their kids. These believers wield a slightly different glossary of loaded terms, some co-opted from feminist politics—like "forced penetration" (which conflates vaccination with sexual assault) and "my body, my choice" (an antivaxx/anti-mask slogan purloined from the pro-choice movement). Because social media algorithms track people's keywords in order to feed them only what they're already interested in, a sprawling spiderweb of customized QAnon offshoots was able to form.

In this manner, with language as its matter and energy, QAnon became like a black hole sucking in every breed of cultish twenty-first-century believer that crossed it. That's part of why its central buzzwords—like the "deep state," "mainstream media," and "paradigm shift"—are so lofty and vague; they work to reel in and bond recruits without revealing too much. It's not unlike how Scientology conceals the language of their bizarre upper levels so as not to lose new followers. Akin to a horoscope, the generic posts allow participants to convince themselves that they're being spoken to uniquely—like this community singularly holds the answers to the world's suffering—all the while camouflaging the fact that a unified belief system doesn't actually exist.

Like most manipulative cults, QAnon's magnetism is largely the promise of special foreknowledge, which is available only to members of its enlightened underground collective. This allure is constructed with (and this will sound quite familiar now) an exhaustive sociolect of insider-y acronyms and keyboard symbols, "us"/"them" labels, and loaded language. In QAnon-speak, CBTS stands for "calm before the storm," "truth seekers" are followers, and ignorant outsiders are "sheeple" or "agents of the elite." #Savethechildren is an innocent-sounding QAnon shibboleth stolen from real child trafficking activists, used to hide in plain sight and attract newcomers. "5D consciousness" is a level of enlightenment that becomes available to insiders during turbulent times, "ascension" is a loaded buzzword used to explain away symptoms of anxiety or cognitive dissonance, and "looking at all viewpoints" is one of many euphemisms equating evidence and fantasy.

The glossary goes on and on. And it's always changing, branching off into different "dialects" of QAnon-ese, in order to accommodate new additions to the belief system . . . and, so that social media algorithms don't catch up, flag the language, and block or shadowban the accounts using it. New code words, hashtags, and rules for how to use them are introduced all the time. QAnon followers (some of whom are influencers with acolytes of their own) stand by for updates, often choosing to post only in their ephemeral Instagram Stories—the social media equivalent of "this message will self-destruct in 24 hours." This creates an even deeper level of exclusivity for the followers following them. To put it crudely, with QAnon, there are cults inside cults inside cults inside cults; it's the ultimate cult-ception, and social media made it possible.

Depending on their subsect of beliefs, QAnon participants feel free to define the broad talk of "sheeple" and "5D" in whatever way "resonates." After all, for them, "truth is subjective." It doesn't matter to them that some interpretations of this language have led to enough real-world violence† that QAnon has become one of the most threatening domestic terror groups of our time. It also doesn't matter that at its core, QAnon is just another madcap apocalyptic cult in a line of them that goes back centuries. The updated cast of characters is new, and so is the medium of social media, but baseless doomsday predictions and ideas of dark forces secretly controlling everything are practically trite.

All this and still, those wrapped up in the QAnon-to-conspirituality "culture of shared understanding" will find a way to keep rolling with it no matter what. Any question or wrinkle can be conveniently dismissed with one of their go-to thought-terminating clichés, like "Trust the plan," "The awakening is bigger than all of this," "The media is propaganda," and "Do your research," which refers to the

---

† Since 2018, QAnon supporters have committed murders, made bombs, destroyed churches, derailed freight trains, livestreamed themselves monologuing about Q while engaged in a high-speed police car chase, and organized deadly pro-Trump mobs (among other nightmarish crimes).

process of falling down an obsessed, confirmation-biased rabbit hole online, revealing a fantasy world of explanations for things that feel inexplicable.

If this all sounds like a dystopian video game, that's part of the "fun." There's a reason Q's original timbre was so conspiratorial it sounded like a made-for-TV movie: "Follow the money," "I've said too much," "Some things must remain classified to the very end." QAnon has been described as "an unusually absorbing alternate-reality game" where online users play their imaginary roles as bakers, hungrily anticipating the puzzle of each new crumb. According to UCLA psychiatrist Dr. Joseph M. Pierre, this sort of virtual treasure hunt creates a form of conditioning called a variable-ratio schedule, where rewards are dispensed at unpredictable intervals. Like online gaming or gambling or even the erratic intoxication of when you'll get your next social media "like"—that feeling that keeps you refreshing your feed—QAnon's immersive experience generates a kind of compulsive behavior similar to addiction. In a cognitive analysis of QAnon for *Psychology Today*, Pierre noted that with QAnon, "the conflation of fantasy and reality isn't so much a risk as a built-in feature."

Some of the psychological quirks thought to drive conspiracy theory belief in general, Pierre writes, include a craving for uniqueness, plus the needs for certainty, control, and closure that feel especially urgent during crisis-ridden times. With all their plot twists and good/evil binaries, conspiracy theories seize our attention, while supplying simple answers to unresolved questions. "Conspiracy theories offer a kind of reassurance that things happen for a reason, and can make believers feel special that they're privy to secrets to which the rest of us 'sheeple' are blind," Pierre explains.

After platforms like Twitter and Instagram started catching on to the dangers of QAnon and cracking down, supporters had to get more creative with their language in order to communicate without getting deleted. This is part of why QAnon messages began appearing in the form of aesthetic quotegrams: graphically designed maxims that blend in with the "keep calm and manifest"–type self-care memes innocently populating most users' Instagram feeds. This development soon became known as "Pastel QAnon."

Quotegrams—with their comely fonts and generic syntax—serve as a form of loaded language themselves, designed to yank on users' heartstrings, to get them to like and repost without much thought. It's what allowed one clever troll in 2013 to get away with Photoshopping Hitler quotes over images of Taylor Swift—obscure ones pulled from *Mein Kampf* ("The only preventable measure one can take is to live irregularly," "Do not compare yourself to others. If you do so, you are insulting yourself"). The memer uploaded his creations to Pinterest and watched smugly as fans reposted them all over the web. The point was to prove the extreme devotion of impressionable young Swifties, and their eagerness to instantly and unquestioningly share all things Tay.

There's a religious power in quotegrams that far predates social media. Our love of a pithy adage in square form is connected to the needlepointed psalms on display in religious aunts' powder rooms. But it even goes back further than that, to—can you guess the era?—the Protestant Reformation, when there was a big shift in focus away from religious imagery (stained glass, Last Supper frescoes) and onto text. "There was an increasing discomfort with the ambiguity you get from images," commented Dr. Marika Rose, a Durham University research fellow in digital theology, in *Grazia* magazine. "So a Protestant valuing of the Bible made it a much more text-based religion." Ever since, our culture has looked to snack-size proverbs for guidance and gospel, convinced that when it comes to written quotes, what you read is what you get. On the internet, however, a mysterious epigram with no clear source can serve as an on-ramp leading seekers to something much more sinister.

With no tangible organizational structure, no single leader, no cohesive doctrine, and no concrete exit costs, QAnon is not exactly in the same cultish category as, say, Heaven's Gate or Jonestown. But a fully immersed QAnon follower couldn't just go cold turkey. For those fully submerged in the world of "the awakening" and "the research," climbing out of the rabbit hole could mean a profound psychological loss: a loss of "something to occupy one's time, of feeling connected to something important, of finally feeling a sense of self-worth and control during uncertain times," elucidates Pierre. Even if former believers come out to denounce QAnon, the existential consequences are enough to keep true die-hards under.

Not everyone finds their way into a QAnon-level internet cult, but platforms from Facebook to Tumblr are what help life feel important and connected for so many of us. The way I see it, while celebrities and conspiritualists create their own cult followings online, the ultimate pseudo-church to which billions of us belong—even (and especially) figures like Dr. Joe Dispenza and Donald Trump—is social media itself.

In a sense, we can't even claim to be growing "less religious" when social media's job is explicitly to generate ideological sects, to pack people's feeds with suggested content that only exaggerates what they already believe. As each of us posts, curating our individual online identities, the apps capture those personas via metadata and reinforce them through irresistible targeted ads and custom feeds. No "cult leader" takes advantage of our psychological drives quite like The Algorithm, which thrives on sending us down rabbit holes, so we never even come across rhetoric we don't agree with unless we actively search for it. The way we make choices—from our clothes all the way to our spiritual and political beliefs—is a direct consequence of these uncanny digital versions of ourselves. In her book *Strange Rites*, Tara Isabella Burton wrote, "America is not secular but simply spiritually self-focused." In a social media–centered society, we've all been rendered at once cult leader and follower.

iii.

It would be easy enough for me to write off all these groups, from SoulCycle to Instagram, as cultish and thus evil. But in the end, I don't think the world would benefit from us all refusing to believe or participate in things. Too much wariness spoils the most enchanting parts of being human. I don't want to live in a world where we can't let our guards down for a few moments to engage in a group chant or mantra. If everyone feared the alternative to the point that they never took even small leaps of faith for the sake of connection and meaning, how lonely would that be?

Studies of famous scientists' personalities and their receptivity to offbeat beliefs show that excessive cynicism actually stymies discovery. Science writer Michael Shermer found that iconic brains like paleontologist Stephen Jay Gould and astronomer Carl Sagan scored off the charts in both conscientiousness and openness to experience, indicating an ideal balance between being pliant enough to accept the occasional kooky claim that turned out to be correct, but not so credulous that they fell for every outlandish theory they stumbled across. "Sagan, for example, was open to the search for extraterrestrial intelligence, which, at the time, was considered a moderately heretical idea," said Shermer. "But he was too conscientious to accept the even more controversial claim that UFOs and aliens have actually landed on earth." Long story short, sometimes when something sounds too wacky to be true, it really is that delightfully—truthfully—wacky.

Some say people who join cults are "lost." But all human beings are lost to some degree. Life is disorderly and confusing for absolutely everyone. A more thoughtful way to think about how people find themselves in precariously cultish scenarios is that these folks are actively searching to be found, and—because of variations in genes and life experiences and all the complicated factors that make up human personalities—they're more open than the average person to finding themselves in unusual places. To stay safe requires just the right combination of fact-checking, cross-checking, and amenability to the idea that spiritual fulfillment may very well come from unexpected sources.

I also don't think it's helpful to decide there's something naturally, defenselessly malevolent about the everyday "cults" to which most humans belong. SoulCycle is not Scientology. Instagram influencers are not Jim Jones. And as we've learned, invoking sensationalized "cult leader" comparisons to denounce any group that rubs us the wrong way can create confusion surrounding what the hazards being critiqued even are. It can create active harm. We know this from the siege of the Branch Davidian compound, when the FBI was so scandalized into believing Waco was bound to become "another Jonestown" that they themselves wound up causing an avoidable calamity. Now Waco acts as perverse inspiration for some of those anarchical right-wing internet groups, who view dying in an FBI standoff as the ultimate martyrdom. Events like this serve as proof that overlooking the nuances of cultish communities only perpetuates a culture of hyperbole and chaos.

The fact is that most modern-day movements leave enough space for us to decide what to believe, what to engage with, and what language to use to express ourselves. Tuning in to the rhetoric these communities use, and how its influence works for both good and not so good, can help us participate, however we choose, with clearer eyes.

Growing up on my dad's Synanon stories—his daily escapes to the forbidden high school in San Francisco, his experiments in the microbiology lab—taught me that as much as good moods and optimism can make a person more susceptible to suspicious influence, they can also lift someone out of a truly dark situation. With the right amount of judicious questioning, taking care never to abandon your logical thoughts or emotional instincts (which are there for a reason), one can ensure they stay connected to themselves through anything from an isolated commune to an oppressive start-up job to a scammy Instagram guru.

Above all else, it's important to maintain a vigilant twinkle in your eye—that tingle in your brain that tells you there's some degree of metaphor and make-believe here, and that your identity comes not from one swami or single-minded ideology but from the vast amalgam of influences, experiences, and language that make up who you are. As long as you hang on to that, I think it's possible to engage with certain cultish groups, knowing that at the end of the day, when you come home or close the app, strip off the group's linguistic uniform, and start speaking like yourself again, you're not all in.

When I began writing this book, I was a touch concerned that by the end, all this cult research would just turn me into an antisocial, misanthropic version of myself. And even though I do feel more hyperaware than ever of the varying dialects of Cultish that imbue our daily lives, I've also gained a stronger sense of compassion. While I'm hardly likelier to move to a Shambhala-esque co-op or put my loyalty into some Instagram conspiritualist myself, I have acquired a newfound ability to suspend harsh judgment of those who might. This comes from knowing that one's out-of-the-box beliefs, experiences, and allegiances are less a mark of individual foolishness and more a reflection of the fact that human beings are (to their advantage and their detriment) physiologically built to be more mystical and communal than I knew.

It's in our DNA to want to believe in something, to feel something, alongside other people seeking the same. I'm confident there's a healthy way to do that. Part of me thinks it's actually by becoming a part of several "cults" at once—like our Jonestown survivor Laura Johnston Kohl exchanging her one-commune lifestyle for involvement in a medley of separate groups. That way, we're free to chant, to hashtag, to talk of manifesting and blessings, to use glossolalia even . . . to speak some form of Cultish . . . all the while ιg tethered to reality.

et's try again: Come along. Join me. Life is much too r to go at it all alone.

Acknowledgments

It takes so many generous people to make a book like this possible. First, a gigantic thank-you to my many sources (including those whose interviews didn't end up in the book but were still invaluable). I appreciate your time, expertise, reflection, and vulnerability more than I can say. What made this book especially neat was that it reconnected me to so many friends and family members I hadn't spoken to in years. Leave it to the oddly universal topic of cults to bring us back together.

To my wonderful editors, Karen Rinaldi and Rebecca Raskin, for your continual belief and investment in me. And to the rest of my fabulous, enthusiastic Harper Wave team: Yelena Nesbit, Sophia Lauriello and Penny Makras.

To my literary agent, Rachel Vogel, who actually belongs to the next evolutionary level above human. I feel so lucky to have you as a representative and friend. Big thanks as well to Olivia Blaustein, for your constant championing. And to my book launch guru Dan Blank, for "just adding the water."

To my inspiring, supportive family, to whom I owe everything: my parents, Craig and Denise, and my brother, Brandon. Thank you for passing on the curiosity and skepticism. Special thanks to you, Mom, for helping with the title. To you, Brandon, for reading and nitpicking. And to you, Dad, for the many riveting cult stories. As always, I wait on the edge of my seat for your memoir.

To my sweet, encouraging friends, mentors, and creative collaborators, especially Racheli Alkobey, Isa Medina, Amanda Kohr, Koa Beck, Camille Perri, Keely Weiss, Azadeh Ghafari, Joey Soloway, and Rachel Wiegand. Rae Mae, can you believe that creepy conversation we had at Pioneer Cemetery in early 2018 actually became a book? Wild.

To my wonderfully engaged community of Instagram "followers": You make the internet feel like a decent place to be.

To Katie Neuhof for the killer author photo, and to Lacausa Clothing and Sargeant PR for the incredible dress.

To my right-hand woman, Kaitlyn McLintock—this book could not have happened without your dedication, reliability, and sunshiny mettle.

To my faithful canine and feline assistants: Fiddle, Claire, and especially my buddy David. I couldn't have gotten through this year without you, my coccolone.

And finally, to Casey Kolb. My soul mate, best friend, duet partner, sounding board, quarantine-mate, and one-man fan club. If there were a cult of CK, I'd join in a heartbeat.

Notes

Part 1: Repeat After Me . . .

i.

4 head of all Western Sikhs: Steven Hassan, "The Disturbing Mainstream Connections of Yogi Bhajan," *Huffington Post*, May 25, 2011, http://huffpost.com/entry/the-disturbing-mainstream_b_667026.

8 their shopping bags: Chloe Metzger, "People Are Freaking Out Over This Shady Hidden Message on Lululemon Bags," *Marie Claire*, October 11, 2017, https://www.marieclaire.com/beauty /a28684/lululemon-tote-bag-sunscreen/.

ii.

10 rubbernecking: SBG-TV, "Can't Look Away from a Car Crash? Here's Why (and How to Stop)," WTOV9, May 1, 2019, https://wtov9.com/features/drive-safe/cant-look-away-from-a-car -crash-heres-why-and-how-to-stop.

iii.

21 Civic engagement is at a record-breaking low": Alain Sylvain, "Why Buying Into Pop Culture and Joining a Cult Is Basically the Same Thing," Quartz, March 10, 2020, https://qz.com/1811751/the -psychology-behind-why-were-so-obsessed-with-pop-culture/.

21 loneliness an "epidemic": Neil Howe, "Millennials and the Loneliness Epidemic," *Forbes*, May 3, 2019, https://www.forbes.com /sites/neilhowe/2019/05/03/millennials-and-the-loneliness-epidemic /?sh=74c901d57676.

21 since the time of ancient humans: M. Shermer and S. J. Gould, *Why People Believe Weird Things* (New York: A. W. H. Freeman/Owl Book, 2007).

21   feel-good chemicals: Jason R. Keeler et al., "The Neurochemistry and Social Flow of Singing: Bonding and Oxytocin," *Frontiers in Human Neuroscience* 9 (September 23, 2015): 518, DOI: 10.3389/fnhum.2015.00518.

21   group chanting and singing: Jacques Launay and Eiluned Pearce, "Choir Singing Improves Health, Happiness—and Is the Perfect Icebreaker," The Conversation, October 28, 2015, https://theconversation.com/choir-singing-improves-health-happiness-and-is-the-perfect-icebreaker-47619.

22   engage in ritualistic dances: Brandon Ambrosino, "Do Humans Have a 'Religion Instinct'?," BBC, May 29, 2019, https://www.bbc.com/future/article/20190529-do-humans-have-a-religion-instinct.

22   a desire for belonging and purpose: Roy F. Baumeister and Mark R. Leary, "The Need to Belong: Desire for Interpersonal Attachments as a Fundamental Human Motivation," *Psychological Bulletin* 117, no. 3 (1995): 497–529, http://persweb.wabash.edu/facstaff/hortonr/articles%20for%20class/baumeister%20and%20leary.pdf.

23   four in ten millennials: "In U.S., Decline of Christianity Continues at Rapid Pace," Pew Research Center's Religion & Public Life Project, June 9, 2020, https://www.pewforum.org/2019/10/17/in-u-s-decline-of-christianity-continues-at-rapid-pace/.

23   up nearly 20 percentage points: "'Nones' on the Rise," Pew Research Center's Religion & Public Life Project, May 30, 2020, https://www.pewforum.org/2012/10/09/nones-on-the-rise/.

23   Harvard Divinity School study: Angie Thurston and Casper ter Kuile, "How We Gather," Harvard Divinity School, https://caspertk.files.wordpress.com/2015/04/how-we-gather1.pdf.

23   the "Nones" and the "Remixed": Tara Isabella Burton, *Strange Rites: New Religions for a Godless World* (New York: PublicAffairs, Hachette Book Group, 2020).

26   encroaching Roman Empire: Holland Lee Hendrix, "Jews and the Roman Empire," PBS, April 1998, https://www.pbs.org/wgbh/pages/frontline/shows/religion/portrait/jews.html.

26   the US is exceptional: Jonathan Evans, "U.S. Adults Are More Religious Than Western Europeans," *Fact Tank* (blog), Pew Research

Center, May 31, 2020, https://www.pewresearch.org/fact-tank/2018/09/05/u-s-adults-are-more-religious-than-western-europeans/.

27 "The Japanese and the Europeans": David Ludden, "Why Do People Believe in God?," *Psychology Today*, August 21, 2018, https://www.psychologytoday.com/us/blog/talking-apes/201808/why-do-people-believe-in-god.

iv.

30 "forever forming associations": Alain Sylvain, "Why Buying Into Pop Culture and Joining a Cult Is Basically the Same Thing," Quartz, March 10, 2020, https://qz.com/1811751/the-psychology-behind-why-were-so-obsessed-with-pop-culture/.

30 "Cults" of the time: Elizabeth Dunn, "5 19th-Century Utopian Communities in the United States," History.com, January 22, 2013, https://www.history.com/news/5-19th-century-utopian-communities-in-the-united-states.

31 "cult film" and "cult classic": Ernest Mathijs and Jamie Sexton, *Cult Cinema: An Introduction* (Hoboken, New Jersey: Wiley-Blackwell, 2011), 234.

34 pledge-hazing rituals: John Marr, "A Brief History of the Brutal and Bizarre World of Fraternity Hazing," Gizmodo, September 20, 2015, https://gizmodo.com/a-brief-history-of-the-brutal-and-bizarre-world-of-frat-1733672835.

35 brainwashing presents an untestable hypothesis: Rebecca Moore, "The Brainwashing Myth," The Conversation, July 18, 2018, https://theconversation.com/the-brainwashing-myth-99272.

35 not all "cults" are depraved or perilous: Laura Elizabeth Woollett, "The C-Word: What Are We Saying When We Talk About Cults?," *Guardian*, November 18, 2018, https://www.theguardian.com/culture/2018/nov/19/the-c-word-what-are-we-saying-when-we-talk-about-cults.

36 didn't set out with murder and mayhem in mind: Jane Borden, "What Is It About California and Cults?," *Vanity Fair*, September 3, 2020, https://www.vanityfair.com/hollywood/2020/09/california-cults-nxivm-the-vow.

36   condemn the Quakers: Eileen Barker, "One Person's Cult Is Another's True Religion," *Guardian*, May 29, 2009, https://www .theguardian.com/commentisfree/belief/2009/may/29/cults-new -religious-movements.

37   "cult + time = religion": Joe Posner and Ezra Klein, "Cults," *Explained*, Netflix.

37   To quote Megan Goodwin: Tara Isabella Burton, "The Waco Tragedy, Explained," Vox, April 19, 2018, https://www.vox.com/2018 /4/19/17246732/waco-tragedy-explained-david-koresh-mount -carmel-branch-davidian-cult-25-year-anniversary.

37   "unworthy of postmortem respect": Woollett, "The C-Word."

v.

46   "If the boundaries between cult and religion": Tara Isabella Burton, "What Is a Cult?," *Aeon*, June 7, 2017, https://aeon.co /essays/theres-no-sharp-distinction-between-cult-and-regular-religion.

46   "reach toward what we did not yet know or understand": Gary Eberle, *Dangerous Words: Talking About God in an Age of Fundamentalism* (Boston: Trumpeter, 2007).

Part 2: Congratulations—You Have Been Chosen to Join the Next Evolutionary Level Above Human

i.

51   "top annoying cliché": James D. Richardson, "The Phrase 'Drank the Kool-Aid' Is Completely Offensive. We Should Stop Saying It Immediately," *Washington Post*, November 18, 2014, https:// www.washingtonpost.com/posteverything/wp/2014/11/18/the -phrase-drank-the-koolaid-is-completely-offensive-we-should-stop -saying-it-immediately/.

52   "so odious": Lesley Kennedy, "Inside Jonestown: How Jim Jones Trapped Followers and Forced 'Suicides'," History.com, A&E Television Networks, November 13, 2018, https://www.history.com /news/jonestown-jim-jones-mass-murder-suicide.

52 "It makes me shudder": Jennie Rothenberg Gritz, "Drinking the Kool-Aid: A Survivor Remembers Jim Jones," *The Atlantic*, November 18, 2011, https://www.theatlantic.com/national/archive/2011/11/drinking-the-kool-aid-a-survivor-remembers-jim-jones/248723/.

54 "revolutionary suicide": Federal Bureau of Investigation, "Q042 Transcript," The Jonestown Institute, San Diego State University Department of Religious Studies, June 16, 2013, https://jonestown.sdsu.edu/?page_id=29081.

55 the "Rainbow Family": Lauren Effron and Monica Delarosa, "40 Years After Jonestown Massacre, Ex-Members Describe Jim Jones as a 'Real Monster,'" ABC News, September 26, 2018, https://abcnews.go.com/US/40-years-jonestown-massacre-members-describe-jim-jones/story?id=57933856.

55 hybristophilia: Eliza Thompson, "3 Experts Explain Why Some People Are Attracted to Serial Killers," *Cosmopolitan*, February 14, 2018, https://www.cosmopolitan.com/entertainment/tv/a17804534/sexual-attraction-to-serial-killers/.

55 "sexual appeal": Melissa Dittmann, "Lessons from Jonestown," *Monitor on Psychology* 34, no. 10 (November 2003): 36, https://www.apa.org/monitor/nov03/jonestown.

56 "He appealed to anyone": David M. Matthews, "Jim Jones' Followers Enthralled by His Skills as a Speaker," CNN, http://edition.cnn.com/2008/US/11/13/jonestown.jim.jones/.

56 his "little Angela Davis": Sikivu Hutchinson, "No More White Saviors: Jonestown and Peoples Temple in the Black Feminist Imagination," The Jonestown Institute, San Diego State University Department of Religious Studies, October 5, 2014 (updated May 30, 2020), https://jonestown.sdsu.edu/?page_id=61499.

57 "the fading promise of the Black Power movement": Sikivu Hutchinson, "Why Did So Many Black Women Die? Jonestown at 35," Religion Dispatches, December 12, 2013, https://religiondispatches.org/why-did-so-many-black-women-die-jonestown-at-35/.

57 "I was just enthralled": Effron and Delarosa, "40 Years After Jonestown Massacre, Ex-Members Describe Jim Jones as a 'Real Monster.'"

57   Known for quotes: Fielding M. McGehee III, "Q932 Summary," The Jonestown Institute, San Diego State University Department of Religious Studies, June 16, 2013, https://jonestown.sdsu.edu/?page_id=28323.

59   Laura Johnston Kohl: Joseph L. Flatley, "Laura Johnston Kohl and the Politics of Peoples Temple," The Jonestown Institute, San Diego State University Department of Religious Studies, October 25, 2017, https://jonestown.sdsu.edu/?page_id=70639.

63   White Nights: "What Are White Nights? How Many of Them Were There?," The Jonestown Institute, San Diego State University Department of Religious Studies, June 15, 2013 (updated October 6, 2013), https://jonestown.sdsu.edu/?page_id=35371.

65   Christine Miller: Michael Bellefountaine, "Christine Miller: A Voice of Independence," The Jonestown Institute, San Diego State University Department of Religious Studies, July 25, 2013, https://jonestown.sdsu.edu/?page_id=32381.

67   the Death Tape: Alternative Considerations of Jonestown & Peoples Temple authors, "The Death Tape", The Jonestown Institute, San Diego State University Department of Religious Studies, July 25, 2013, https://jonestown.sdsu.edu/?page_id=29084.

ii.

69   Jonestown mass death: Lauren Effron and Monica Delarosa, "40 Years After Jonestown Massacre, Ex-Members Describe Jim Jones as a 'Real Monster,'" ABC News, September 26, 2018, https://abc news.go.com/US/40-years-jonestown-massacre-members-describe -jim-jones/story?id=57933856.

72   ended in the suffix –ody: u/Apatamoose, "Is there a list anywhere tying the -ody names of the Heaven's Gate members with their legal names?," Reddit, February 26, 2018, https://www.reddit.com /r/Heavensgate/comments/80fmt5/is_there_a_list_anywhere_tying _the_ody_names_of/.

72   who belonged to Heaven's Gate: Frank Lyford, "About My New Book," Facilitating You, http://facilitatingu.com/book/.

73   "severe inability to speak": Margeaux Sippell and Tony Maglio, "'Heaven's Gate' Docuseries: Why Does Frank Lyford's Voice Sound

Like That?" TheWrap, December 3, 2020, https://www.thewrap
.com/heavens-gate-docuseries-hbo-max-frank-lyford-voice.

75 You can see it yourself: Heavens Gate Remastered, "Heav-
en's Gate Class Exit Videos," YouTube, April 9, 2016, https://www
.youtube.com/watch?v=U2D4wUF1EKQ.

iii.

77 Michelle Carter court case: "Woman Who Convinced Friend
to Commit Suicide Released from Jail," *CBS This Morning*, You-
Tube, January 24, 2020, https://www.youtube.com/watch?v=aPX
57hWAKo8.

77 conversion, conditioning, and coercion: Rebecca Moore, "The
Brainwashing Myth," The Conversation, July 18, 2018, https://the
conversation.com/the-brainwashing-myth-99272.

78 what makes people stick: Laura Elizabeth Woollett, "What
I Learned About the Jonestown Cult by Spending Time with Survivors," Refinery29, February 26, 2019, https://www.refinery29.com
/en-gb/jonestown-massacre-book.

81 problematic populist: Cas Mudde, "The Problem with Pop-
ulism," *Guardian*, February 17, 2015, https://www.theguardian.com
/commentisfree/2015/feb/17/problem-populism-syriza-podemos
-dark-side-europe.

81 similarities between Trump and Jim Jones: Steven Hassan, *The
Cult of Trump* (New York: Simon & Schuster, 2019).

81 zingy, incendiary nicknames: Caroline Howe, "Exclusive: Fake
Enemies, Loaded Language, Grandiosity, Belittling Critics: Cults
Expert Claims Donald Trump's Tactics Are Taken Straight from
Playbook of Sun Myung Moon, David Koresh and Jim Jones," *Daily
Mail*, October 9, 2019, https://www.dailymail.co.uk/news/article
-7552231/Trumps-tactics-taken-playbook-cult-leaders-like-Jim
-Jones-David-Koresh-says-author.html.

82 Trump's populist language: George Packer, "The Left Needs a
Language Potent Enough to Counter Trump," *The Atlantic*, August 6,
2019, https://www.theatlantic.com/ideas/archive/2019/08/language
-trump-era/595570/.

84   with these stock sayings: Robert J. Lifton, *Thought Reform and the Psychology of Totalism: A Study of "Brainwashing" in China* (New York: W. W. Norton & Company, 1961).

84   calling someone "brainwashed": Alla V. Tovares, "Reframing the Frame: Peoples Temple and the Power of Words," The Jonestown Institute, San Diego State University Department of Religious Studies, July 25, 2013, https://jonestown.sdsu.edu/?page_id=31454.

87   Jones enforced a "quiet rule": Lesley Kennedy, "Inside Jonestown: How Jim Jones Trapped Followers and Forced 'Suicides,'" History .com, February 20, 2020, https://www.history.com/news/jonestown -jim-jones-mass-murder-suicide.

iv.

88   known style of delivery labeled "the voice of God": Jessica Bennett, "What Do We Hear When Women Speak?," *New York Times*, November 20, 2019, https://www.nytimes.com/2019/11/20 /us/politics/women-voices-authority.html.

89   not the most useful way to evaluate their specific danger: Rebecca Moore, "Godwin's Law and Jones' Corollary: The Problem of Using Extremes to Make Predictions," *Nova Religio* 22, no. 2 (2018): 145–54.

90   Teal Swan: Jennings Brown, *The Gateway*, Gizmodo, May 21, 2018, https://www.stitcher.com/podcast/the-gateway-teal-swan.

93   "I can't stop thinking about her pores": Maureen O'Connor, "I Think About This a Lot: The Beauty Habits of This Possible Cult Leader," *The Cut*, August 27, 2018, https://www.thecut .com/2018/08/i-think-about-this-a-lot-teal-swan-beauty-habits.html.

v.

97   Moonie careers: Eileen Barker, "Charismatization: The Social Production of an 'Ethos Propitious to the Mobilisation of Sentiments,'" in *Secularization, Rationalism, and Sectarianism: Essays in Honour of Bryan R. Wilson*, eds. Eileen Barker, James A. Beckford, and Karel Dobbelaere (Oxford, UK: Clarendon Press, 1993), 181–201.

97   "we selectively recruited": Steven Hassan, *Combatting Cult Mind Control* (Rochester, Vermont: Park Street Press, 1988).

98 the reason why Black women: Sikivu Hutchinson, "No More White Saviors: Jonestown and Peoples Temple in the Black Feminist Imagination," The Jonestown Institute, San Diego State University Department of Religious Studies, October 5, 2014 (updated May 30, 2020), https://jonestown.sdsu.edu/?page_id=61499.

99 classic confirmation bias: Elizabeth Kolbert, "Why Facts Don't Change Our Minds," The New Yorker, February 27, 2017, https://www.newyorker.com/magazine/2017/02/27/why-facts-dont-change-our-minds.

99 hypochondria, prejudice, and paranoia: M. Shermer and J. S. Gould, Why People Believe Weird Things (New York: A. W. H. Freeman/Owl Book, 2007).

Part 3: Even YOU Can Learn to Speak in Tongues

i.

110 an interview for the role of Tom Cruise's girlfriend: Molly Horan, "This Actress Auditioned To Be Tom Cruise's Girlfriend — But Never Wanted The Part," Refinery29, August 1, 2016, https://www.refinery29.com/en-us/2016/08/118620/tom-cruise-girlfriend-audition-cathy-schenkelberg.

110 the device "itself does nothing": David S. Touretzky, "Inside the Mark Super VII," Secrets of Scientology: The E-Meter, Carnegie Mellon University School of Computer Science, https://www.cs.cmu.edu/~dst/Secrets/E-Meter/Mark-VII/.

ii.

119 the door locked behind me: Steve Mango, "Inside the Scientology Celebrity Centre: An Ex-Parishioner Reveals All," YouTube, January 26, 2014, https://www.youtube.com/watch?v=LfKqOUMrCw8&t=.

120 Billion-Year Contract: Margery Wakefield, "The Sea Org—'For the Next Billion Years . . . ,'" in Understanding Scientology: The Demon Cult (Lulu, 2009).

121 It's called TR-L: Margery Wakefield, "Declaration of Margery Wakefield," Operation Clambake, June 23, 1993, https://www.xenu.net/archive/go/legal/wakefiel.htm.

122 A "dynamic" in Scientology: "The Eight Dynamics," Scientology .org, https://www.scientology.org/what-is-scientology/basic-principles -of-scientology/eight-dynamics.html.

iii.

123 "religious language 'performs' rather than 'informs'": Gary Eberle, *Dangerous Words: Talking About God in an Age of Fundamentalism* (Boston: Trumpeter, 2007).

127 Christian-affiliated direct sales: Nicole Woolsey Biggart, *Charismatic Capitalism: Direct Selling Organizations in America* (Chicago: University of Chicago Press, 1993).

127 Jesus as a marketing ploy: "How a Dream Becomes a Nightmare," *The Dream*, Stitcher, October 22, 2018, https://www.stitcher .com/podcast/stitcher/the-dream/e/56830345.

iv.

129 Chögyam Trungpa: Paul Wagner, "Chögyam Trungpa: Poetry, Crazy Wisdom, and Radical Shambhala," Gaia, January 21, 2020, https://www.gaia.com/article/chogyam-trungpa-poetry-crazy-wisdom -and-radical-shambhala.

131 Hubbard was obsessed with space fantasy: "Written Works of L. Ron Hubbard," Wikipedia, August 17, 2020 copycat "cult leaders", https://en.wikipedia.org/wiki/Written_works_of_L._Ron _Hubbard.

131 you can look up portions of the Technical Dictionary online: Scientology Glossary: UVWXYZ, Scientology Critical Information Directory, https://www.xenu-directory.net/glossary/glossary _uvwxyz.htm.

132 copycat "cult leaders": Kenzie Bryant, "How NXIVM Used the Strange Power of Patents to Build Its 'Sex Cult,'" *Vanity Fair*, June 27, 2018, https://www.vanityfair.com/style/2018/06/keith -raniere-nxivm-patents-luciferian; Gina Tron, "ESP, DOS, Proctors, and More: NXIVM Terminology, Explained," Oxygen, August 27, 2020, https://www.oxygen.com/true-crime-buzz/what-does-nxivm -terminology-like-dos-esp-mean.

133 in Scientology, it has but one solitary definition: Margery Wake-field, *Understanding Scientology: The Demon Cult* (Self-Published, Lulu, 2009).

134 insider-y acronyms and abbreviations: Margery Wakefield, "The Language of Scientology—ARC, SPS, PTPS and BTS," June 23, 1993, https://www.xenu.net/archive/go/legal/wakefiel.htm.

134 an entirely plausible conversation between Scientologists: Wakefield, *Understanding Scientology.*

135 "bypassed charge": Clerk, "Bypassed Charge; Bypassed Charge Assessment," January 1, 1975, http://www.carolineletkeman.org/c /archives/1439.

139 for his blog: Mike Rinder, "The Horrors of Wordclearing," *Something Can Be Done About It*, July 27, 2016, https://www.mike rindersblog.org/the-horrors-of-wordclearing/.

v.

143 signs of stress reduction: Christopher Dana Lynn et al., "Sal-ivary Alpha-Amylase and Cortisol Among Pentecostals on a Wor-ship and Nonworship Day," *American Journal of Human Biology* 22, no 6 (November–December 2010): 819–22, DOI: 10.1002/ajhb .21088.

143 lack of self-consciousness and feelings of transcendent bliss: Junling Gao et al., "The Neurophysiological Correlates of Religious Chanting," *Scientific Reports* 9, no. 4262 (March 12, 2019), DOI: 10.1038/s41598-019-40200-w.

143 glossolalia seemed to provoke greater intensity of faith: Ed-ward B. Fiske, "Speaking in Tongues Is Viewed by Psychologist as 'Learned,'" *New York Times*, January 21, 1974, https://www.nytimes .com/1974/01/21/archives/speaking-in-tongues-is-viewed-by -psychologist-as-learned-some.html.

144 a form of dissociation: Dirk Hanson, "Speaking in Tongues: Glossolalia and Stress Reduction," Dana Foundation, October 23, 2013, https://www.dana.org/article/speaking-in-tongues-glossolalia -and-stress-reduction/.

145 "required to speak in tongues in front of everyone": "True Story: My Family Was in a Cult," *Yes and Yes*, https://www.yesandyes.org/2010/11/true-story-my-family-was-in-cu.html.

146 Flor spent most of her '80s-era childhood in Thailand: Flor Edwards, "I Grew Up in the Children of God, a Doomsday Cult. Here's How I Finally Got Out," *Huffington Post*, December 6, 2018, https://www.huffpost.com/entry/children-of-god-cult_n_5bfee4a3e4b0e254c926f325.

vi.

149 "the supplication for the Sakyong": Russell Rodgers, "Longevity Supplication for Sakyong Mipham Rinpoche," *Shambhala Times*, April 3, 2009, https://shambhalatimes.org/2009/04/03/the-longevity-supplication-for-sakyong-mipham-rinpoche/.

149 a series of grievous reports: Andy Newman, "The 'King' of Shambhala Buddhism Is Undone by Abuse Report," *New York Times*, July 11, 2018, https://www.nytimes.com/2018/07/11/nyregion/shambhala-sexual-misconduct.html.

Part 4: Do You Wanna Be a #BossBabe?

i.

155 "Have you ever thought about turning that energy into a side hustle?": Eric Worre, "The Hottest Recruiting Scripts in MLM," Network Marketing Pro, https://networkmarketingpro.com/pdf/the_hottest_recruiting_scripts_in_mlm_by_eric_worre_networkmarketingpro.com.pdf.

157 LuLaRoe: Charisse Jones, "LuLaRoe Was Little More Than a Scam, a Washington State Lawsuit Claims," *USA Today*, January 28, 2019, https://www.usatoday.com/story/money/2019/01/28/lularoe-pyramid-scheme-duped-consumers-washington-suit-says/2700412002/.

157 Tupperware: Cristen Conger, "How Tupperware Works," HowStuffWorks, July 25, 2011, https://people.howstuffworks.com/tupperware2.htm.

159 The Federal Trade Commission sent warnings: Lisette Voytko, "FTC Warns 16 Multi-Level Marketing Companies About Coronavirus

Fraud." *Forbes*, June 9, 2020, https://www.forbes.com/sites/lisette voytko/2020/06/09/ftc-warns-16-multi-level-marketing-companies -about-coronavirus-fraud/?sh=12d56c827b9d.

160 to throw plastic confetti: Lawrence Specker, "It Wasn't Easy, But Mobile Now Has a 21st Century Confetti Policy," *Mobile Real-Time News*, August 7, 2018, https://www.al.com/news/mobile/2018 /08/it_wasnt_easy_but_mobile_now_h.html.

160 schemes both pyramid and Ponzi: Christopher Jarvis, "The Rise and Fall of Albania's Pyramid Schemes," *Finance & Development* 37, no. 1 (March 2000), https://www.imf.org/external/pubs/ft /fandd/2000/03/jarvis.htm; Antony Sguazzin, "How a 'Giant Ponzi Scheme' Destroyed a Nation's Economy," *Bloomberg*, February 27, 2019, https://www.bloomberg.com/news/articles/2019-02-28/how -a-giant-ponzi-scheme-destroyed-a-nation-s-economy.

160 pyramid schemes don't announce themselves as such: Bridget Casey, "Your Gifting Circle Is a Pyramid Scheme," Money After Graduation, August 24, 2015, https://www.moneyaftergraduation .com/gifting-circle-is-a-pyramid-scheme/.

164 MLM recruits: "Do You Party?," *The Dream*, October 15, 2018, https://www.stitcher.com/podcast/stitcher/the-dream/e/5672 2353.

166 a "morally superior way of being in the economy": Nicole Woolsey Biggart, *Charismatic Capitalism: Direct Selling Organizations in America* (Chicago: University of Chicago Press, 1993).

167 "MLM Quotes": Chuck Holmes, "Top 50 MLM Quotes of All Time," OnlineMLMCommunity.com, October 10, 2013, https:// onlinemlmcommunity.com/my-top-50-favorite-mlm-quotes/.

167 "mental warfare": Alley Pascoe, "5 Women Reveal the Moment They Realised They Were in a Pyramid Scheme," *Marie Claire*, November 29, 2019, https://www.marieclaire.com.au/multi-level -marketing-pyramid-schemes-women-survivors.

ii.

173 Mormons, as direct sales leaders have discovered, are an ideal sales force: "Leave a Message," *The Dream*, podcast, November 2018, https://open.spotify.com/episode/14QU34m1rYlF9xliSWlM5l.

174 "nose to the grindstone": Amelia Theodorakis, "Why Would 'You Keep Nose to the Grindstone' Anyway?," Your Life Choices, December 8, 2016, https://www.yourlifechoices.com.au/fun/enter tainment/keep-your-nose-to-the-grindstone.

175 big American business: "The Rise of Big Business," in *1912: Competing Visions for America*, eHISTORY, Ohio State University, https://ehistory.osu.edu/exhibitions/1912/trusts/RiseBigBusiness.

178 values and rituals: Michael G. Pratt, "The Good, the Bad, and the Ambivalent: Managing Identification Among Amway Distributors," *Administrative Science Quarterly* 45, no. 3 (September 2000): 456–93, DOI: 10.2307/2667106.

179 the very meaning of life: Nathalie Luca, "Multi-Level Marketing: At the Crossroads of Economy and Religion," in *The Economics of Religion: Anthropological Approaches*, vol. 31, eds. Lionel Obadia and Donald C. Wood (Bingley, UK: Emerald Group Publishing Limited, 2011).

179 spiritually charged promises: C. Groß, "Spiritual Cleansing: A Case Study on How Spirituality Can Be Mis/used by a Company," *Management Revu* 21, no. 1 (2010): 60–81, DOI: 10.5771/0935 -9915-2010-1-60.

iii.

184 "heavenly deception": Steve Keohane, "Sun Myung Moon's Unification Church," *Bible Probe*, April 2007, https://www.bibleprobe .com/moonies.htm.

184 get involved without their husbands' "permission": "The Husband Unawareness Plan," F.A.C.E.S (Families Against Cult-like Exploitation in Sales), https://marykayvictims.com/predatory-tactics/the -husband-unawareness-plan/.

187 "God's laws": "Amway Speaks: Memorable Quotes," Cult Education Institute, https://culteducation.com/group/815-amway/1674 -amway-speaks-memorable-quotess.html.

187 Trump made a killing from his endorsements of several MLMs: James V. Grimaldi and Mark Maremont, "Donald Trump Made Millions from Multilevel Marketing Firm," *Wall Street Journal*, Au-

gust 13, 2015, https://www.wsj.com/articles/trump-made-millions -from-multilevel-marketing-firm-1439481128.

188 Trump and his three children could be sued for fraud: Lisette Voytko, "Judge Rules Trump Can Be Sued for Marketing Scheme Fraud," *Forbes*, July 25, 2019, https://www.forbes.com/sites/lisette voytko/2019/07/25/judge-rules-trump-can-be-sued-for-marketing -scheme-fraud/?sh=7448b2516395.

iv.

192 gullibility: Joseph Paul Forgas, "Why Are Some People More Gullible Than Others?," The Conversation, March 30, 2017, https:// theconversation.com/why-are-some-people-more-gullible-than -others-72412; Daniel Kahneman, "The Sveriges Riksbank Prize in Economic Sciences in Memory of Alfred Nobel 2002," NobelPrize .org, https://www.nobelprize.org/prizes/economic-sciences/2002 /kahneman/biographical/.

193 human-reasoning flaws: Elizabeth Kolbert, "Why Facts Don't Change Our Minds," *The New Yorker*, February 27, 2017, https:// www.newyorker.com/magazine/2017/02/27/why-facts-dont-change -our-minds.

194 differences in trust: "Trust: The Development of Trust," Marriage and Family Encyclopedia, JRank, https://family.jrank.org/pages /1713/Trust-Development-Trust.html.

194 better at sensing deception: Joseph P. Forgas, "On Being Happy and Gullible: Mood Effects on Skepticism and the Detection of Deception," *Journal of Experimental Social Psychology* 44, no. 5 (September 2008): 1362–67, DOI: 10.1016/j.jesp.2008.04.010.

v.

196 reeked of the stock exchange: Molly Young, "Garbage Language: Why Do Corporations Speak the Way They Do?," Vulture, February 20, 2020, https://www.vulture.com/2020/02/spread-of -corporate-speak.html.

197 psychopathic tendencies: Tomas Chamorro-Premuzic, "1 in 5 Business Leaders May Have Psychopathic Tendencies—Here's Why,

According to a Psychology Professor," CNBC, April 8, 2019, https://www.cnbc.com/2019/04/08/the-science-behind-why-so-many-successful-millionaires-are-psychopaths-and-why-it-doesnt-have-to-be-a-bad-thing.html.

197 Leadership Principles: Jodi Kantor and David Streitfeld, "Inside Amazon: Wrestling Big Ideas in a Bruising Workplace," *New York Times*, August 15, 2015, https://www.nytimes.com/2015/08/16/technology/inside-amazon-wrestling-big-ideas-in-a-bruising-workplace.html.

vi.

200 "strangest politician": Staff, "The Troubled World of William Penn Patrick," *Los Angeles Times*, August 16, 1967.

200 "Tell [recruits] they're going to be happier": *The Dream*, Stitcher, October 22, 2018, https://www.stitcher.com/podcast/stitcher/the-dream

Part 5: This Hour Is Going to Change Your Life . . . and Make You LOOK AWESOME

i.

207 cult-favorite workout: Rose Surnow, "Love, Sweat and Tears: Intensati Kicks Your Ass and Cleanses Your Soul," *Cosmopolitan*, July 16, 2013, https://www.cosmopolitan.com/health-fitness/advice/a4579/patricia-moreno-finds-thinner-peace/.

210 do it in groups: David Nield, "Working Out in a Group Could Be Better for You Than Exercising Alone," Science Alert, November 5, 2017, https://www.sciencealert.com/working-out-in-groups-better-than-exercising-alone.

210 endorphins surge even more powerfully: "Group Exercise 'Boosts Happiness,'" BBC News, September 15, 2009, http://news.bbc.co.uk/2/hi/health/8257716.stm.

210 yoga had already existed for millennia: "Yoga: How Did It Conquer the World and What's Changed?," BBC, June 22, 2017, https://www.bbc.com/news/world-40354525.

212 outing himself as a shameless racist: "CrossFit: CEO Greg Glassman Steps Down After Racist Tweet," *Diario AS*, October 6, 2020, https://en.as.com/en/2020/06/10/other_sports/1591791315 _063019.html.

212 health and fitness industry was worth over $32 billion in 2018: Jenny Weller, "Why the Fitness Industry Is Growing," Glofox, November 15, 2019, https://www.glofox.com/blog/fitness -industry/.

214 millennials are unsatisfied with their healthcare: "How Millennials are Redefining Healthcare Today: Are You Behind?" Multiple Chronic Conditions Resource Center, 2018, https://www.multiple chronicconditions.org/assets/pdf/Aging%20in%20America/How _Millennials_are_Redefining_Healthcare%20(1).pdf.

214 "radio calisthentics": "The Japanese Morning Exercise Routine— Rajio-Taiso —JAPANKURU." *Japankuru Let's share our Japanese Stories!*, March 29, 2020, https://www.japankuru.com/en/culture/e2263 .html.

214 young people's disillusionment with traditional faith: "'Nones' on the Rise," Pew Research Center, October 9, 2012, https://www .pewforum.org/2012/10/09/nones-on-the-rise/.

214 the ways millennials find community and transcendence: Tom Layman, "CrossFit as Church? Examining How We Gather," Harvard Divinity School, November 4, 2015, https://hds.harvard.edu /news/2015/11/04/crossfit-church-examining-how-we-gather#.

215 El Monte's "Zumba Ladies": Carribean Fragoza, "All the Zumba Ladies: Reclaiming Bodies and Space through Serious Booty-Shaking." KCET, January 1, 2017, https://www.kcet.org/history-society/all -the-zumba-ladies-reclaiming-bodies-and-space-through-serious-booty -shaking.

216 The fitness "movement": Meaghen Brown, "Fitness Isn't a Lifestyle Anymore. Sometimes It's a Cult," *Wired*, June 30, 2016, https:// www.wired.com/2016/06/fitness-isnt-lifestyle-anymore-sometimes -cult/.

216 devout Peloton user: Amy Larocca, "Riding the Unicorn: Peloton Accidentally Built a Fitness Cult. A Business Is a Little More

Complicated," *The Cut*, October 17, 2019, https://www.thecut.com /2019/10/peloton-is-spinning-faster-than-ever.html.

216 "dark times": Zan Romanoff, "The Consumerist Church of Fitness Classes," *The Atlantic*, December 4, 2017, https://www.the atlantic.com/health/archive/2017/12/my-body-is-a-temple/547346/.

217 "SoulCycle is like my cult": Casper ter Kuile and Angie Thurston, "How We Gather (Part 2): SoulCycle as Soul Sanctuary," *On Being* (blog), July 9, 2016, https://onbeing.org/blog/how-we-gather -part-2-soulcycle-as-soul-sanctuary/.

217 "I want the next breath to be an exorcism": Alex Morris, "The Carefully Cultivated Soul of SoulCycle." The Cut, January 7, 2013. https://www.thecut.com/2013/01/evolution-of-soulcycle.html.

ii.

224 "hills" monologues: "Soul Cycle Instructor and Motivational Coach Angela Davis Reminds You That You Are More Than Enough!," Facebook Watch, SuperSoul, April 23, 2018, https://www. facebook.com/watch/?v=1612129545501226.

225 "Enthusiasm" comes from the Greek: OWN, "Enthusiasm: With Angela Davis: 21 Days of Motivation & Movement," YouTube, August 8, 2016, https://www.youtube.com/watch?v=bhVfjuwptJY&ab _channel=OWN.

225 "created in purpose": OWN, "Angela Davis: Finding Your Purpose: SuperSoul Sessions," YouTube, May 10, 2017, https://www .youtube.com/watch?v=DnwdpC0Omk4&ab_channel=OWN.

225 Manuel-Davis resigned from SoulCycle: Chris Gardner, "Celebrity Soul-Cycle Instructor Angela Davis Joins Akin Akman as Co-Founder of AARMY Fitness Studio," *Hollywood Reporter*, November 21, 2019, https://www.hollywoodreporter.com/rambling-reporter /celebrity-soulcycle-instructor-angela-davis-joins-akin-akman-as -founder-aarmy-fitness-studio-1256636.

226 "I go to hear a message": Erin Magner, "How to Create a Powerful, Purposeful Life, According to LA's Most Inspiring Fitness Instructor," Well+Good, July 14, 2016, https://www.welland good.com/how-to-create-a-powerful-purposeful-life-angela-davis -soulcycle/.

iii.

232 Broadway theater–esque auditions: Victoria Hoff, "Inside the Ultra-Competitive 'Auditions' to Become a Cycling Instructor," The Thirty, March 8, 2018, https://thethirty.whowhatwear.com/how-to-become-a-spin-instructor/slide2.

iv.

235 exercise and American Protestantism: R. Marie Griffith, *Born Again Bodies: Flesh and Spirit in American Christianity* (Berkeley, California: University of California Press, 2004).

236 "CrossFit is not like church": Connor Gwin, "My Church Is Not CrossFit," Mockingbird, September 12, 2018, https://mbird.com/2018/09/my-church-is-not-crossfit/.

237 eerily Amwayian: Zan Romanoff, "The Consumerist Church of Fitness Classes," *The Atlantic*, December 4, 2017, https://www.theatlantic.com/health/archive/2017/12/my-body-is-a-temple/547346/.

237 "You can get inner peace and flat abs in an hour": Alice Hines, "Inside CorePower Yoga Teacher Training," *New York Times*, April 6, 2019, https://www.nytimes.com/2019/04/06/style/corepower-yoga-teacher-training.html.

237 fallen members of the military: Robbie Wild Hudson, "Hero CrossFit Workouts to Honour Fallen American Soldiers," *Boxrox Competitive Fitness Magazine*, February 17, 2020, https://www.boxrox.com/hero-crossfit-workouts-to-honour-fallen-american-soldiers/.

237 the personal politics of its founder, Greg Glassman: Elizabeth Nolan Brown, "CrossFit Founder Greg Glassman: 'I Don't Mind Being Told What to Do. I Just Won't Do It,'" *Reason*, August 28, 2017, https://reason.com/2017/08/28/crossfits-conscious-capitalism/.

238 ex-CrossFitter: Jason Kessler, "Why I Quit CrossFit," Medium, July 15, 2013, https://medium.com/this-happened-to-me/why-i-quit-crossfit-f4882edd1e21.

238 rhabdomyolysis: Janet Morrison et al., "The Benefits and Risks of CrossFit: A Systematic Review," *Workplace Health and Safety* 65, no. 12 (March 31, 2017): 612–18, DOI: 10.1177/2165079916685568.

238 Uncle Rhabdo: Eric Robertson, "CrossFit's Dirty Little Secret," Medium, September 20, 2013, https://medium.com/@ericrobertson/crossfits-dirty-little-secret-97bcce70356d.

238 "Pukie": Mark Hay, "Some CrossFit Gyms Feature Pictures of These Puking, Bleeding Clowns," *Vice*, June 21, 2018, https://www.vice.com/en/article/yweqg7/these-puking-bleeding-clowns-are-a-forgotten-part-of-crossfits-past.

240 Commodifying the language of Eastern and Indigenous spiritual practices: Rina Deshpande, "Yoga in America Often Exploits My Culture—but You May Not Even Realize It," *SELF*, October 27, 2017, https://www.self.com/story/yoga-indian-cultural-appropriation.

240 CrossFit HQ denied any suggestion: Gene Demby, "Who's Really Left Out of the CrossFit Circle," Code Switch, NPR, September 15, 2013, https://www.npr.org/sections/codeswitch/2013/09/15/222574436/whos-really-left-out-of-the-crossfit-circle.

241 track records of toxicity: Alex Abad-Santos, "How SoulCycle Lost Its Soul." Vox, December 23, 2020, https://www.vox.com/the-goods/22195549/soulcycle-decline-reopening-bullying-bike-explained.

241 allegedly sleeping with: Matt Turner, "SoulCycle's Top Instructors Had Sex with Clients, 'Fat-Shamed' Coworkers, and Used Homophobic and Racist Language, Insiders Say." *Business Insider*, November 22, 2020, https://www.businessinsider.com/soulcycle-instructors-mistreated-staff-slept-with-riders-2020-11.

241 studio drama: Bridget Read, "The Cult of SoulCycle Is Even Darker Than You Thought." The Cut, December 23, 2020, https://www.thecut.com/2020/12/the-cult-of-soulcycle-is-even-darker-than-you-thought.html.

241 covering up complaints: Katie Warren, "SoulCycle's top instructors had sex with clients, 'fat-shamed' coworkers, and used homophobic and racist language, but the company treated them like Hollywood stars anyway, insiders say." *Business Insider*, November 17, 2020, https://www.businessinsider.com/soulcycle-instructors-celebrities-misbehavior-2020-11.

v.

244 Walter White of yoga: Lisa Swan, "The Untold Truth of Bikram Yoga," The List, March 20, 2017, https://www.thelist.com/50233/untold-truth-bikram-yoga/.

246 rape allegations: Jenavieve Hatch, "Bikram Yoga Creator Loses It When Asked About Sexual Assault Allegations," *Huffington Post*, October 28, 2016, https://www.huffpost.com/entry/bikram-choudhury-loses-it-when-asked-about-sexual-assault-allegations_n_58139871e4b0390e69d0014a.

Part 6: Follow for Follow

i.

257 "Thinking about something": Be Scofield, "Tech Bro Guru: Inside the Sedona Cult of Bentinho Massaro," *The Guru Magazine*, December 26, 2018, https://gurumag.com/tech-bro-guru-inside-the-sedona-cult-of-bentinho-massaro/.

258 "tech bro guru": Be Scofield, "Tech Bro Guru: Inside the Sedona Cult of Bentinho Massaro," Integral World, December 26, 2018, http://www.integralworld.net/scofield8.html.

258 quack spiritual consortium: Jesse Hyde, "When Spirituality Goes Viral," *Playboy*, February 18, 2019, https://www.playboy.com/read/spirituality-goes-viral.

259 social media interactions contribute to depression, anxiety, and suicide: David D. Luxton, Jennifer D. June, and Jonathan M. Fairall, "Social Media and Suicide: A Public Health Perspective," *American Journal of Public Health* (May 2012), https://www.ncbi.nlm.nih.gov/pmc/articles/PMC3477910/.

260 the cult of social media attention: Oscar Schwartz, "My Journey into the Dark, Hypnotic World of a Millennial Guru," *Guardian*, January 9, 2020, https://www.theguardian.com/world/2020/jan/09/strange-hypnotic-world-millennial-guru-bentinho-massaro-youtube.

ii.

261 "the evils of the Internet": Mark Dery, "Technology Makes Us Escapist; The Cult of the Mind," *New York Times Magazine*, September 28, 1997, https://www.nytimes.com/1997/09/28/magazine/technology-makes-us-escapist-the-cult-of-the-mind.html.

261 "Spiritual predators? Give me a break": Josh Quittner, "Life and Death on the Web," *Time*, April 7, 1997, http://content.time.com/time/magazine/article/0,9171,986141,00.html.

262 "modern-day campfire": Alain Sylvain, "Why Buying Into Pop Culture and Joining a Cult Is Basically the Same Thing," *Quartz*, March 10, 2020, https://qz.com/1811751/the-psychology-behind-why-were-so-obsessed-with-pop-culture/.

263 the word "influencer": Jane Solomon, "What Is An 'Influencer' And How Has This Word Changed?" Dictionary.com, January 6, 2021, https://www.dictionary.com/e/influencer/#:~:text=The%20word%20influencer%20has%20been,wasn't%20a%20job%20title.

263 "if Buddha or Jesus lived today": Jesse Hyde, "When Spirituality Goes Viral," *Playboy*, February 18, 2019, https://www.playboy.com/read/spirituality-goes- viral.

264 quotegrams: Sophie Wilkinson, "Could Inspirational Quotes Be Instagram's Biggest Invisible Cult?," *Grazia*, September 30, 2015, https://graziadaily.co.uk/life/real-life/inspirational-quotes-instagrams-biggest-invisible-cult/.

267 controversial New Age circle called Ramtha: Lisa Pemberton, "Behind the Gates at Ramtha's School," *Olympian*, July 15, 2013, https://www.theolympian.com/news/local/article25225543.html.

270 the correlation between intelligence and belief in "weird ideas": M. Shermer and J. S. Gould, *Why People Believe Weird Things* (New York: A. W. H. Freeman/Owl Book, 2007).

270 "immune to superstition": Stuart A Vyse, Believing in Magic: the Psychology of Superstition (New York: Oxford University Press, 1997).

272 the term "conspirituality": Charlotte Ward and David Voas, "The Emergence of Conspirituality." Taylor & Francis, Journal of Con-

temporary Religion, January 7, 2011, https://www.tandfonline.com /doi/abs/10.1080/13537903.2011.539846?journalCode=cjcr20&.

272 whitewashed yoga classes: Anusha Wijeyakumar, "We Need to Talk about the Rise of White Supremacy in Yoga." InStyle, October 6, 2020, https://www.instyle.com/beauty/health-fitness/yoga -racism-white-supremacy.

273 over half of the Republicans surveyed: Tommy Beer, "Majority of Republicans Believe the QAnon Conspiracy Theory Is Partly or Mostly True, Survey Finds," *Forbes*, September 2, 2020, https://www .forbes.com/sites/tommybeer/2020/09/02/majority-of-republicans -believe-the-qanon-conspiracy-theory-is-partly-or-mostly-true-survey -finds/?sh=3d8d165b5231.

275 The glossary goes on and on: "Conspirituality-To-QAnon (CS-to-Q) Keywords and Phrases," Conspirituality.net, https://con spirituality.net/keywords-and-phrases/

276 nightmarish crimes: Lois Beckett, "QAnon: a Timeline of Violence Linked to the Conspiracy Theory." *Guardian*. October 16, 2020, https://www.theguardian.com/us-news/2020/oct/15/qanon-violence -crimes-timeline.

277 dystopian video game: Alyssa Rosenberg, "I Understand the Temptation to Dismiss QAnon. Here's Why We Can't," *Washington Post*, August 7, 2019, https://www.washingtonpost.com/opinions /2019/08/07/qanon-isnt-just-conspiracy-theory-its-highly-effective -game/.

277 a cognitive analysis of QAnon: Joe Pierre, "The Psychological Needs That QAnon Feeds," *Psychology Today*, August 12, 2020, https://www.psychologytoday.com/us/blog/psych-unseen/202008 /the-psychological-needs-qanon-feeds.

About
the Author

Amanda Montell is a writer and language scholar from Baltimore, Maryland. She is the author of the critically acclaimed *Wordslut: A Feminist Guide to Taking Back the English Language*, which she is developing for television with FX. Her writing has appeared in *Marie Claire*, *Cosmopolitan*, *Glamour*, The Rumpus, Nylon, Byrdie, and Who What Wear, where she formerly served as the features and beauty editor. Amanda holds a degree in linguistics from NYU and lives in Los Angeles' Silver Lake neighborhood with her partner, plants, and pets.